Transnationalism
FROM BELOW

Comparative Urban and Community Research

Series Editor, Michael Peter Smith

Volume 6

COMPARATIVE URBAN & COMMUNITY RESEARCH

Transnationalism
FROM BELOW

Edited by

MICHAEL PETER
SMITH

LUIS EDUARDO
GUARNIZO

Transaction Publishers
New Brunswick (U.S.A.) and London (U.K.)

Sixth printing 2006

Library of Congress Catalog Number: 97-28327
ISSN: 0892-5569
ISBN: 1-56000-990-X
Printed in the United States of America

Library of Congress Cataloging-in-Publication Data

Transnationalism from below / edited by Michael Peter Smith and Luis
Eduardo Guarnizo.
       p. cm.—(Comparative urban community research, ISSN 0892-
       5569 ; v. 6)
    Includes bibliographical references.
    ISBN 1-56000-990-X (pbk. : alk. paper)
          1. Social movements. 2. International economic relations.
    3. Nationalism. 4. Group identity. 5. National characteristics.
    I. Smith, Michael P. II. Guarnizo, Luis. III. Series.

HT110.C65 vol. 6
[HN17.5]
307.76 s   97-28327
[307]—dc21   CIP

Contents

Comparative Urban and Community Research is an annual review devoted to theoretical, empirical and applied research on the processes of urbanization and community change throughout the world. The format of *Comparative Urban and Community Research* enables the publication of manuscripts that are longer and more richly textured than the articles a quarterly journal can feature.

Editorial correspondence and manuscript submissions should be addressed to *Comparative Urban and Community Research*, Department of Human and Community Development, University of California, Davis, CA 95616-8523. Submission requirements: (1) papers should be double-spaced; and (2) author's name, affiliation, address and telephone number should appear on a separate sheet.

Michael Peter Smith, Editor
University of California, Davis

Alexis Ohran, Editorial Assistant

I

Theorizing Transnationalism

1

The Locations of Transnationalism[1]

Luis Eduardo Guarnizo
Michael Peter Smith

Transnationalism is clearly in the air. Expansion of transnational capital and mass media to even the remotest of hinterlands has provoked a spate of discourses on "globalization," "transnationalism," and the "crisis of the nation state." A core theme in these discourses is the penetration of national cultures and political systems by global and local driving forces. The nation-state is seen as weakened "from above" by transnational capital, global media, and emergent supra-national political institutions. "From below" it faces the decentering "local" resistances of the informal economy, ethnic nationalism, and grassroots activism. These developments are sometimes viewed in celebratory terms. For some they bring market rationality and liberalism to a disorderly world "from above." For others they generate conditions conducive to the creation of new liberatory practices and spaces "from below" like transnational migration and its attendant cultural hybridity. In more pessimistic readings, these developments are seen as preludes to a new form of capitalist modernization that is bound to convert the entire planet to "global consumerism." This volume of *Comparative Urban and Community Research* brings together a rich combination of theoretical reflections and grounded studies of transnational processes and practices that offer a more nuanced reading of "transnationalism from below" that is neither celebratory nor dystopian.

Meanings and Metaphors of Transnationalism

In the past decade the concept of transnationalism has swiftly migrated across disciplinary boundaries. It has been rapidly "assimilated," indeed appropriated and consumed by anthropologists, sociologists, political scientists, geographers and other scholars. The concept's sudden prominence has been accompanied by its increasing ambiguity. Transnationalism thus runs the risk of

3

becoming an empty conceptual vessel. The articles in this volume should temper such skepticism. They show that transnationalism is a useful concept that represents phenomena which, although not entirely new, have reached particular intensity at a global scale at the end of the 20th century. This volume centers on the development and consequences of transnational practices linked to the processes of mass migration, economic expansion, and political organization across national spaces. Moving deftly between micro- and macro-analyses, the studies in this volume expand the boundaries of the current scholarship on transnationalism, locate new forms of transnational agency, and pose provocative questions that challenge prevailing interpretations of globalization.

The convergence of several historically specific factors all help explain the complexity of transnationalism. This is a new complexity not only in terms of scale, but also because of the scope of effects that contemporary transnational flows have upon the societies involved. These include:

- the globalization of capitalism with its destabilizing effects on less industrialized countries;
- the technological revolution in the means of transportation and communication;
- global political transformations such as decolonization and the universalization of human rights; and
- the expansion of social networks that facilitate the reproduction of transnational migration, economic organization, and politics.

Cultural studies scholars have been at the forefront in the analysis of transnational practices and processes (Appadurai 1990, 1996; Buell 1994; Clifford 1992; Bhabha 1990; Hannerz 1996). Their leadership has imprinted the field with a peculiar cultural bent and a distinctive normative, postmodern discursive flavor. A variety of alternative visions of transnationalism, often specifically linked to transmigration, have also emerged in the social sciences (Glick Schiller and associates 1994, 1995; Kearney 1991; Rouse 1992; Portes 1996; M.P. Smith 1994; and authors in this volume). However different in their theoretical starting points, a sense of convergence between approaches in cultural studies and the social sciences is arising. One sign of this convergence is the tendency to conceive of transnationalism as something to celebrate, as an expression of a subversive popular resistance "from below." Cultural hybridity, multi-positional identities, border-crossing by marginal "others," and transnational business practices by migrant entrepreneurs are depicted as conscious and successful efforts by ordinary people to escape control and domination "from above" by capital and the state.

Authors celebrating the liberatory character of transnational practices often represent transnationals as engaged in a dialectic of opposition and resistance to the hegemonic logic of multinational capital. Given the declining political influence of working-class movements in the face of the global reorganization of capitalism, all sorts of new social actors on the transnational stage are now being invested with oppositional possibilities, despite the fact that their practices are neither self-consciously resistant nor even loosely political in character. For example, recent work inscribes the activities of transnational immigrant entrepreneurs with a series of attributes which socially construct small capitalists as common people whose entrepreneurial practices amount to an expression of popular resistance (Portes 1996). In a similar vein, Bhabha (1990: 300) characterizes the practices and identities of transmigrants as "counter-narratives of the nation" which continually evoke and erase their totalizing boundaries and "disturb those ideological manoeuvres through which 'imagined communities' are given essentialist identities" (see also Anderson 1983). An example of this use of transnationalism as a counter-hegemonic political space is found in the work of Michael Kearney (1991) who represents Mixtec migrant farm workers, despite their poverty, as having created autonomous spaces in southern California and Oregon in which, he claims, neither the United States nor the Mexican state have access or control.

The totalizing emancipatory character of transnationalism in these discourses is questionable. While transnational practices and hybrid identities are indeed potentially counter-hegemonic, they are by no means always resistant. As Katharyne Mitchell (1993, 1996) and Aihwa Ong (1996) have demonstrated in their studies of the Chinese diaspora in Canada and the United States, respectively, the liminal sites of transnational practices and discourses can be used for the purposes of capital accumulation quite as effectively as for the purpose of contesting hegemonic narratives of race, ethnicity, class, and nation. The dialectic of domination and resistance needs a more nuanced analysis than the celebratory vision allows. At the risk of disrupting these hopeful, albeit utopian, visions, this volume attempts to bring back into focus the enduring asymmetries of domination, inequality, racism, sexism, class conflict, and uneven development in which transnational practices are embedded and which they sometimes even perpetuate.

Transnationalism is a multifaceted, multi-local process. A main concern guiding *Transnationalism from Below* is to discern how this process affects power relations, cultural constructions, economic interactions, and, more generally, social organization at the level of the locality. We try to unpack the deceptive local-global binary that dominates a significant segment of current academic discourse. This task requires us to construct an analytical optic for viewing transnationalism and for exploring the most useful methods for investigating transnational practices and processes from below. Five main analytical themes weave together the nine essays that form this volume: the political organization of transnational space; the centrality of "locality" in a historicized sense; the constitution and reproduction of transnational networks through material and symbolic exchange; transnationalism and identity politics; and the development of viable approaches for studying transnationalism.

Political Organization of Transnational Spaces

Transnational political organization and mobilization take place at multiple levels (M.P. Smith 1994). Constructing transnational political spaces should be treated as the resultant of separate, sometimes parallel, sometimes competing projects at all levels of the global system—from the "global governance" agenda of international organizations and multinational corporations to the most local "survival strategies," by which transnational migrant networks are socially constructed. At the most global level, specific multilateral collectivities—such as the United Nations (UN), the International Monetary Fund (IMF), the World Bank, international non-governmental organizations (NGOs), and the global capitalist class—seek to construct a global neoliberal contextual space, a "new world order," to regulate transnational flows of capital, trade, people, and culture. In the process, they supplant the disintegrating nationally-managed regimes of Keynesianism and Fordism (Drainville, this volume). Again, at the most local level, it is specific collectivities—local households, kin networks, elite fractions, and other emergent local formations—which actively pursue transnational migration to create and reproduce another kind of transnational social space, the "trans-locality," to sustain material and cultural resources in the face of the neo-liberal storm.

Does this mean, as some (e.g., Appadurai 1996: Part III) have claimed, that transnationalism "from above" and "from below" are ushering in a new period of weakened nationalism, a "postnational" global cultural economy? There are several reasons to doubt this claim. First, historically, states and nations seeking statehood have often kept the transnational connections of their overseas diasporas alive, as in the classical examples of the Jewish, Greek, and Armenian social formations (Tölölyan 1996). Second, and relatedly, contributors to this volume underline the continuing significance of nationalist projects and identities and their articulation with competing identities and projects, such as feminism, environmentalism and globalism in the formation of "transnational grassroots movements" (M.P. Smith 1994). These issues are thoughtfully explored in Sarah Mahler's analysis of alternative modes of political mobilization of "deterritorialized" migrants as well as in André Drainville's discussion of the implications of enduring national and local political identities in the new transnational political coalitions that have sprung up to resist the hegemonic ideology and austerity policies imposed "from above" by the global neo-liberal regime.

Third, in the present period of mass migration many nation-states that have experienced substantial out-migration are entering into a process of actively promoting "transnational reincorporation" of migrants into their state-centered projects. Why is this so?

As suggested above, global economic restructuring and the repositioning of states, especially less industrialized ones, in the world economy, have increased the economic dependency of these countries on foreign investment. Political elites and managerial strata in these societies have found that as emigration to advanced capitalist countries has increased, the monetary transfers provided by transmigrant investors have made crucial contributions to their national economies (Lessinger 1992), and family remittances have promoted social stability (Mahler 1996; M.P. Smith 1994). Thus, their growing dependence on transmigrants' stable remittances has prompted sending states to try to incorporate their "nationals" abroad into both their national market and their national polity by a variety of measures including: naming "honorary ambassadors" from among transmigrant entrepreneurs in the hope that they will promote "national" interests vis-à-vis receiving countries; subsidizing transnational migrant "home-town" and "home-state" associations (Goldring, R. Smith, and Mahler, this volume); creating formal channels for communicating with these "constituencies" across national borders (Glick Schiller and Fouron, this volume; Guarnizo 1996); passing dual citizenship laws; and even, in the bizarre case of the state apparatus in El Salvador, providing free legal assistance to political refugees so that they may obtain asylum in the United States on the grounds that they have been persecuted by the state that is now paying their legal expenses (Mahler, this volume).

In short, far from withering away in the epoch of transnationalism, sending states once presumed to be "peripheral," are promoting the reproduction of transnational subjects; and, in the process reinventing their own role in the "new world order" (see Glick Schiller and Fouron, this volume). They are officially incorporating their "nationals" residing abroad into their newly configured trans-territorial nation-state. This political process has been called "deterritorialized" nation-state formation by Nina Glick Schiller and her associates (Basch, Glick Schiller, and Szanton-Blanc 1994). The role of the sending state and state-centered social movements in the production of transnational social formations is thoughtfully explored below in Glick Schiller and Fouron's study of the political organization of the Haitian diaspora in New York and other U.S. cities since the restoration of the Aristide regime in Haiti.

This process of trans-territorialization raises intriguing questions concerning human agency. The sending states are insuring their own survival by contributing to the constitution of new bifocal subjects with dual citizenships and multiple political identities. Inadvertently, this very process opens up interstitial social spaces which create multiple possibilities for novel forms of human agency. These spaces provide possibilities for resistance as well as accommodation to power "from above." For example, by accommodating to their newly-legitimated dual status, bi-national subjects are able to enjoy the benefits of citizenship, the opportunities for household reproduction, as well as the costs these entail in two nation-states. They may be doubly empowered or doubly subordinated, depending on historically-specific local circumstances (compare, for instance the multiple empowerment of Ticuanenses in New York City and Ticuani, Puebla with the multiple subordination of Garifuna in Los Angeles and Belize City in the studies by R. Smith and L. Matthei and D. Smith, this volume).

Fourth, in light of these new interstitial possibilities, it is important to recall that the agents of "receiving states" remain relevant actors. States still monopolize the legitimate means of coercive power within their borders. Thus, it is problematic to conceptualize as a "deterritorialization of the state" the expansion of the reach of "states of origin" beyond their own national territorial jurisdiction into other state formations. Rather, the "foreign" territory in which transmigrants reside and their "state of origin" comes to "visit" has a material force that cannot be ignored. When politicians come to proselitize, officials to promote their programs and plans, or business people to open or maintain markets, their influence is exercised in a particular territorial domain, formally controlled by the "receiving" state. This juridical construction of transnational social formations is one which denies their "globality" and re-territorializes their meaning as a "boundary penetration," as a "transgression" of its own jurisdiction. The recent political controversy in the United States concerning the "penetration of Asian money" into U.S. national political campaigns suggests that the political elites ruling nation-states do not merely react to, but actually act to constitute the scope and meaning of "transnationalism" within their territories. In terms of racialization, this example could be taken as a gross overgeneralization of the notion of illegitimate border-crossing from the level of the individual to that of entire states and regions of the globe. It does illustrate, however, the key role of state-initiated discourses in the reinscription of nationalist ideologies and national subjects.

Paradoxically, the expansion of transnational practices from above and from below has resulted in outbursts of entrenched, essentialist nationalism in both "sending" and "receiving" countries. In receiving nation-states, movements aimed at recuperating and reifying a mythical national identity are expanding as a way to eliminate the penetration of alien "others." States of origin, on the other hand, are re-essentializing their national identity and extending it to their nationals abroad as a way to maintain their loyalty and flow of resources "back home." By granting them dual citizenship, these states are encouraging transmigrants' instrumental accomodation to "receiving" societies, while simultaneously inhibiting their cultural assimilation and thereby promoting the preservation of their own national culture.

Our effort to differentiate the local from the national and the global political organization of transnational spaces points to the growing interdependence of geographical scales. It suggests a weakness in the prevailing postmodernist metaphors of "deterritorialization" and "unboundedness." Undoubtedly, the boundaries limiting people cut across the politically instituted boundaries of nation-states. But transnational actions are bounded in two senses—first, by the understandings of "grounded reality" socially constructed within the transnational networks that people form and move through, and second, by the policies and practices of territorially-based sending and receiving local and national states and communities. We now turn to a closer examination of this double-grounding.

Grounding Transnationalism

Transnational practices do not take place in an imaginary "third space" (Bhabha 1990; Soja 1996) abstractly located "in-between" national territories. Thus, the image of transnational migrants as deterritorialized, free-floating people represented by the now popular academic adage "neither here nor there" deserves closer scrutiny. Intermittent spatial mobility, dense social ties, and intense exchanges fostered by transmigrants across national borders have indeed reached unprecedented levels. This has fed the formulation of metaphors of transnationalism as a "boundless" and therefore liberatory process. However, transnational practices cannot be construed as if they were free from the constraints and opportunities that contextuality imposes. Transnational practices, while connecting collectivities located in more than one national territory, are embodied in specific social relations established between specific people, situated in unequivocal localities, at historically determined times. The "locality" thus needs to be further conceptualized.

For classical modernist theory the local, as opposed to the cosmopolitan, is conceived as a bounded "property or diacritic of social life" (Appadurai 1996: 179). In this light, the local is seen as a derogatory site that compounds backwardness, as the realm of stagnation against the dynamism of the industrial civilization of capitalism, as the realm of idiosyncratic culture at odds with scientific rationality, "as the obstacle to full realization of that political form of modernity, the nation-state" (Dirlik 1996: 23). One of the main contributions of postmodern ethnography and critical theory has been the redefinition of the local as a dynamic source of alternative cosmopolitanisms and contestation (See M.P. Smith 1992; Robbins 1993; Schein, this volume). Recently, Appadurai (1996: 185) has argued that, embedded in the contingencies of history, local subjects reproduce their locality (which he calls neighborhood) in interaction with the environment in which it is embedded. This is, in his view, "how the subjects of history become historical subjects, so that no human community, however apparently stable, static, bounded, or isolated, can usefully be regarded as cool or outside [of] history."

Despite the high level of fragmentation in the literature on transnationalism, the concepts of "deterritorialization" and "unboundedness" have gone unquestioned. Here we take issue with the concept of transmigrants as unbounded social actors. We wish to examine the applicability of the concept of unboundedness to the practices of transmigrants as though implying their total disconnection from local constraints and social moorings. If we were to believe that transmigrants are socially, politically, and culturally unbound, the question then is how can we define who is and who is not a transmigrant? In other words, what are the boundaries of transnationality? This is a central issue to resolve to determine whether transnational practices are evanescent or a new structural feature of society.

We wish to underline the actual mooring and, thus, boundedness of transnationalism by the opportunities and constraints found in particular localities where transnational practices occur. For example, consider the question of the role of cities in transnational studies. Cities are not merely empty containers of transnational articulations. Is a transnational flow, such as a capital investment, migratory stream, or IMF policy, simply imposed on cities? Or does it matter whether Hong Kong capital flows go to Shenzhen or Vancouver; IMF austerity policies are implemented in San Jose, Costa Rica or Mexico City; Haitian, Mexican, Dominican, and Salvadoran migrants move to New York or Miami, Los Angeles or Madrid, Long Island or San Francisco, respectively? The studies in this volume and other studies (compare Mahler, this volume with Smith and Tarallo 1993 and Tardanico 1995, with Barkin, Ortiz, and Rosen 1997) suggest that the local sites of global processes do matter. The social construction of "place" is still a process of local meaning-making, territorial specificity, juridical control, and economic development, however complexly articulated these localities become in transnational economic, political, and cultural flows.

The complexity does not stop here, however. The research of our contributors further illustrates that the specific context in which transnational actions take place is not just local, but also "trans-local" (i.e., local to local). Luin Goldring and Robert Smith call these contexts "translocalities." In these social fields (see Glick Schiller et al. 1992) transnational practices are vested with particular meanings. Translocal relations are constituted within historically and geographically specific points of origin and migration established by transmigrants. Such relations are dynamic, mutable, and dialectical. They form a triadic connection that links transmigrants, the localities to which they migrate, and their locality of origin. The locality of migration provides a specific context of opportunities and constraints (e.g., labor market conditions, popular and official perceptions of the migrant group, the presence or absence of other co-nationals) into which migrants enter. The fit between specific kinds of migrants and specific local and national contexts abroad shapes not only the likelihood of generating, maintaining or forsaking transnational ties, but also the very nature of the ties that migrants can forge with their place of origin. While transnational practices extend beyond two or more national territories, they are built within the confines of specific social, economic, and political relations which are bound together by perceived shared interests and meanings. Without such social closure, without a basic sense of shared meanings and a sense of predictability of results bounding together the actors involved (i.e., social control), it would be unthinkable for any person to try to establish any kind of relations across national territories, whether a transnational migrant network, economic project, or political movement.

The diverse effects of this triadic translocal relation are clearly illustrated in Ninna Sørensen's article comparing the disparate experiences of Dominican migrants in New York and Madrid. While in both situations transmigrants have built transnational relations with their native land, the type, scale, and scope of these relations differ. The differences stem not only from the contextual differences abroad, but also from a selective social and regional composition of transmigrants in both locations. Those going to Madrid tend to be drawn from among those who could not afford to migrate to New York—because of their regional or class origin, because of their gender, or, most importantly, because of their lack of the appropriate social capital connecting them with the migration networks linked to the Big Apple. In this case, class, gender, and regional origin emerge as critical determinants of migrants' destination, attainment, and transnationality. The limited power of the generic "Dominican" label as a homogenizing national identifier and predictor of migrants' performance is clearly demonstrated.

This case well illustrates the generalization that migration from the same country is formed by a heterogenous rather than unitary group of people, possessing distinct personal and social endowments (human capital and social capital), migrating under disparate circumstances, and professing significant, if subtle, regional cultural differences. Heterogeneity, in turn, results in disparate rates of access to opportunities in the receiving labor market and society, which in part explains why not all migrants are able to afford the maintenance of active transnational ties (see Mahler, this volume)—and why the transnational practices of those who do maintain them are also diverse. In general, different "receiving" localities offer migrants dissimilar contexts of reception, and thus dissimilar opportunities and constraints.[2]

The contribution by Alan Smart and Josephine Smart illustrates another dimension of locality and translocality, namely, that the historically particular forging of translocal relations significantly mediates the patterns of global investment as well as migration. Their study of the formation of social networks by entrepreneurial Hong Kong capitalists and Chinese workers starts from the well taken assumption that an exclusive focus on international migration in studying transnationalism is too restrictive (for an alternative argument see Mahler, this volume). In the contemporary period, national boundaries are being constantly criss-crossed by processes of communication and exchange that do not include actual bodily movement, such as capital expansion, Internet, and other telecommunications. Other modes of transnational bodily movement, such as tourism and expatriate consulting and entrepreneurship, do not entail migration. All of these relationships are mediated by trans-local understandings. Smart and Smart's study of the constitution and mobilization of transnational social networks traversing the soon-to-be-erased Hong Kong-China border reveals a particular pattern of "situated ethnicity" as a basis for translocal network solidarity and exclusion that differs markedly from the kinds of translocal ties forged by corporate Hong Kong Chinese capitalists investing in Vancouver (Mitchell 1993, 1996). In order to successfully penetrate different localities in the world economy, the transnational capitalist fractions from Hong Kong have to justify their activities within prevailing local cultural understandings. The entrepreneurial Hong Kong capitalists studied by Smart and Smart foregrounded their Chineseness in China, while the corporate capitalists from Hong Kong in Vancouver accommodated to a different setting by downplaying their Chineseness and foregrounding their capitalist economic position within a dominant multicultural public discourse. Thus transnationalism, far from erasing the local identifications and meaning systems, actually relies on them to sustain transnational ties.

The reproduction of transnational ties is clearly sensitive to contextual conditions. However, contextual conditions are not static, and must be historicized. Over time, for example, labor market conditions can improve or deteriorate; state policies can become friendlier (see for example Schein and Smart and Smart this volume); or additional opportunities may arise from an emergent aggregate demand for goods and services generated by increasing numbers of people arriving from the same country or region. This latter process may also provoke class restructuring within the group, as well as social transformations within the receiving city and society (Sassen-Koob 1987; Sassen 1991). Given the many possibilities for social transformation generated by all of these flows, how are transnational networks currently constituted and reproduced? Just how new are these processes?

Constituting and Reproducing Transnational Networks

A critical unanswered question raised by scholars of transnational migration is whether transnational practices and relations are merely an evanescent phenomenon which will not last beyond first

generation migrants. Or, by contrast, are transnational social practices becoming an enduring structural characteristic of global
social organization? Critics of transnationalism argue that the
attention devoted to transnational practices is misplaced, for such
relations have always existed. In fact, the well-known "dual frame
of reference" phenomenon has been a typical trait of first
generation immigrants. At first glance, the historical record
supports this interpretation.

Despite the relative paucity and inconsistency of existing data,
there is consensus among scholars about a high incidence of
transnational mobility among European immigrants, before and
after the turn of the century. During the 1899-1952 period, for
example, a full one-third of all immigrants to the United States,
either returned or moved on. Between 1925 and 1943, almost two-
fifths of all migrants remigrated (Hoerder 1985: 353-54; see also
Rosenblum 1973). Moreover, some studies at the turn of the
century found that return rates tended to be higher among newer
immigrants. Some have attributed this to changes in the United
States labor market and society which made it harder for the
newcomers to adapt, and to the national composition of the
newcomers, most of whom were Southern and Eastern Europeans
who, apparently, returned in larger numbers than those from
Northern and Western Europe (Rosenblum 1973: 125-26). Yet,
according to received assimilationist wisdom, the dual frame of
reference of the first generation died with it. Accordingly, the
withering away of transnational ties, language, and most cultural
practices and values brought by immigrants from the old country
was almost completed by the third generation (Portes and Rumbaut
1990: 183).

Are transnational relations exclusively a first generation practice? Did European immigrants actually sever their connections
with their old country once the first generation passed on? While
these questions need further examination, recent scholarship suggests otherwise. It shows that old world immigrants' transnational
orientation did not die with them. For example, Irish, Polish, and
Jewish "immigrant nationalisms did not simply go to the grave
with the members of the migrating generation; on the contrary, a

cultural thread links the diasporic political vision of the immigrants with the ethnic gestures of their grandchildren and great-grand-children" (Jacobson 1995: 5). More than 100 years after the arrival of their forbearers, the enduring transnational linkages between the politics of the homeland and the culture of European diasporas still persist. Polish Americans, Jewish Americans, and Irish Americans still profess political identity and allegiance to their distant, and, for many, unknown homeland. During the struggle of the Solidarity movement in Poland, for example, thousands of Polish Americans sang the Polish national anthem in demonstrations in Chicago and other major U.S. cities. St. Patrick's Day parades are celebrated nationwide and Irish Americans' support of Irish independence and the IRA's struggle remains strong. Meanwhile, the defense of Israel remains the paramount task and unifying force for many Jews in the United States. Similar patterns are also found among other Americans of Southern and Eastern European descent.

This still leaves unanswered the question of what, if anything, is different about current transnational practices? Critics of the reconstitution of immigration studies as transnational studies argue that cross-generational language retention remains problematic, that different receiving state practices (e.g., ethnic pluralism in the United States versus full assimilation in France) still tilt the balance in favor of assimilation over time, and that renewed anti-immigrant hysteria creates further pressures for "immigrants" to assimilate or "go home" rather than maintaining the double-consciousness required of transmigrants. Thus, what is the likelihood that contemporary transnational practices will be reproduced beyond first generation migrants?

In order to answer this question we will address three factors connected to the processes of migration, namely: the micro-dynamics of migration; the globalization of capitalism and economic reorganization of the economy; and the technological revolution. With regard to the micro-dynamics of migration we must differentiate the reproduction of networks and households. The social diffusion of a given social practice, like transnationalism, may be either kin- or non-kin-based. Village-based migration, for example, has become a fact of life for many Mexican localities where thousands of migrants to the United States have originated. However historically resilient, the actual process of migration is not reproduced exclusively by kinship networks. Migrants from the same family often do emigrate North generation after generation. Yet, because of the locality-based character of circular migration from Mexico, many families, whose members had not ever emigrated before may join the process at any particular time (Massey et. al. 1987). In other words, the reproduction of migration is social, not just familial.

This is what Robert Smith and Luin Goldring (this volume) mean by the concept of "transnational communities." Smith, for example, appropriates Alarcon's (1994) depiction of such locality-based structures of reproduction as "rural Mexican communities that specialize in the production and reproduction of international migrant workers." Such transnational social structures are sustained by social networks in migration and their attendant modes of social organization—home town associations, economic remittances, social clubs, celebrations and other bi-national social processes as well as by more indirect technological means of transportation and communication now available to facilitate the reproduction of transnational social fields such as jet airplanes, sattelite dishes, telephones, faxes, and e-mail.

The examples provided in all of our case studies of transmigration well illustrate the interaction of global economic restructuring, the technological revolution, and the microdynamics of migrant social practices in reproducing transnational social fields. Global restructuring has created contextual conditions in the form of labor demand and labor market conditions in both rural agriculture (Zabin 1995) and in manufacturing and services in global cities like New York (Sassen-Koob 1984) favorable to transnational migration. The technological revolution in transportation and communications has facilitated the simultaneous maintenance of bi-national connections by migrating members of the new transnational working class. But it is the everyday practices of migrants that provide a structure of meaning to the acts of crossing borders, living in bi-national households, and reproducing transnational social relations. Such meanings are not exhausted by the economistic rubric represented in the concept of "household reproduction." Rather, they may involve the production of local or global status positions (compare Goldring with Matthei and D. Smith, this volume), the reconfiguration of local power relations (R. Smith, this volume) or the transgression of racial and gendered boundaries (Sørensen, this volume). Politically organized transnational networks and movements also weld together transnational connections by constituting structures of meaning. Historically specific examples include coalitions forged by international political and economic organizations (Drainville, this volume), cross-border labor organizing and "principled issue networks" advancing the cause of human rights, environmental justice, political democratization, and gender or racial equality (Sikkink 1993; Brysk 1993; M.P. Smith,1994; Mahler this volume). Once established, the maintenance and reproduction of relations of power, status, gender, race, and ethnicity become inextricably enmeshed in the reproduction of transnational social fields.

Moreover, recall that transational flows are not limited to transmigrants bodily geographic mobility. They also include multiple exchanges of monetary and non-monetary resources, material and symbolic objects, commodities and cultural values. Even in the highly unlikely event that every new immigrant became "settled" and severed all her or his connections with their country of origin, a continuous flow of new arrivals and material goods may reproduce a transnational social field. So too may the continuous flow of ideas and information provided by global media, ethnic tourism, and religious or secular festivals and rituals. All of these mechanisms have played a role in the re-emergence of transnational ties. Even in cases in which the sense of connectedness with the old country appear to have vanished, we find second and even third generation immigrants to the United States and other nation-states retaking the banner of ethnic pride and nationalism—e.g., the new nationalism vis-à-vis the Balkans and the Baltic states. Louisa Schein's case study of the invention of Hmong transnational ties with the Miao ethnic minority in China shows that it is now even possible to completely reinvent one's ethnic origins by the production, diffusion, and consumption of culturally oriented ethnic videos laden with geographical images and cultural icons. By these means, Hmong refugees from Laos are currently constructing a myth of cultural origins linked not to Laos but to Miao regions of China. Does this intriguing example mean, as some postmodernists would contend, that personal and social identity are completely malleable and that, in our postmodern world, anybody can become anybody else? We think not, but, as we shall see, the answer to this question is not as simple as it seems.

Transnationalism and Identity Politics

There is a tension in the literature on transnationalism between postmodern cultural studies' conception of identity construction as a free-floating, if not voluntaristic, process of individual self-formation and the many empirical studies of bi-national migrants, transnational social movements, and international organizational networks which envisage personal identity as embedded in socially structured and politically mediated processes of group formation and collective action. How can personal identity be seen as both hybrid and channeled, multipositional and network-bound, transgressive and affiliative, freely formed yet socially determined?

In a chapter of *Reading the Postmodern Polity* (1990: 70-72), entitled "American Fictions and Political Culture," social theorist Michael Shapiro offers an insightful way to reconcile this apparent contradiction. Building on the work of Foucault, but moving beyond his conceptual categories, Shapiro calls for a mapping of the "competing situations, local spaces, discourses, media, and genres...which affect the building of a person's consciousness of self and others." Among the different venues "through which people move as they form and reform their character and identity over time," Shapiro singles out such historicized and socially structured discursive fields as "educational space, military space, metropolitan space, [and] foreign ideational space." Shapiro makes a persuasive case for the post-structuralist view of subjectivity in which the "self" is envisaged as "fragmented and in contention as it is dispersed over a variety of dominant and peripheral discursive practices rather than existing as a homogeneous, centered steering mechanism." Yet the decentered subject is not a free-floating subjectivity. Rather, the discursive fields through which people travel as they move through life constitute alternative, socially structured bases for the inner tension and contention over selfhood and identity. In this way various "social spaces" like trans-local migrant networks, transnational working arrangements, and globalized neo-liberal ideology, can be viewed as affecting the formation of character, identity, and acting subjects at the same time that identity can be seen as fluctuating and contingent, as the contexts through which people move in time-space change and are appropriated and/or resisted by acting subjects.

The implications of the foregoing analysis for the study of transnational processes are intriguing. The discursive spaces through which transnational actors move are socially structured and shape character and identity—as do more general and enduring features of social structure, such as patriarchical gender relations, racial hierarchies, and economic inequality. Yet, as we have argued, the localized contexts of social action are important and differentiated, thus making possible a wider space for identity formation and "made character" than social structural inequalities and power/knowledge venues alone would predict. The loyalties and oppositions forged by transnational social networks, the ideological projects of transnational political actors, and the metropolitan cultures in which transnational processes are located, are more often in a state of "becoming" rather than "arrival." They constitute opportunities as well as constraints. In short, personal identity formation in transnational social spaces can best be understood as a dialectic of embedding and disembedding which, over time, involves an unavoidable encumbering, dis-encumbering, and re-encumbering of situated selves. Identity is contextual but not radically discontinuous. People seek to be situated, to have a stable mooring, an anchor amidst the tempest. Ticuanese moving between New York and Ticuani may conceive of themselves differently than they did before migration but they do not conceive of themselves as postmodern role-players on the global stage.

The complexities of transnational-identity politics are well illustrated in several of the contributions to this volume. These case studies lucidly capture emergent spaces of group loyalty and identity formation ushered in by transnational investment, migration, and political mobilization, both between and within various scales of state and community. One of the most obvious discourses of identity centers around the group loyalties and affiliations fostered by localities and by the state. In the case studies by Louisa Schein and Alan Smart and Josephine Smart political elites of the local state in different Chinese regions forge links and construct a cultural sense of "weness" with U.S.-based Hmong cultural brokers and Hong Kong-based entrepreneurs, respectively, that bypass national party loyalties and the ideology of the Chinese state. The Chinese state, eager to attract foreign remmitances and investment, tolerates these trans-local ties within its borders, but remains watchful, worried about the risks of ethnic separatism and the erosion of the ruling party's control of local politics. Unlike Robert Smith's and Luin Goldring's Mexican transmigrants who are concerned with reconfiguring power and status relations within their villages of origin and maintaining a reconfigured home-town identity, the Smarts' Hong Kong small capitalists carefully avoid establishing economic ties in their villages of origin in China for fear of the "excess"—i.e, non-business related—expectations and demands that might be thrust upon them if they did invest there, thus minimizing the cost of negative social capital. Their basis for building transnational economic and social relations is "situated ethnicity" (i.e., a constructed "transnational Chineseness") rather than home town loyalty. Despite their differences, each of these cases illustrates the persistent pull of "locality" as a social space of identity formation in transnational social fields.

Similarly, the experiences of Dominicans in New York City and Madrid and Haitians and Belizians in the United States discussed in this volume question the hopeful expectations of those who argue that transnational practices and identities constitute "counter-narratives of the nation" that subvert essentialist nationalist identities (Bhabha 1990: 300). If anything, these cases suggest the reinscription of group identities by transnational actors "from below" as efforts to recapture a lost sense of belonging by recreating imagined communities. These identities forged from below are often no less essentialized than the hegemonic projects of nation states. Identities forged "from below" are not inherently subversive or counter-hegemonic. Yet they are different from hegemonic identities imposed from above. The process of subaltern identity formation is a process of constant struggle—a struggle in which discursive communities produce narratives of belonging, resistance, or escape. In these grand narratives of personal meaning, the spaces available for forming non-essentialist identities, while not entirely absent, are interstitial—i.e., they open up between such dominant discursive venues as the "nation-state," the "local community," and the "ethno-racial community."

The process of marking differences within these essentialized identities is no easy task, however necessary and desirable it may be. Power, including the power to resist hegemonic projects, exists latently at all levels of the global system. But to materialize, it must be socially organized, and cannot be taken for granted as inherently embedded in phantom discourses "from below." The literature on transnational grassroots movements reviewed by Mahler underlines this point. Resistance to the kind of hegemonic neo-liberal project discussed by Drainville is more than merely spontaneous or episodic. Despite their scattered successes, these transnational movements are nonetheless systematically organized by the intentional human agency of human rights organizations (Sikkink 1993), solidarity networks of indigenous peoples (Nagengast and Kearney 1990; Smith 1994), grassroots political leaders (e.g., the Central American Solidarity and Zapatista movements), cross-border labor organizers (e.g., the tri-lateral labor struggle against NAFTA), and other issue-oriented interest groups (see, for example, Eisenstadt and Thorup 1994).

Furthermore, while transnational practices may reduce power asymmetries based on gender and race, and even promote solidarity based on these dimensions, such asymmetries often tend to persist not only as a steady source of struggle, but also of identity. For example, Ticuanense in New York, while marginalized by mainstream society, affirm and recreate an essentialized group identity by positioning themselves as racially superior to their equally impoverished Puerto Rican and African American neighbors. Analogously, Mixtec immigrants remain discriminated against and marginalized by their fellow mestizo Mexicans in the United States, while women's subordination vis-à-vis men endures, although to a lesser degree than in their communities of origin (Sørensen, this volume; Guarnizo 1997; Hondangneu-Sotelo 1994; Levitt 1994; Pessar 1994).

Future Directions for Transnational Studies

It should be apparent from what we have already said that there is a need to "stretch" the study of "transnationalism from below" to encompass the scope of global processes, as well as to focus empirical research upon the "local" specificity of various socio-spatial transformations. This means that the traditional methods for studying people in local communities—ethnography, life histories, and historical case studies, must be contextualized and historicized to take into account four central dimensions of transnational socio-economic and political transformation:

1. the globalization of capitalism and the repositioning of states, nations, and class, gender and ethno-racial formations within this global restructuring;
2. the transnational dimension of global political transformations like decolonization, the universalization of human rights, and the rise of cross-national institutional networks;
3. the transnational social relations made possible by the technological revolution in the means of transportation and communication; and
4. the spatial expansion of social networks "from below" that facilitate the reproduction of migration, business practices, cultural beliefs, and political agency.

The challenge then is twofold, namely: to integrate macro- and micro-determinants into analysis, and to develop an appropriate research strategy capable of capturing the complexity of transnational processes. In undertaking this task it should be kept in mind that it is impossible to study unmediated agency; structural factors are omnipresent. The definition of an appropriate unit of analysis is thus central to the exercise of situating transnationalism. Should the unit be the individual, the household, transnational organizations, the global system, or all of the above?

Three major shortcomings have limited the explanatory power and reliability of existing theories of transnationalism. We will discuss each of these in turn. The first is the use of disparate and not always clearly stated levels of analysis. If scholars of transnationalism were to state at the outset the level of analysis they were using, particularly whether it was macro-, meso-, or micro-structural, this would help define not only the unit of analysis, but also the most suitable research methods to use. Each level of analysis has advantages and limitations not only for what can be examined, but more importantly, for the extent to which the researcher can generalize from her or his inquiry.

Given the complexity of transnational processes, we think that a fruitful approach for future transnational research would be to start from a meso-structural vantage point, the point at which institutions interact with structural and instrumental processes. This would facilitate incorporating into one's analysis both the effects of macrostructural processes and those generated by micro-structures and practices. In contrast, starting from the macro-structural vantage point may lead to the kind of overgeneralization that produces the self-fulfilling "grand theories" that have been the postmodern object of derision. This is particularly problematic when scholars become so wrapped up in the theoretical elegance of their formulations, e.g., "late capitalism," or time-space "distantiation" or "compression," that they altogether ignore empirical analysis of the world "out there" (See for example, Jameson 1984; Giddens 1991; Harvey 1990). The contribution to this volume by André Drainville nicely avoids this pitfall by grounding the analysis of the social production of the hegemonic ideology of neo-liberalism in the political practices of historically specific macro-level actors "from above" as well as the particular forms of resistance that are emerging "from-below."

Other contributors to this volume have avoided the equally problematic pitfall of starting analysis at the micro-structural level, namely, that in privileging "personal knowledge," researchers may develop a kind of solipsistic tunnel vision that altogether fails to connect human intentions to social structure and historical change. One of the most complicated components to investigate is that of the micro-dimension of transnationalism. To understand transnationalism from below as well as from above, it is crucial to systematically study the translocal micro-reproduction of transnational ties. Specifically, it is crucial to determine how transnational networks work, and in that sense, how principles of trust and solidarity are constructed across national territories as compared to those which are locally based and maintained. What discourses and practices hold these principles in place? How are social closure and control organized across borders to guarantee loyalty and curtail malfeasance? How do transnational relations interact with local power structures, including class, gender and racial hierarchies? More generally, how does translocality affect the sociocultural basis supporting transnational relations and ties?

This task presents serious challenges as well as new opportunities for creative scholarship. All of the contributors to this volume who have used field research have been required by the character of the transnational processes of investment, migration, and political organization to pursue a multi-locational research strategy that crisscrosses national, cultural, and institutional boundaries. For example, Louisa Schien's inventive deployment of unorthodox ethnographic methods moves back and forth between text and context, observation and participation, the United States and China, acting out her self described role as an ethnographic nomad. This flexible and reflexive approach is also apparent in the postmodern reading of Dominican migrant women's identities provided by Ninna Sørensen in the Dominican Republic, the United States and Spain. The study of rural Mexican and Salvadoran transnationals, members of the Haitian diaspora, Belizian transnational households, and Hong Kong Chinese transnational entrepreneurs all require multipositionality. As James Clifford (1992) has suggested, the study of "travelling cultures" requires travelling researchers.[3]

The second common conceptual pitfall in transnational studies has been a conflation that confuses transnational social relations with the effects of these relations on social organization and regrouping in the nations involved. Often, analytical conceptualizations of *how* transnational relations take place, such as through a "transnational social network"or by means of a "transnational circuit," are interchangeably used with other concepts that speak to the social organization emerging from transnational practices, e.g., "transnational communities" or "binational societies." Moreover, the theorized transnational spaces in which these actions occur, i.e., "transnational social fields" (Glick Schiller et. al. 1992, 1995), are often rather carelessly thrown into the cauldron of transnationalism. Regardless of the theoretical richness and utility that researchers have given to each of these conceptualizations, it is important to keep in mind the theoretical differences among each of these types of conceptualization and to consider the implications of each.

It is important to try to sort out which of these conceptualizations carries the most promise for future research directions. A useful starting point in this exercise is to ask which captures more of the discernable consequences of transnationalism on social organization and restructuring. Given the complexity and unevenness of this emerging social organization, the concept of "transnational social formation," seems to offer some promise of capturing what is actually happening. This is because this conceptualization signifies the transterritorialization of a complex array of socioeconomic and political asymmetries, hegemonic discourses, and contradictory cultural practices and identities, which center around the formation and reconstitution of the nation-state. It implies a process in which what has conventionally been seen as belonging within well defined territorial boundaries (i.e, political institutions and practices as well as social and cultural relations), has spilled over national borders, producing something new, namely new social formations.

The third limitation of existing knowledge about transnationalism is the lack of comparative studies. Future research centered on the comparative analysis of diverse cases of transnationalism would clearly advance the field. Comparative studies are needed at different scales and may take different forms. Several examples of particularly useful comparisons come to mind:

    a)   comparing the practices of the same group in different lo-
           calities, whether it is a migrant group or a participating
           component of a transnational social movement, to deter-
           mine the effect of localities;
    b)   comparing and contrasting forms of transnational practices
           undertaken by different groups in similar locations, to ex-
           amine the effect of group differences;
    c)   comparing the practices of migrants and states vis-à-vis
           transmigration in different broadly geo-political regions
           (e.g., Latin America and the Asian-Pacific) to determine if
           differences within regions are greater than differences be-
           tween regions;
    d)   comparing the consequences of neo-liberal policies in dif-
           ferent places where they have been "localized" to tease
           out new spaces of domination, accommodation, and
           resistance.

In all of these cases systematic comparative examination can shed light on key differences and similarities of contemporary transnationalism.

In studying transnational processes, as Mahler has suggested, a sense of scale, and thus some common indicators, are needed to determine the weight and prevalence, as well as the frequency, density, and intensity of transnational relations in the societies and communities involved. We believe, however, that this search for empirical measures of scale, scope, and impact should be undertaken with caution. Quantitative measurement cannot replace qualitative investigation of social, economic, and political processes. Quantitative and qualitative analysis are complementary. Thus, quantitative evidence of transnational processes should be qualified by interpreting it in the context of ethnographic insights which quantitative methods cannot capture.

In doing this, it must be kept in mind that positivist taxonomies can lead to the erroneous conceptualization of transnationalisms as "things" that can be readily "measured" such that a person or group may be conceived as being "more or less transnational." Transnationalism is neither a thing nor a continuum of events that can be easily quantified. It is a complex process involving macro-

and micro-dynamics. In our view, a main concern guiding transnational research should be the study of the causes of transnationalism and the effects that transnational practices and discourses have on preexisting power structures, identities, and social organization. Put differently, the causes and consequences of transnationalism, from above and below, ought to form the center of the transnational research agenda. Both quantitative and qualitative methods ought to focus on elucidating these questions.

Whether using ethnographic, quantitative, or comparative-historical methods, transnational studies must clearly identify social and political agency—i.e., who initiates and thus who determines the direction of any transnational action under study. In investigating the "above" and the "below" of transnational action, we should guard against the common mistake of equating "above" exclusively with global structures or agents. Categorizing transnational actions as coming from "above" and from "below" aims at capturing the dynamics of power relations in the transnational arena. By definition, these categories are contextual and relational. Thus they cannot be taken as essential, immutable categories. As Schein's study so pointedly shows, Hmong cultural brokers act "from below" vis-à-vis the United States and Chinese states by transgressing traditional borders while simultaneously they act "from above" vis-à-vis the Miao objects of their tourist gaze. Similarly, the explicit or implicit intentionality of the agent undertaking an action carries tremendous sociological weight, regardless of the final intended and unintended consequences of the action. Thus, we must avoid, at all costs, confusing intentionality with consequences, as when actors are designated "resistant" or "oppositional" because their practices produce some social change, even when it was not one they intended, fought for, or socially organized. In the last instance, as we have shown, "transnationalism from below" must be located and historicized if its is to have any meaningful referent capable of being studied now or in the future.

Notes

1. We wish to thank Alexis Ohran for her able editorial support at all stages of our work on this volume, John Dale for his editorial scrutiny of the final manuscript, and Anita LaViolette for her expert assistance in preparing the final manuscript for publication. We are indebted to the insightful work of each of the authors contributing to this volume as well as to the anonymous reviewers who assisted us in the difficult task of selecting articles from among the many fine manuscripts submitted in response to our call for papers for Volume 6.

2. With respect to class structuration, the queuing of migrants into particular socioeconomic positions abroad is maintained not only by such contextual forces as labor market conditions and employers' recruitment patterns, but also by the inertia of social networks. Ethnic labor niche formation, based on social networking, has been widely documented by migration scholars (Waldinger 1994, 1996; Model 1993; Portes and Borocsz 1989; Lieberson 1980). However, aggregate data tend to overlook the effects of regionalism and ethnic stratification among people coming from the same country, with all the inequalities they imply. For example, the subordination of and discrimination against indigeneous peoples in countries of origin are reproduced upon immigration, as in the case of Mexican Mixtecs in California (See Zabin 1995).

3. This approach is greatly facilitated by contemporary means of transportation and communication. However, emergent patterns of transnational mobility place significant limitations on this research approach. Transmigrants from the same country of origin are now leaving from more regions and are following a more diverse and more diasporic migratory path than in the past. For example, in addition to the United States, significant and increasing numbers of Caribbean, Latin American and Asian populations are also migrating within their own regions and to Europe and Japan. More often than not these migrants are moving to more than one location in the countries of destination making their geographical dispersion more intense and more difficult to track by lone researchers. To counter these limitations, the ethno-centric and sometimes even imperialistic approach traditionally used by scholars from core countries should be revised and transnational, collaborative projects with scholars in countries of origin should be explored.

References

Alarcon, Rafael. (1994). "Labor Migration from Mexico and Free Trade: Lessons from a Transnational Commuity," Berkeley: Chicano/Latino Policy Project Working Paper 1: 1.

Anderson, Benedict. (1983). *Imagined Communities: Reflections on the Growth and Spread of Nationalism*. New York and London: Verso. Reprinted 1991.

Appadurai, Arjun. (1990). "Disjuncture and Difference in the Global Culture Economy." *Theory,Culture and Society* 7: 295-310.

————. (1996). *Modernity at Large: Cultural Dimensions of Globalization*. Minneapolis: University of Minnesota Press.

Barkin, David, Ortiz, Irene, and Rosen, Fred. (1997). "Globalization and Resistance: The Remaking of Mexico." *NACLA Report on the Americas* 30:4: 14-27.

Linda Basch, Nina Glick Schiller, and Cristina Szanton Blanc. (1994). *Nations Unbound: Transnational Projects, Postcolonial Predicaments and the Deterritorialized Nation-State*. New York: Gordon and Breach Publishers.

Bhabha, Homi K. (1990). "DissemiNation: Time, Narrative and the Margins of the Modern Nation." Homi K. Bhabha (ed.), *Nation and Narration*. New York: Routledge. Pp. 291-322.

Brysk, Allison. (1993). "From Above and Below: Social Movements, the International System, and Human Rights in Argentina." *Comparative Political Studies* 26:3: 259-285.

Buell, Frederick. (1994). *National Culture and the New Global System*. Baltimore: The Johns Hopkins University.

Clifford, James. (1992). "Traveling Cultures." In Grossberg et al (eds.), *Cultural Studies*. New York: Routledge. Pp. 96-116.

Dirlik, Arif. (1996). "The Global in the Local." In Rob Wilson and Wimal Dissanayake (eds.), *Global/Local: Cultural Production and the Transnational Imaginary*. Durham: Duke University Press.

Eisenstadt, T.A. and C. L. Thorup. (1994). *Caring Capacity versus Carrying Capacity: Community Responses to Mexican Immigration in San Diego's North County*. San Diego: Center for U.S.-Mexican Studies, University of California, Monograph Series, No. 39.

Giddens, Anthony. (1991). *Modernity and Self-Identity: Self and Society in the Late Modern Age*. Stanford: Stanford University Press.

Glick Schiller, Nina, Linda Basch, and Cristina Szanton Blanc. (1995). "From Immigrant to Transmigrant: Theorizing Transnational Migration." *Anthropological Quarterly* 68:1: 48-63.

————. (1992). "Transnationalism: A New Analytical Framework for Understanding Migraton." In Glick Schiller, et al (eds.), *Toward a Transnational Perspective on Migration: Race, Class, Ethnicity and Nationalism Reconsidered* New York: New York Academy of Sciences. Pp. 1-24.

Guarnizo, Luis E. (1996). "The Nation-State and Grassroots Transnationalism: Comparing Mexican and Dominican Transmigration." Paper presented at 118th Annual American Ethnological Association Meeting, San Juan, Puerto Rico, April.

————. (1997). "Going Home: Class, Gender and Household Transformation Among Dominican Return Migrants." In Patricia R. Pessar (ed.), *Caribbean Circuits: New Directions in the Study of Caribbean Migration*. New York: Center for Migration Studies.

Hannerz, Ulf. (1989). "Notes on the Global Ecumene." *Public Culture* 1:2: 66-75.

————. (1996). *Transnational Connections*. London and New York: Routledge.

Harvey, David. (1990). *The Condition of Postmodernity: An Inquiry into the Origins of Cultural Change*. Cambridge, MA: Blackwell.

Hoerder, Dirk. (1985). "Acculturation Twice: Return Migration." In Dirk Hoerder (ed.), *Labor Migration in the Atlantic Economies: The European and North American Working Classes During the Period of Industrialization.* Wesport, Connecticut: Greenwood Press.

Hondagneu-Sotelo, Pierrette (1994). *Gendered Transitions: Mexican Experiences of Immigration.* Berkeley: University of California Press.

Jacobson, Matthew F. (1995). *Special Sorrows: The Diasporic Imagination of Irish, Polish, and Jewish Immigrants in the United States.* Cambridge, MA: Harvard University Press.

Jameson, Frederic. (1984). "Postmodernism, or the Cultural Logic of Late Capitalism," *New Left Review,* 146: 53-92.

Kearney, Michael. (1991). "Borders and Boundaries of State and Self at the End of Empire." *Journal of Historical Sociology,* Volume 4, March.

Lessinger, Johanna. (1992). "Investing or Going Home? A Transnational Strategy Among Indian Immigrants in the United States." In Nina Glick Schiller, Linda Basch, and Cristina Szanton Blanc (eds.), *Toward a Transnational Perspective on Migration: Race, Class, Ethnicity, and Nationalism Reconsidered.* New York: Annals of the New York Academy of Sciences 645. Pp. 53-80.

Levitt, Peggy. (1994). "God and Country: How the Transnationalization of Politics and Religion Affects Women." Paper presented at the Annual Meeting of the American Sociological Association, Los Angeles. August.

Lieberson, Stanley. (1980). *A Piece of the Pie.* Berkeley: University of California Press.

Mahler, Sarah J. (1996). *American Dreaming: Immigrant Life on the Margins.* Princeton, NJ: Princeton University Press.

Massey, Douglas, Rafael Alarcon, Jorge Durand, Humberto Gonzalez. (1987). *Return to Aztlan: The Social Process Of International Migration from Western Mexico.* Berkeley: University of California Press.

Mitchell, Katharyne. (1993). "Multiculturalism, or the United Colors of Capitalism?" *Antipode* 25: 263-94.

———. (1996). "In Whose Interest? Transnational Capital and the Production of Multiculturalism in Canada." In Rob Wilson and Wimal Dissanayake (eds.), *Global/Local: Cultural Production and the Transnational Imaginary.* Pp. 219-254.

Model, Suzanne. (1993). "The Ethnic Niche and the Structure of Opportunity: Immigrants and Minorities in New York City." In Michael B. Katz (ed.), *The "Underclass" Debate: Views from History.* Princeton: Princeton University Press.

Nagengast, Carole and Kearny, Michael. (1990). "Mixtec Ethnicity: Social Identity, Political Consciousness, and Political Activism." *Latin American Research Review* 25: 2: 61-91.

Ong, Aihwa. (1996). "Chinese Modernities: Narratives of Nation and of Capitalism." In A. Ong and D. Nonini, (eds.), *Ungrounded Empires: The Cultural Politics of Modern Chinese Transnationalism.* New York: Routledge. Pp. 171-203.

Pessar, Patricia. (1994). "Sweatshop Workers and Domestic Ideologies: Dominican Women in New York's Apparel Industry." *International Journal of Urban and Regional Research* 18:1: 127-42.

Portes, Alejandro. (1995). "Transnational Communities: Their Emergence and Significance in the Contemporary World System." Working Papers Series, No. 16. Program in Comparative and International Development, Department of Sociology, The Johns Hopkins University. July.

————. (1996). "Global Villagers: The Rise of Transnational Communities." *The American Prospect* 2: 74-77.

Portes, Alejandro and Joseph Borocz. (1989). "Contemporary Immigration: Theoretical Perspectives on its Determinants and Modes of Incorporation." *International Migration Review* 23:3: 606-30.

Portes, Alejandro and Ruben G. Rumbaut. (1990). *Immigrant America: A Portrait*. Berkeley: University of California Press.

Robbins, Bruce. (1993). "Comparative Cosmopolitanisms." In Bruce Robbins *Secular Vocations: Intellectuals, Professionalism, Culture*. London: Verso. Pp. 180-211.

Rosenblum, Gerald. (1973). *Immigrant Workers: Their Impact on American Labor Relations*. New York: Basic Books.

Rouse, Roger. (1992). "Making Sense of Settlement: Class Transformation, Cultural Struggle, and Transnationalism Among Mexican Migrants in the United States." In Nina Glick Schiller, Linda Basch, and Cristina Szanton Blanc (eds.), *Toward a Transnational Perspective on Migration: Race, Class, Ethnicity, and Nationalism Reconsidered*. New York: Annals of the New York Academy of Sciences 645. Pp. 22-55.

Sassen, Saskia. (1991). *The Global City: New York, London, and Tokyo*. Princeton, NJ: Princeton University Press.

Sassen-Koob, Saskia. (1984). "The New Labor Demand in Global Cities." In Michael Peter Smith (ed.), *Cities in Transformation: Class, Capital, and the State*. Beverly Hills: Sage.

————. (1987) "Growth and Informalization at the Core: A Preliminary Report on New York City," In Michael Peter Smith and Joe R. Feagin (eds.), *The Capitalist City: Global Restructuring and Community Politics*: Oxford: Blackwell. Pp. 138-154.

Shapiro, Michael. (1992). *Reading the Postmodern Polity*. Minneapolis: University of Minnesota Press.

Sikkink, Kathryn. (1993). "Human Rights, Principled Issue Networks, and Sovereignty in Latin America," *International Organization* 47:3: 411-441.

Smith, Michael Peter. (1992). "Postmodernism, Urban Ethnography, and the New Social Space of Ethnic Identity," *Theory and Society* 21: 493-531.

————. (1994). "Can You Imagine? Transnational Migration and the Globalization of Grassroots Politics." *Social Text* 39: 15-33.

Smith, Michael Peter and Bernadette Tarallo. (1993). *California's Changing Faces: New Immigrant Survival Strategies and State Policy*. Berkeley: California Policy Seminar.

Soja, Edward. (1996). *Thirdspace: Journeys to Los Angeles and Other Real-and-Imagined Places*. Cambridge, MA: Blackwell.

Tardanico, Richard. (1995). "Economic Crisis and Structural Adjustment: The Changing Labor Market of San Jose, Costa Rica." In M.P. Smith (ed.), *After Modernism: Global Restructuring and the Changing Boundaries of City Life. Comparative Urban and Community Research* 4. New Brunswick: Transaction .

Tölölyan, Khachig. (1996). "Rethinking Diaspora(s): Stateless Power in the Transnational Moment." *Diaspora* 5:1: 3-36.

Waldinger, Roger. (1994). "The Making of an Immigrant Niche." *International Migration Review* 28:1: 3-30.

———. (1996). *Still the Promised City? African Americans and New Immigrants in Postindustrial New York.* Cambridge, MA: Harvard University Press.

Zabin, Carol. (1995). "Mixtecs and Mestizos in California Agriculture: Ethnic Displacement and Hierarchy among Mexican Farm Workers." In Michael Peter Smith (ed.) *Marginal Spaces. Comparative Urban and Community Research* 5. New Brunswick, N.J.: Transaction. Pp. 114-143.

2

The Fetishism of Global Civil Society:
Global Governance, Transnational Urbanism and Sustainable Capitalism in the World Economy

André C. Drainville

> *This book opens with a city that was, symbolically, a world: it closes with a world that has become, in many practical aspects, a city.*
> —Lewis Mumford, The City in History

In the last chapter of *Age of Extremes*, Eric Hobsbawm looked to the new millennium and reflected on a world "entirely lack[ing] any international system or structure" and moving towards "a global disorder whose nature [is] unclear, and without an obvious mechanism for either ending it or keeping it under control" (Hobsbawm 1994: 559, 562).

Had he sought to "forecast" the new millennium rather than gain historical perspective on a decomposing century, Hobsbawm might rather have emphasized the emergence, in the last 20 years or so, of transnational attempts to devise new mechanisms of order in the world economy and keep social relations under control.[1] Rather than write of the world's "slide into instability" (Hobsbawm 1994: 562), he might have drawn historical parallels (as does the UN's Commission on Global Governance, the CGG) between, on the one hand, the Westphalian peace conferences of 1648 (which signaled the birth of the modern inter-state system) and the 1815 Congress of Vienna (which inaugurated the hundred years peace of the 19th century) and, on the other hand, the upcoming "Conference on Global Reform" (projected for 1998), which will aim to define the boundaries of transnational order in the post-Westphalian period.

A short history of transnational projects for global order at the close of the twentieth century would have to begin with monetarism in the years immediately following the collapse of the Bretton Woods system, and include later calls to order: debt restructuring in the 1980s, the new world order of the Gulf War, and the "new global economic partnership" forecasted by G7 countries at the London summit of 1991. Finally, and perhaps most importantly, this history would have to contend with, as we propose to do, the rise of "global governance" in the world economy.

As we shall see, global governance represents an attempt to move transnationally-constructed order beyond the coercive enforcement of managerial devices towards a politically more enduring and consensual "global framework for actions and policies..." (Commission on Global Governance 1995: 5). Revealingly, this attempt has framed politics in the world economy in distinctly civic terms. In the spirit of global governance, both international organizations whose task it is to manage and reproduce the world economy and groups and popular movements which purport to change it, have begun speaking of "global civic ethics," "global neighborhoods," and of a global civil society in the making. In the spirit of governance as well, authors such as Paul Ekin (1992), Richard Falk (1995), David Held (1992), Paul Wapner (1995) and Thomas Weiss (Weiss and Gordenker 1996a), amongst many others who have begun documenting what Wapner called "world civic politics, which takes place in global civil society" (Wapner 1995: 153), have written of globalizing citizenship and civility, and they have drawn a direct historical connection between politics in the Greek *polis* and in the contemporary world economy. Enthusiastic about global urbanism, but misunderstanding the abstract/ideological nature of governance's civic calls, some commentators have even gone so far as to call for such a concretely urban initiative as a *Pacte fédéral pour les chantiers urbains du XXIe siècle* reminiscent of the *grands projets* of Haussmann or Le Corbusier's *Plan Voisin*.[2]

Such images of civic covenants on a global scale should not be dismissed lightly as either rhetorical flights of fancy masking the coerciveness of transnational *conjuratios*, or as the romantic notions of presumed internationalists who imagine themselves at the center of a global agora in the making. As we shall see, they tell us something essential about contemporary attempts to manage and transform the contemporary world economy, and to re-create on a global scale the political cohesiveness of the *polis*.

This article proposes to take civic imagery of global governance—rather more literally than it was intended to be—as a heuristic device. It is, in fact, an attempt to explore the relationship between what Fernand Braudel called the defining cities of *économies-mondes* (in historical succession: Venice, Genoa, Amsterdam, London and New York) and the rather more abstract, ideologically-created, global city of global governance. It aims to better situate global governance as a moment in the history of organized capitalism on a world scale.

The article can be read as the continuation of a critical exploration of the ideology of global governance I began in a recent article entitled "Of Social Spaces, Citizenship and the Nature of Power in the World Economy." There, I emphasized that governance's global city was in fact more of a private enclave of transnational capital, and that the principal political process at work in its making was the ostracisation of social relationships to the peripheral spaces of national social formations. In conclusion, I also emphasized the role of states as political gatekeepers of the world economy:

> it appears...that political transformation in the world economy...relies both on the confinement of political and social relationships to the space of national social formations, and on the capacity of states to structure political participation.... [International organizations and states have] in effect build a wall around the space [they] are attempting to manage (Drainville 1995b).

However, as Weber emphasized, there is more to cities than walls, and our analysis of the dynamics of order in the contemporary world economy ought not to stop at exclusionary processes, but should also look at the making of a compliant citizenry. This is the intention of this article. It is divided into three sections. The first section documents the short history of transnational efforts to re-define the terms of order in the world economy. This history leads from fragmentary and coercive ideas of transnational order to the transnational urbanism of global governance, ostensibly negotiated with an emerging global civil society. In the second section, cosmopolitan claims concerning the emergence of this "global civil society" are situated historically and contrasted with the rise of the more modest transnationalism of social movements. The last section of the article attempts to put the first two together and examine the politics of the cosmopolitan calls to order issued by the organs of global governance.

Two Phases of Order in the World Economy

The short history of transnational blueprints for order in the post-Bretton Woods period can be told in two chapters. First, in the decade after the convertibility of the American dollar was suspended in 1971, an implosion of power took place in the world economy which announced what Lewis Mumford would have called the "concentrated act of will" needed to steer the birth of new urban forms. In this period, a specifically transnational response to the crisis took shape in organizations such as the International Monetary Fund, the World Bank and the Organization for Economic Cooperation and Development, as well as in private transnational organizations (most notably in the Trilateral Commission). For the most part, these institutions had been part of the nationally-centered edifice of *Pax Americana*, but became increasingly autonomous (and increasingly transnational) during the first phase of the Bretton Woods crisis. This first transnational act of will begot monetarism, hard conditionality and other coercive measures quickly shown to be politically unsustainable. As we shall see, transnational strategies constructed in the beginning of the Bretton Woods crisis dealt with crises (of monetary equivalences, national debtor solvency, payment imbalances, etc.) in a piecemeal fashion. Furthermore, they had no social moorings in the world economy itself, and relied either on transnational coercion or on nationally-constructed consensus. Monetarism, and the IMF's policy of "strict conditionality," to take but two early examples of post-crisis transnational policy frameworks, were about enforcing a transnational order constructed *ex cathedra*, beyond the national level where was woven the fabric of civil society. They took for granted the soundness of global capitalism itself, and spoke of the unremitting exigencies of global accumulation, and of unnegotiable transnationally-constructed imperatives. As I have argued elsewhere (Drainville 1995b), these early-crisis strategies showed the world economy to be the preserved domain of transnational capital, and world order to be a shallow and unsustainable bourgeois covenant imposed onto the world.

In the second chapter of the short history of post-Bretton Woods plans for order, the strategy of global governance attempts to define global notions of civility and settle matters with selected transnational partners. It is in this period that appears the discourse of global civility and that non-governmental organizations become both relevant social interlocutors of transnational capital, and essential components of a global civil society tailor-made from above in the convivial salons of the United Nations.

Transnational Order in the Immediate Post-Bretton Woods Period

From the point of view of its political configuration, the world economy in the age of *Pax Americana* looked more like a conduit between nationally-structured social relations than an autonomous social sphere: Keynesianism and Fordism were principally about the national management of the conditions of accumulation; the Bretton Woods monetary regime was inter-national in the strictest sense of the term, as were GATT trading rules, ILO codes of conduct, OECD reviews and prescriptions and efforts to regulate international migrations and trans-border pollution, limit human rights abuses, and defend human security (issues later to be at the heart of "good governance"). As Nicos Poulantzas put it, the national state was the organizing principle of capitalist accumulation in the post-war period (Poulantzas 1971: 40-41). Yet, *Pax Americana* was also a period of historically unprecedented ideological homogeneity in the center of the world economy, which facilitated what Robert Cox called a "process of inter-state consensus formation regarding the needs or requirements of the world economy..." (Cox 1987: 254) and Stephen Gill identified as the "growth of transnational networks of interests and identity" (Gill 1991).

In the years immediately following the beginning of the Bretton Woods crisis, this transnational network acquired a cohesiveness of its own and gained an increasing measure of autonomy from structured inter-state relationships. To borrow again from Poulantzas, we could say that a "reading" of the conditions of accumulation took place more and more at the transnational level, both in familiar institutions such as the World Bank, the IMF and the OECD, but also, increasingly, in more discrete locales, such as the Bank for International Settlements, which played a key role in the rise of monetarism in the immediate post-Bretton Woods period (Drainville 1995a), the Trilateral Commission, G7 meetings, and in such private regulatory institutions as debt securities and bond rating agencies.[3] About the increasing autonomy and authority of this transnational network in relations to states (even those at the center of the world economy), and about its privileged relationship with transnational capital, little need be said here. As the principal topic of interest of what Craig N. Murphy and Roger Tooze (1991) called the "New International Political Economy," these questions have been well documented and theorized.

What has not been as well theorized, however, is the relationship between this increasingly autonomous transnational network, and the later rise of global governance in the world economy. Without examining this relationship, the civic imagery and consensual discourse of global governance look unprecedented and, indeed, radical.

Using the distinctively cosmopolitan vernacular of global governance to explore both its historical lineage and its future trajectory, we could say that the growth of transnational regulation in the years immediately following the beginning of the Bretton Woods crisis corresponds to what Lewis Mumford called the "founding moment" of cities: the implosion of power which transformed the pre-urban notions of community togetherness and consensus that prevailed in hamlets and villages into urban civility. This implosion, according to Mumford, was the product of the simultaneous extension of inter-village intercourse "through raidings and tradings, through seizures and commandeerings, through migrations and enslavement, through tax gatherings and the wholesale conscription of labor" (Mumford 1961: 46) and of the increasing concentration of power resulting from the consolidation of temporal and religious power into the institution of kingship from which stemmed the "concentrated act of will" required to transform the decentralized village economy into an organized and hierarchical urban economy. The first movement increased the importance of those walled hamlets which served as relay stations in a broadening material space, and the second increased the role of cities as centers of power. Together, they engendered urban civilization: "that peculiar combination of creativity and control, of expression and repression, of tension and release" (Mumford 1961: 41). For Mumford, city walls contained the implosion that begot urban civility.

As the Parisian *école de la régulation* emphasized, post-war capitalism was organized principally at the level of nation-states. There were negotiated what Robert Boyer (1986) called the four institutional forms which gave its distinctive configuration to the fordist regime of accumulation (the forms of money, wage relations, competition, as well as the organized relationship between nationally-centered regimes and the world economy as a whole), and there was the principal focal point of structured political struggles. Thus, at a first level, the world economy in the Bretton Woods period, grew as an internationally-structured economy where even export-oriented economies (that of Japan for example) remained very much their own centers of gravity.

This was also a period when global intercourse grew at an unprecedented rate, and when a truly transnational economy took shape between, and increasingly *above*, nationally-centered economies. A great many indicators point to this growth of global intercourse: strategic alliances between multinational corporations, world exports and international productive investments all grew in an unprecedented fashion and gelled into what Eric Hobsbawm (1994) called a "transnational process of manufacture" and the Lisbon group (Groupe de Lisbonne 1995) a "Made in the World" production process. Furthermore, what Pierre Salama (1989) labeled the "dollarisation" of national currencies (that is to say the process whereby national currencies became the local expression of an increasingly transnational monetary equivalent) also underlined the transnational redefinition of monetary relationships, as did the transnational monetary standards that began emerging from the hulk of the Bretton Woods monetary regime: Eurodollars, Petrodollars, Special Drawing Rights, and the like.

The growth of inter-national intercourse continued apace through the first phases of the Bretton Woods crisis. Though it appeared to its contemporaries (Amin et al. 1982, for example) as a crisis of capitalism itself, the Bretton Woods crisis was rather that of the particular inter-national regime which had steered global accumulation since the end of the second world war. It is this inter-national dimension of the crisis which was signaled by the suspension of the convertibility of the American dollar (and its subsequent devaluation), and continues to this day to be highlighted by national monetary and debt crises (the Pound's crisis of September 1992 and the Pesos devaluation of December 1994 to mention but two salient examples). The intensification of global intercourse (what fashionable vernacular calls "globalization") continued to progress at its considerable post-war pace through the first phase of the Bretton Woods crisis and beyond. From this transnational growth came what Kees Van der Pijl called the *esprit de corps* of the Atlantic managerial class (van der Pijl 1989).

In the first phase of the Bretton Woods crisis inter-national organizations such as the OECD, the World Bank, the IMF, the BIS and the Trilateral Commission became, as the "New International Political Economy" emphasized, increasingly autonomous centers of power. This increased autonomy was the result both of a structural progression and of very conjunctural conditions. To speak of structural developments is to link the increasing autonomy and coherence of transnational organizations managing the world economy to the historical growth of transnational capitalism and of a transnational capital *pour soi*, and to their separateness from nationally-centered economies. To speak of the conjunctural elements is to emphasize that the autonomy and coherence of international organizations was also linked to the political role they played both as meeting-places where was organized the specifically transnational political response to the crisis of (national) Fordism/Keynesianism in the center of the world economy, and as organizers of the response of advanced capitalist countries to G7 demands for a New International Economic Order based on the defense of the "common heritage of humankind." To these demands, which took shape in specialized organizations and conferences of the United Nations principally at the UNCTAD, UNCLOS and the UNESCO but also through producers' associations such as OPEC, advanced capitalist countries at the center of the world economy and, increasingly, international organizations such as the World Bank and the OECD, opposed an increasingly coherent neoliberal cosmopolitanism, centered on the long-term interest of transnational financial capital. Thus, the manifold political dynamics of the Bretton Woods crisis (at once a crisis of national modes of regulation in advanced capitalist countries; of the structuring of inter-national relations between countries at the center of the world economy, and between them and peripheral countries) created a context where inter-national institutions born in the post-war period under the hegemonical leadership of core countries at the center of the traditional inter-national division of labor re-centered an increasingly transnational division of labor around new, transnational, social forces with no national moorings.

This re-centering was profoundly important to global governance. Inasmuch as it signaled the birth of a new, transnational capital *pour soi*, removed from the national level at which social relations had hitherto been organized, the first phase of the Bretton Woods crisis is to the ideology of governance, and the global city it projects, what the development of the institution of kingship represented to Mumford: it is an implosion of power, that is to say a systemic revolution from within that begot a transnationally-concentrated act of will, which will later presume to transform what Marshall McLuhan called "global togetherness" into a codified and bounded transnational civic ethics.

As I have argued elsewhere, this global city of transnational capital took shape, in this first moment, as a private enclave first noticeable by the coercive measures taken to shelter its residents from social relations. These measures included the strengthening of national ties of citizenship and states-bound political processes, the ostracization of citizens to national territories, as well as the shrinking of their political capabilities (linked to what Stephen Gill called "neo-liberal constitutionalism").[4] Thus, though the literature on "global cities" that started becoming popular in the beginning of the 1980s referred, almost matter-of-factly, to transnational capitalists as citizens of the world, Thomas Wolfe's image of self-conscious "Master of the Universe," or Lewis Mumford's "powerful gods" who succeeded in bringing captive farm populations to order (Mumford 1961: 63) are more appropriate to this first period.[5]

Global Governance

Borrowing still from Mumford and from the civic language prevalent in contemporary discourses on transnational order, we could say that global governance represents an attempt to summon law and order and create "social comity" from above (Mumford 1961: 63). For Mumford, this summing up is an effort at reconciliation and accommodation with the involuntary residents of cities, and is a decisive moment in the crystallization of urban forms and the making of urban civility. Where the king had all the power to keep farm populations captive and institute law and order, the settling of emerging social relations, and the collective transcendence distinctive of true civility, though they can be hastened—and, to a certain extent, framed—by royal intervention, are the result of relatively autonomous processes.

Similar processes are at work in the ideology of global governance, which began to take shape in the latter parts of the 1980s and continues to guide the work of increasingly autonomous transnational organizations which are managing and reproducing the conditions of global accumulation. It is in relation to these efforts that we can make sense of cosmopolitan appeals to global civic values.

Appeals to international law and order were particularly visible in the beginning of this period, when invocation of what Peter Gowan (writing about the Gulf war) labeled a "depoliticized process of crime and judicial punishment" defined the discourse of the New World Order (Gowan 1991). As George Bush put it in one of the first speeches of the New World Order, "renegade states" would be disciplined.[6] In terms of the short history of global governance, this is the importance of the Gulf War, fought on behalf of the sanctity of UN Security Council resolutions by troops only nominally under its supervision. It is also in relation to this political building up of law and order that we can situate, amongst others, "Operation Just Cause" (the invasion of Panama on December 20, 1989), American efforts (starting in December 1992) to resolve the famine in Somalia through the enforcement of law and order, and the judicial discourse that framed U.S. relations with Libya throughout the 1980s (which accompanied a policy which explicitly excluded appeals to the International Court of Justice). More broadly, we can also include here the principle of "humanitarian interference" defended by Boutros Boutros-Ghali since his arrival as Secretary General of the UN, UN-election monitoring (in El Salvador, Liberia, South Africa and elsewhere) and the increased engagement of UN peacekeeping troops and calls (from the CGG) "for Charter recognition of the UN's right to intervene in domestic situations when there are egregious violations of human security."

More recent efforts to judicialize transnational politics include plans (by, among others, the UN Development Programme, the Independent Working Group on the Future of the United Nations, as well as the CGG) to restructure the United Nations around "Economic Security" and "Development" councils that would be responsible for the coordination of global economic policy and bring development policy under legislated control. A related process is also at work on the issue of the "Tobin tax" on international currency transactions. This is one of the key policy initiatives to have come out of discussions over global governance. At once, the Tobin tax is a global revenue-raising scheme that would give the organs of global governance a source of revenue relatively sheltered from vagaries of inter-state politics, and an attempt to bring global financial markets under transnational political control.

Beyond their appeals to law and order, organs of global governance have also attempted to foster transnational comity by inviting designated agents of an ostensibly emerging global civil society to gather together in order to either deliberate the institutional renewal of UN institutions or, more generally, help solve global problems and define the terms of a sustainable transnational social contract. Thus, in the spirit of governance, international organizations have worked more closely with selected non- or para-governmental organizations to solve global problems. According to their policy objectives and resources at their disposals, governance institutions have set up an architecture of collaboration with chosen NGOs (the "Partners in Action" programme of the UNHCR, and the NGO Resource Center of the UN Department of Public Information for example), or they have increased resource allocation to chosen NGOs. As Leon Gordenker and Thomas Weiss note, the volume of public development aid channeled through NGOs now surpasses that of the combined UN system save the World Bank and the IMF (Weiss 1993: 25).

The double attempt to construct global civil society and settle with it the terms of transnational civility is most clearly at work in the global social and economic summits organized by the United Nations. There have been six summits held so far in the 1990s: the United Nations Conference on Environment and Development (Rio de Janeiro, June 1992), the World Conference on Human Rights (Vienna 1993), the International Conference on Population and Development (ICPD, Cairo 1994), the World Summit for Social Development (Copenhagen, March 1995), the Fourth World Conference on Women (WCW, Beijing, September 1995), and Habitat II (Istanbul 1996). If the Conference on Global Reform called for by the CGG indeed takes place as anticipated in 1998, it will close this chapter in the construction of transnational civility.

As we shall see, summits are to global governance what world fairs were to free-trade internationalism from the second half of the 19th century to the second world war: they are idealized representations of a projected order and (to borrow from Walter Benjamin's critique of Universal Exhibits), "phantasmagorical" destinations of transnational pilgrims who come to fetishise order on display. Starting with the "Great Exhibition of the Industry of all Nations" (London, 1851), universal exhibits displayed the best of merchandise promised by free-trade capitalism and celebrated the universalist appeal of exchange value rather than the particularisms of use value. Global summits in the 1990s attempt to put on display a scale-model of global civil society that transcends (local, regional, national, gender or class) specificities and complements "world-class cities" and "technopoles" that have become the landing points of transnational capital.7

At stake in debates over global civil society is the relationship between these cosmopolitan phantasmagorias being created in, or in the vicinity, of the salons of global governance, and politics elsewhere in the world economy. This is the subject of the last two sections of this text.

Global Civil Society and the
Transnationalism of Social Movements:
From International Solidarity to Transnational Civility

As I have argued elsewhere, the history of popular internationalism can be read as a collection of encounters between universalist-cosmopolitan projects to reinvent social relations from above, and a more reluctant "internationalism from below" which sees internationalism as a sometimes-necessary means to continue struggles rooted in particular conditions and in specific sites of the world economy. While the former offer an immediate answer to bourgeois cosmopolitanism in the form of an alternative cosmopolitanism, transnationalism from below takes the form of a collection of episodic moments of internationalist solidarity with little programmatic, strategic or political coherence (Drainville 1995a).

In the period between the beginning of what F. van Hoolthon and Marcel van der Linden called the 'classical age' of Left internationalism and the end of the cold war, Left internationalism was principally structured from above as a cosmopolitan alternative to bourgeois internationalism (van Hoolthon and van der Linden 1988: vii). Two factors in particular contributed to this. One was the fractionning of Left internationalism (especially after the Berlin congress of 1922), which transformed episodes of internationalist solidarity (the Spanish civil war and the trial and execution of Sacco and Vanzetti to take but two examples), into terrains of struggles between different cosmopolitan programmes, which left little room for internationalist movements not defined in terms of party or state allegiance. The second factor was the preponderance of inter-national politics within the Left's agenda. The Russian civil war, the cold war and related peripheral conflicts in Korea, Indo-China, Egypt, Yemen, etc., as well as the debates over a New International Economic Order and the debt crisis, were all profoundly defining moments of the Left which turned international solidarity into state-bound allegiances and internationalism into an inter-state affair.

In the 20 years since the beginning of the Bretton Woods crisis, the structures shaping internationalism from above have lost much of their ability to over-determine internationalist politics. The end of the cold war has meant the virtual disappearance of the political dynamics of inter-state, inter-party and inter-Internationals relations that had shaped Left internationalism since Marx and Bakhunin split up the First International. As well, the crisis of national frameworks of regulation and the growth of a genuinely transnational division of labor (as well as the corresponding disappearance of an inter-national division of labor centered on a geographically-identifiable center and an outlying periphery), have both diminished the political salience of the cosmopolitan strategies of organizations such as the AFL-CIO and the International Confederation of Free Trade Unions, which were constructed as the projection onto the world economy of national-corporatist alliance, and increased the room for maneuver of transnationalism from below.

It is now possible to speak of two distinct internationalist movements in the contemporary world economy. The first movement is made up of such organizations as Greenpeace, Amnesty International, Peace Brigades International, etc. that have organized decidedly cosmopolitan campaigns and programmes. Theirs is a problem-solving internationalism which (as the *Amici della terra* put it) shuns "extreme and vociferous radicalism" in an attempt to become "crucial partners for any official action on the issues of environment and development" (Amici della Terra 1993). It seeks to transcend specificities and address the problems of humanity as a whole. Amnesty International, for example, functions on a principle of "strict impartiality and independence" which requires of its members (who number more than one million worldwide) that they not become involved in cases in their own countries (Amnesty International 1996).

In this cosmopolitan spirit, NGOs have responded to invitations of global governance in two ways. First they have convened rallies, demonstrations, international caucuses, participated in preparatory meetings and gathered in designated cosmopolitan sites. UN summits in particular have attracted an increasingly greater number of erstwhile citizens of the world economy. In terms of the number of participants, the summits have become amongst the largest internationalist gatherings, comparable to the thousands who fought with the International Brigades in the Spanish civil war, the tens of thousands who gathered worldwide to protest the execution of Sacco and Vanzetti (but not, however to the millions who visited universal exhibits in the 19th century). The smallest of the six summits was the Cairo ICPD, which attracted an estimated 20,000 government delegates, UN, NGO and media representatives. The largest summit was the Beijing WCW, which attracted over 50,000 people. The WCW also formalized and widened the separation between formal Inter-Governmental and informal NGO summits, which had coexisted since the recent renewal of cosmopolitan summits. In Rio, the 1,400 NGO representatives were assembled in a "Global Forum" which they "informally" could leave to lobby government representatives attending the main summit. In Vienna, "representatives of 171 governments met 'upstairs,' and thousands of NGO representatives (some 2,700 representatives from more than 1,500 organizations) passed through the 'downstairs' meeting rooms." In Beijing, the NGO forum took place in Huairou, 50 kilometers from the site of the official heads of state summit.[8]

Secondly, NGOs have responded to invitations issued by international institutions managing the world economy by creating a cosmopolitan phantasmagoria of their own. Just as they denounce "transnational corporations" for having "no allegiance to any single nation," they attempt to assemble transnational groupings of universalist, cosmopolitan forces transcending local specificities: "transnational corporations, with no allegiance to any single nation, must...be accountable to the people of all nations."9 In this spirit, the "Fifty Years is Enough" coalition celebrated the half-century anniversary of Bretton Woods institutions by drawing a "People's Plan for the Twenty-First Century," and popular groups that have shadowed G7 summits since their beginning in 1975 have increasingly taken to fashioning alternative plans of world order ostensibly presented on behalf on "women and men from around the world." At the G7 summit in Halifax, for example, the P7 (People's Summit) issued the "Halifax initiative" on behalf of "the people of all nations." It called, among other broad requests, for the affirmation that...all constituencies, be they First Nations, peoples of color or women, must join as equal partners with federal and provincial governments in debates about fiscal restraint, allocation of resources and social reform;...[the] reduction of inequalities of power and income along gender, race, class and ability lines;...[the] affirmation that we urgently need to formulate restorative economic concepts and institutions centered on ecological principles and human needs; (and the) the introduction of life, not business, as the center of the educational agenda in all settings where children, youth and adults learn about our damaged world, and how it can be renewed.

This first type of movement has grown alongside global governance, and it offers a cosmopolitanism from below that, as we shall see, complements rather than challenges liberal cosmopolitanism. It is not, however, the only transnational movement of the contemporary period. Indeed, below the level at which cosmopolitan internationalists attempt to make a world order on the basis of problem-solving ventures, a distinct movement has begun taking shape that brings together a wide variety of social movements touched directly by the increasingly transnational management of the world economy. In an earlier article, I wrote of this movement as a movement of resistance:

> ...not brought about by shared allegiances to political programs and ideologies, or by a particularly developed humanist consciousness, but by the shared social and historical experience of life in the world economy (Drainville 1995a).

This new "grassroots" transnationalism is made up of locally and strategically-bounded actors dragged onto the terrain of the world economy by the increasingly transnational conditions of existence, and forced to organize what the Mexican *Frente Auténtico de Trabajadores*, an important participant in continental coalitions against free-trade integration in the Americas, called "strategic organizing alliances" with counterparts elsewhere in the world economy (Drainville 1997). In the post-Bretton Woods period in particular, these alliances have brought together mainly local and nationally-centered social forces into transnational coalitions with essentially defensive purposes. Thus, to take but three recent illustrations: union-members in different countries fighting the same multinational employer and linked together in an increasingly transnational division of labor fight together (as in the case of Bridgestone workers (Fumiaki 1995) to limit out-sourcing from non-union shops; women of different worlds link up to fight sexual tourism, which, as Cynthia Enloe, Thanh-dam Truong, Laurie Shrage and others underlined, takes as many different shapes as there are sexual inclinations and ideas about what is foreign and exotic (Enloe 1989; Shrage 1994; Truong 1990); and nationally-centered groups in Canada, the United States and Mexico join in temporary alliances against the North American Free Trade Agreement to defend distinct nationally-centered notions of popular sovereignty (Drainville 1996).

Inasmuch as it is assembled from below, with little programmatic or strategic coherence, this reluctant transnationalist movement is, in fact, neither explicitly internationalist nor a movement in the strictest sense. It is closer to a transnational mob in revolt against the injustices of the new order than to the *a priori* internationalism of erstwhile citizens of the world gathering at UN summits. It appears, in fact, to be a motley collection of particularistic fights possessing little more than a fragile contrapuntal unity and having little do with the making of global civil society. Indeed, these temporary transnational coalitions are about defending specific positions, values, projects and interests inside the general framework of capitalist accumulation in the world economy. These particular struggles are most certainly not those from which emerge what Marx would have called world-historical, empirically-universal individuals.

There is, however, more to this new phenomenon than meets the eye. Beyond its disavowal of "global governance," it harbors a truly radical conception of internationalism and, indeed, of civility in the world economy.

Transnational Urbanism and Beyond

When Le Corbusier saluted the birth of modern urbanism in 1923, he was applauding the appearance of an orderly answer to the chaotic and contingent growth of European cities in the 19th century (Le Corbusier 1994: 241). What this new science provided for Le Corbusier was a way to solve the problems of uncontrolled urban growth and a means to "straighten the donkey's path into a boulevard," that is to say plan the future course of city life. Thus, for Le Corbusier (and indeed for Le Nôtre, L'Enfant, Haussmann or even Hippodamos before him—for urbanism is not such a modern science), urbanism was both a rather technical effort to resolve inherited problems and a radical social science dedicated to building "freedom through order": *l'ordre, humain, géométrique règne dans les villes* (Le Corbusier 1994: 22-23, 203). For Le Corbusier, the new order (which was nothing more than the logical arrangement of social cells) would come about as the result of master plans drawn above the level at which city-dwellers live, in consultation with those powerful enough to have both a comprehensive vision of city growth and the means to realize the *grands projets* needed to transform ancient neighborhoods into clear and orderly living (and working) machines: *boulevards, places publiques*, through streets, centralized shopping and living areas.

Carrying the spirit of urbanism to the world economy, global governance proposes to "bring more orderly and reliable responses to social and political issues that go beyond capacities of states to address individually" (Weiss and Gordenker 1996b: 17). In the first instance, the grand plans of global governance are about resolving human problems conjuncturally related to the management of capitalism on a world scale but once (or twice, or thrice) removed from it: overpopulation, trans-border pollution, human rights abuses, etc. When, for example, the CGG asked NGOs to move "beyond advocacy" towards a more convivial—and more malleable—neighborliness, when the Cairo conference informed women that control over their fertility had become an essential condition of sustainable development in the world economy, or when the World Bank invited NGO representatives to sit in the newly created "NGO-World Bank Committee," it is in an effort to find solutions to global human problems as concrete, and as pressing, as those facing European cities in the 19th century.

Beyond problem-solving, global governance is also about putting in place the social and political infrastructure of a new (and sustainable) transnational order. Such schemes as the "Agenda 21," the "World Social Charter" (which begins thus: "We the people of the world solemnly pledge to build a new global civil society..."), and "the 20/20 development compact," are not just piecemeal problem-solving ventures, they are also cosmopolitan *grands projects* of global order.10

As the *plan directeur* of a new order, global governance is as politically dependent on finding social interlocutors with both a comprehensive—that is to say transnational—vision of the world economy, and the means to realize the necessary *grands travaux* as was Le Corbusier on sponsors capable of surveying cities as if for the first time, with as much detachment as a surgeon *vis à vis* a patient on the operating table.

Herein lies a key to understanding such appeals to global civil society as those issued recently by the "Human Development Reports" of the United Nations Development Programme, the Report of the CGG, and (increasingly) the annual reports of the World Bank. They are, as Gordenker and Weiss put it, about connecting the local to the global (Weiss and Gordenker 1996b: 17). Thus, the "multitude of institutions, voluntary associations, and networks—women's groups, trade unions, chambers of commerce, farming and housing cooperatives, neighborhood watch associations, religion-based organizations, and so on..." who are at the center of an ostensibly emerging global civil society are anchoring points of global order (Commission on Global Governance 1995: 32). These are privileged interlocutors of governance, whose civic-minded cosmopolitanism complements that of transnational capital, and with whom global governance can attempt to negotiate what IMF Managing Director Michel Camdessus called "the widespread acceptance of a set of general propositions about the most effective way of achieving sustainable growth [and] good governance."[11] In the same spirit, Boutros Boutros-Ghali recognized that:

> Nongovernmental organizations have a crucial role to play.... They can help develop effective ways of spreading the ideas of peace and democracy...(Boutros-Ghali 1996).

At the heart of this attempt at linkage and dissemination of global blueprints of order are found processes of task-specialization and site-designation that bring to light the cadastral logic with which global governance approaches the global city it wishes to settle. The physical separation between NGOs and IGOs summits, the broader "sensible division of labor" between NGOs and IGO's sought by global governance, as well as the panoply of new and specialized global fora either called for or put into place by the organs of global governance, all speak of this attempt at political grid-planning. Governance is about problem-solving, and it is the logic of problem-solving which discipline its relationship to social forces in the world economy. Like universal exhibits (divided in standard quarters: machinery, fine arts, raw materials, anthropological displays of natives), colonial capitals of the 17th and 18th centuries (Savannah, New Haven, New Orleans and Charleston, for example) or peripheral cities later colonized by transnational capital (Djakarta, Calcutta, Nairobi, Mexico City, Lima), the transnational city projected by global governance is a gridded, bounded, pre-planned, containers of social life. In it structured relations of power are compartmentalized, politics takes on the appearance of a collection of managerial problems to be solved and where the broad political attempt to settle a new order goes unexamined.

In contrast, social movements whose visit to the phantasmal global city of transnational capital are not pre-planned by organs of global governance or driven by cosmopolitan desires to settle matters at the level of the world economy but rather required by the exigencies of their campaigns, go into it reluctantly. So do people in search of (material, cultural or spiritual) sustenance, be they farmers selling produce in city markets, foreign guest workers, or cultural tourists visiting heartlands of civilization who leave the periphery for established centers. They see it as an adjacent, familiar and hazardous terrain to be explored, circumstantially and purposefully, one step at a time, looking for like groups to exchange with and draw from and protective societal relationships to build.

This approach is not that of the mayors, kings and cosmopolites who draw grandiose plans of urban renewal and treat cities as material homage to civic visions of order. Nor is it that of urban planners wishing to build sustainable cities, or of secure and abiding citizens who take inherited cities for granted and wear their civility on their sleeve. Rather, it is the approach of those who must think in defensive and instrumental terms, who must create their own kin groups, their networks of protection, influence and social intercourse, who invent social equivalences and codes of reciprocity from within the confines of an established city, as they negotiate the relationship between their specific humanity and the generic civility of cities. In contrast to the cadastral approach of governance, which is explicitly about created civility but treats the world economy as a territory to be surveyed, segmented and settled at once, this process is actually one of constant creation of civility, woven together cautiously, defensively, from below.

That most created civility of cosmopolitan centers provides a good illustration of this creative process at work. Notwithstanding grandiloquent discourses of city-boosters wishing to invent world-class cities and cosmopolitan urbanity from above, what actually makes the specific civility of cosmopolitan cities is the people who negotiate their relationship with the city they reside in, and resist attempts to establish transcending codes of civility. Magrebans in Paris, Turks in Amsterdam, and Haitians in New York neither cease to be Magrebans, Turks and Haitians from the moment they enter city limits, nor do they confine their distinctiveness to designated sites and events. Rather, they carry their specific humanity with them, and use it to find their way in the city as they transform it.

Cities that confine this process succeed in becoming as generic and hollow in social terms as shopping centers, or theme-park recreations of ideal cities. They are the opposite of cosmopolitan centers. In the end, cosmopolitan civility is an involuntary collective undertaking from below which does not transcend, but traverses and transforms established social relationships.

So it is with transnational civility, which also happens behind the back of social forces in movement. Rooted in the most immediate of contexts, they enter the world economy in search of strategic and tactical support in particular campaigns and struggles. It is from these evanescent linkages, from occasional transnational campaigns and punctual networks that are fashioned new social relationships and that the fabric of transnational collective life is woven.

Thus, in a sense, the instant transnational communities at the center of what I have called "resistance internationalism" are as much concerned with solving problems as are organs of global governance and cosmopolitan NGOs. They take to the world economy in search of material, tactical and strategic support from kin groups elsewhere in the world economy; they organize joint campaigns, and call transnational organizations and cosmopolitan NGOs as witnesses to their struggles (for internationalisms from above and below are certainly not mutually exclusive). However, social movements do not bring to the world economy the managerial problems raised by global governance, which evacuate politics by taking existing orders as their starting point and invite technical, indeed urbanist, solutions that reproduce (or sustain in the fashionable vernacular of governance) established relationship. In the end, these end up attempting to reconcile (to borrow from Richard Falk's definition of global governance) "market influences and populist demands" (Falk 1995: 7). Social movements carry their politics to the world economy like immigrants to a new city carry their distinctive civility. They drag along immediate preoccupations that speak for themselves, have a urgency of their own, and remain quite indifferent to managerial concerns. The civility thus created is not the finished and generic civility of urbanists, who project an existing logic of order onto a new site. It is a distinct

civility woven from new issues and from obliged meeting concerned with tactical and strategic questions.

About the specific content of this transnational civility, little can
be said for the moment. Notwithstanding cosmopolitan phantasmagorias shared by the organs of management of the world economy who have conveyed global parliaments and universal exhibits
of global civil society and by NGOs who attend them, what Alberto
Mellucci called the *"planétarisation"* of human experience, has
barely begun dragging the ordinary and rather quotidian politics
of social movements into the world economy, and the ensuing process of obliged creation remains in very much in its infancy
(Melucci 1995). The social forces it will bring together, its future
trajectory, and, indeed, the avenues of transnational civility it might
open have not yet taken their distinct shape.

What has begun to take an intelligible shape, though, is the
relationship between, on the one hand, this uncelebrated and
indeterminate process of obliged creation and, on the other, the
cosmopolitan appeals made by the organs of global governance to
an ostensibly emerging global civil society, as well as the "revival
of compassionate capitalism" herein promised (Falk 1995: 136).
As this article has attempted to illustrate, these cosmopolitan
appeals to settle social relationships in the world economy are
efforts to contain and shape the transnationalism from below that
we have elsewhere called "resistance internationalism." They
constitute, in fact, just as direct an answer to this resistance as
Charles de Wailly's *Projet d'utilité et d'embellissement pour la
ville de Paris* (unveiled at the 1789 *salon* of the Louvre, as the
revolution was beginning) and, later, Haussmann's *grands projets,*
were responses to Parisian barricades.

Conclusion

Global governance takes as its point of departure a critique of
actually existing capitalism that has an undeniable radical appeal.
This broad, multi-front critique has taken issue at once with what
Shridath Ramphal, co-chairman of the CGG called the "G7's in-
adequacies as the world's economic directorate;" with the consequences of what Richard Falk, one of the leading academic

advocates of global governance called "market-oriented authoritarianism" and, more generally, with what the Lisbon group called "national capitalism."[12] The organs of governance have also been at the forefront of a humanitarian critique of global disparities "in wealth between countries and between social groups within them," and they have put forth a critique of the social costs of unregulated capital flows, which invites, according to Richard Falk, political change of a "revolutionary nature."[13]

This radicalism of global governance, accounts, in part, for both the ascendance of cosmopolitan ideals among political activists increasingly called upon to manage the global commons and the seriousness with which such improbable proposals as Daniele Archibugi's idea of a UN People's Assembly and David Held's model of cosmopolitan democracy have been received (Archibugi 1995).

In an important way, Archibugi, Held and would-be citizens of the world gathering to celebrate their common humanity in UN conferences on global reform, are inheritors of a cosmopolitan tradition which links such different historical actors as Diogenes, Mesdames de Sevigné and Geoffrin (whose *salons* welcomed such self-conscious citizens of the world as Benjamin Franklin and Thomas Jefferson); Denis Diderot (the *encyclopédiste* who wrote to David Hume boasting of their shared status as "citizens of a great universal city"); Jean-Jacques Rousseau (that most cosmopolite of *philosophes* who thought cities "anthill[s], the abyss of the human species, breeding infirmities of the body and vices of the soul"); French revolutionary utopians who drew a plan to rename Parisian streets and public squares after famous sites throughout the world (thus transforming Paris into "a living map of the world"); the forced internationalization of Paris wished for by Le Corbusier (who saw "beyond petty lives"); that "united human community" triumphantly displayed by the League of Nations at its pavilion of the New York World Fair of 1939 (six weeks after German troops invaded Czechoslovakia); and that most constructed and malleable of sociability found in cybernetic "cities of bits."[14]

To be sure, the significance of cosmopolitan appeals varies according both to the social forces who make them and to the particular circumstances in which they are made. Diderot's cosmopolitan pledges at the close of the eighteenth century have neither the same meaning, nor the same importance, as those of the World Bank, the CGG or the Trilateral Commission on the eve of a new world order. Beyond reminding us of the philosophical lineage of contemporary cosmopolitanism, taking the civic imagery of global governance at face value has also allowed us to begin exploring its political dynamics more critically than do fashionable celebrations of human unity and, perhaps to forecast its future course with more acuity. In the world economy and elsewhere, civic imageries are explicit (and thus useful) prefigurations of political projects in the making. Ideologies and utopias from Plato, Saint Augustine, Thomas Moore and Saint-Simon to contemporary ecologists take material shape as ideal cities.[15] So does the revolutionary urbanism of global governance, whose most conservative radicalism aims to preserve existing order and project it onto a new world, moving, as the Lisbon group put it, beyond "a weakening national capitalism [towards] a growing transnational capitalism" (Groupe de Lisbonne 1995: 65).

Notes

1. On historical forecasting, see Eric Hobsbawm, "Looking Forward: History and the Future," New Left Review, (No. 125 January-February 1981): 3-20.
2. Riccardo Petrella, "Pour un contrat social mondial," *Monde Diplomatique*, (July 1994). The *Monde Diplomatique*, is available on the WWW at http://www.ina.fr/CP/MondeDiplo/.
3. On private rating agencies, see also Timothy J. Sinclair's "Passing Judgement: Credit Rating Processes as Regulatory Mechanisms of Governance in the EmergingWorld Order," in *Review of International Political Economy*, Vol. 1:1: 133-159, Spring.
4. Drainville, André C. 1995. Of Social Spaces, Citizenship, and the Nature of Power in the World Economy. *Alternatives* 20: 51-79, Spring. Stephen Gill defined neo-liberal constitutionalism thus: "...the move towards construction of legal or constitutional devices to remove or insulate substantially the new economic institutions from popular scrutiny or democratic accountability" in Stephen Gill 1992. The Emerging World Order and European Change. In *New World Order?*, edited by L. Panitch and R. Miliband. London: Merlin Press. In a later article, Gill clarified the link between these new constitutional practices and "the reconstitution of capital (and labor) on a

world scale." See Gill, Stephen. 1995. The Global Panopticon? The Neoliberal State, Economic Life, and Democratic Surveillance. *Alternatives* 1995:2:1-49.

5. Anthony D. King documents the growing interest in "globally-oriented urban research" in the second chapter of King, Anthony D. 1990. *Global Cities: Post-Imperialism and the Internationalisation of London, The International Library of Sociology.* London: Routledge. See also Sassen, Saskia. 1994. *Cities in a World Economy.* Thousand Oaks, California: Pine Forge Press. and Castells, Manuel, and Peter Hall 1994. *Technopoles of the World: The Making of 21st Century Industrial Complexes.* London: Routledge. for good introductions to this literature.

6. Bush quoted from a discourse given to the U.S. Coast Guard Academy in New-London Connecticut, 24 May 1989, cited by Michael T. Klare, in "Le Golfe, banc d'essai des guerres de demain," in *Monde Diplomatique*, (Vol. 1.: 18-19 January 1991). The legal points of reference of the new world order discourse were established in two key speeches in September 1990. The first speech was made by George Bush before both Houses of Congress on September 12. This speech is recognized as the keynote address of the new world order. See "Le Président Bush exalte la vision d'un nouveau monde," in *Le Monde*, Thursday, September 13, 1990: 3. The major themes of the speech were repeated at the Bush-Gorbachev summit in Helsinky summit on the 17th of September 1990 (and then a week later by Deputy Foreign Minister Vladimir F. Petrovsky of the Soviet Union, at the first post- cold war gathering of the UN general Assembly). See Paul Lewis, "U.N. as Well, is Entering the Post-Cold War Era," *New York Times,* 24 September 1990, A2.

7. On technopoles and their relation to globally-organized capitalism, see Castells, Manuel, and Peter Hall. 1994. *Technopoles of the World: The Making of 21st Century Industrial Complexes.* London: Routledge.

8. Figures from NGO participation in UN summits were drawn from: "A Summary Report on the International Conference on Population and Development (ICPD)" (Vol. 6 No. 39, September 14, 1994); "Summary issue of the Fourth World Conference on Women," in the *Earth Negociation Bulletin*, (Vol. 14 No. 21). The Earth Negotiations Bulletin (enb@igc.apc.org) is published by the International Institute For Sustainable Development (iisd@web.apc.org); and, principally, from Weiss, Thomas G., and Leon Gordenker, eds. 1996. *NGO's, the UN, and Global Governance.* Boulder: Lynne Rienner.

9. Quoted from the P7's "Halifax initiative." The People's Summit took place in Halifax, Canada from June 11 to 18, 1995, in the shadow of the G7 meeting. The text of the Halifax initiative, and all documents related to the P7 summit, can be found at http://cfn.cs.dal.ca/Current/P7/summ_news/p7-comm.html.

10. Agenda 21 is the global programme of action on sustainable development drawn up at the 1992 Earth Summit in Rio. The World Social Charter began taking shape at the UNDP in preparation for the Copenhagen summit. The 20/20 development compact (under which 20 percent of developing country budgets and 20 percent of industrial country aid are allocated for human prior-

ity expenditures) was drawn up in preparation for the World Summit for Social Development in Copenhagen.

11. Michel Camdessus, "Opening Adddress," in *Central and Eastern Europe: Roads to Growth* (Washington: International Monetary Fund and the Austrian National Bank, 1992): 16. With this address, Camdessus opened a seminar on "Central and Eastern Europe: Roads to Growth" jointly organized by the Austrian National Bank and the IMF. The seminar was held at Baden, Austria in April 1991.

12. Shridath Ramphal cited from "Global Neighbourhood Values," The 1995 Aurelio Peccei Lecture, delivered at Spoleto, Italy, July 1995.

13. The Independent Working Group on the Future of the United Nations quoted from "Report," part 3. Richard Falk, cited from "Vers une Domination politique mondiale de nouveau type," in Vol. 5, *Monde Diplomatique*, May 1996: 17.

14. Diderot cited from Coulmas, Peter. 1995. *Les citoyens du monde: histoire du cosmopolitisme*. Translated by Jeanne Étoré. 1 ed, *Idées*. Paris: Albin Michel. (On *salons* and cosmopolitanism, see "Les salons, l'esprit, le commerce du monde, la conversation," pp. 214-219). Rousseau quoted from Roland Grimsley, "Rousseau's Paris," in *City and Society in the Eigthghteenth Century*, cited in Leith, James A. 1991. *Space and Revolution. Projects for Monuments, Square and Public Buildings in France 1789-1799*. Montréal: McGill-Queen's University Press. The reference to plans to rename Paris streets is from Mercier Pinkerton and C.F. Cramer, *Ansichten der Hauptstadt des französischen Kaiserreich vom jahre 1806 an*, cited in Benjamin, Walter. 1993. *Paris, capitale du XIXe siècle (Le livre des passages)*. Translated by Jean Lacoste. Paris: Cerf. Le Corbusier from Le Corbusier. 1994. *Urbanisme (1925), Champs*. Paris: Flammarion. The reference to the League of Nations is from Pierre-Gerlier Forest and Brigitte Schroeder-Gudehus, "L'internationalisme et les expositions universelles dans les années trente," in Cahiers, *Laboratoire d'Études Politiques et Administratives*, Université Laval, #90-06, October 1990. On citivily and the Internet, see Mitchell, William J. 1995. *City of Bits: Space, Place, and the Infobahn*. Cambridge: The MIT Press.

15. In "Moderniser ou écologiser? À la recherche de la <<Septième>> Cité" Bruno Latour, ponders the political significance of social and political ecology by contrasting *la cité de l'écologie*, with other models of social orders: *la cité marchande, la cité industrielle, la cité domestique, la cité civique*, etc. , in *Écologie et Politique*, (No. 13: 5-27, Spring 1995). Latour's guiding models are taken from Boltanski, Luc, and Laurent Thévenot. 1991. *De la Justification. Les économies de la grandeur*. Paris: Gallimard.

References

Amici della Terra. (1993). *A New Policy for Environmentalists*. Rome.

Amnesty International. (1996). "Amnesty International Facts and Figures." http://www.organic.com/Non.profits/Amnesty/Info/facts.html.

62 Transnationalism from Below

Archibugi, Daniele. (1995). "From the United Nations to Cosmopolitan Democracy." In D. Archibugi and D. Held (eds.), *Cosmopolitan Democracy: An Agenda for a New World Order*. New York: Polity Press.

Benjamin, Walter. (1993). *Paris, Capitale du XIXe Siècle (Le Livre des Passages)*. Translated by Jean Lacoste. Paris: Cerf.

Boltanski, Luc and Laurent Thévenot. (1991). *De la Justification. Les Economies de la Grandeur*. Paris: Gallimard.

Boutros-Ghali, Boutros. (1996). "Foreword." In T. G. Weiss and L. Gordenker (eds.), *NGOs, The UN, and Global Governance,*. Boulder: Lynne Rienner.

Boyer, Robert. (1986). *La Théorie de la Régulation: Une Analyse Critique*. Paris: Agalma/La Découverte.

Castells, Manuel and Peter Hall. (1994). *Technopoles of the World: The Making of 21st Century Industrial Complexes*. London: Routledge.

Commission on Global Governance. (1995). *Our Global Neighbourhood*. Oxford: Oxford University Press.

Coulmas, Peter. (1995) *Les Citoyens du Monde: Histoire du Cosmopolitisme*. Paris: Albin Michel. Translated by Jeanne Étoré. Firt edition , *Idées*.

Cox, Robert W. (1987). *Production, Power and World Order: Social Forces in the Making of History*. New York: Columbia University Press.

Drainville, André C. (1995a). "Left Internationalism and the Politics of Resistance in the New World Order." In D. Smith and J. Böröcz (eds.), *A New World Order: Global Transformation in the Late Twentieth Century*. Westport: Praeger.

———. (1995b). "Of Social Spaces, Citizenship, and the Nature of Power in the World Economy." *Alternatives* 20 (Spring): 51-79.

———. (1996). *Resisting Integration in the Americas: Internationalism in One Country?* Québec: Laval University.

———. (1997). "Continental Integration and Civil Society in the Americas." *Social Justice* (forthcoming).

Ekins, Paul. (1992). *A New World Order: Grassroots Movements for Global Change*. London: Routledge.

Enloe, Cyhthia. (1989). *Bananas, Beaches, and Bases*. Berkeley: University of California Press.

Falk, Richard. (1995). *On Humane Governance: Towards a New Global Politics*. University Park, PA: The Pennsylvania State University Press/World Order Models Project.

Fumiaki, Mariya. (1995). "United Power of Japan-U.S. Workers' Solidarity Attack Bridgestone Corp." *APWSL- JAPAN*. Newsletter from Japan Committee of Asian Pacific Workers Solidarity Links: 1-3.

Gill, Stephen. (1991). "Reflections of Global Order and Socio-Historical Time." *Alternatives* 16.

———. (1992). "The Emerging World Order and European Change." In L. Panitch and R. Miliband (eds.), *New World Order?* London: Merlin Press.

———. (1995). "The Global Panopticon? The Neoliberal State, Economic Life, and Democratic Surveillance." *Alternatives* 2: 1-49.

Gowan, Peter. (1991). "The Gulf War, Iraq, and Western Liberalism." *New Left Review* 187 (May/June): 29-71.

Groupe de Lisbonne. (1995). *Limites à la compétitivité: Vers un Nouveau Contrat Mondial.* Montréal: Boréal.

Held, David. (1992). "Democracy: from City-States to a Cosmopolitan Order." *Political Studies* XL (Special Issue): 10-39.

Hobsbawm, Eric L. (1994). *Age of Extremes: The Short Twentieth Century ,1914-1991.* London: Abacus.

King, Anthony D. (1990). *Global Cities: Post-Imperialism and the Internationalisation of London..* The International Library of Sociology. London: Routledge.

Le Corbusier. (1994). *Urbanisme (1925), Champs.* Paris: Flammarion.

Leith, James A. (1991). *Space and Revolution. Projects for Monuments, Square and Public Buildings in France 1789-1799.* Montréal: McGill-Queen's University Press.

Melucci, Alberto. (1995). "Individualisation et Globalisation; Perspectives Théoriques." *Cahiers de Recherche Sociologique* 24: 184-205.

Mitchell, William J. (1995). *City of Bits: Space, Place, and the Infobahn.* Cambridge: The MIT Press.

Mumford, Lewis. (1961) *The City in History.* London: Penguin Books.

Murphy, Craig N. and Roger Tooze. (1991). "The New International Political Economy." *International Political Economy Yearbook.* Vol. 6. Boulder: Lynne Rienner Publisher.

Poulantzas, Nicos. (1971). *Pouvoir politique et classes sociales.* Paris: François Maspero.

Salama, Pierre. (1989). *La Dollarisation.* Paris: Agalma/La Découverte.

Sassen, Saskia. (1994). *Cities in a World Economy.* Thousand Oaks, California: Pine Forge Press.

Shrage, Laurie. (1994). *Moral Dilemmas of Feminism: Prostitution, Adultery, and Abortion.* London: Routledge.

Truong, Thanh-dam. (1990). *Sex, Money, and Morality: Prostitution and Tourism in Southeast Asia.* London: Zed.

Van der Pijl, Kees. (1989). "The International Level." In T. Bottomore and R. J. Brym (eds.), *The Capitalist Class: An International Study.* New York: New York University Press.

Van Hoolthon, F. and Marcel van der Linden. (1988). *Internationalism in the Labour Movement 1830-1940.* Vol. II. Leiden: E.J. Brill.

Wapner, Paul. (1995). "Politics Beyond the State: Environmental Activism and World Civic Politics." *World Politics* 47:1: 311-340. April.

Weiss, Thomas G. (1993). "New Challenges for UN Military Operations: Implementing an Agenda for Peace." *Washington Quarterly* 16: 51-66.

Weiss, Thomas G. and Leon Gordenker (eds). (1996a). *NGOs, The UN, and Global Governance.* Boulder: Lynne Rienner.

———. (1996b). "Pluralizing Global Governance: Analytical Approaches and Dimensions." In T. G. Weiss and L. Gordenker (eds.), *NGOs, The UN, and Global Governance.* Boulder: Lynne Rienner.

3

Theoretical and Empirical Contributions
Toward a Research Agenda for Transnationalism[1]

Sarah J. Mahler

In recent years, social scientists have contemplated the nature of the growing[2] interconnectedness of the world as a consequence of global capitalism, the flows of money, labor, images, and ideas. Will this emergent world order be an increasingly homogeneous "global village" or will the forces of conformity be counter-weighted by local interpretations—by creolizations into a "global ecumene" (Foster 1991; Hannerz 1987, 1989)? The debate promises to be protracted though there is a groundswell of support for an ecumenical future. This paradigm shift has been promoted by observers of cultural hybridity (Appadurai 1990, 1991; Foster 1991; Hannerz 1987) and also by critics of meta-narratives (e.g., modernization, dependency and world systems theories). They argue that such theories privilege the West and capitalism as Prime Movers of social change and as monopolies of exploitation and repression, while localities are stereotyped as static (Appadurai 1990; Basch, Glick Schiller and Szanton Blanc 1994; Featherstone 1990; Grewal and Kaplan 1994; Kearney 1995a; M.P. Smith 1994). Some promote an alternative image to the meta-narrative, one in which power, domination and control do not radiate from one central source toward peripheries, but radiate from myriad loci and permeate multiple levels of social organization—familial, local, regional, national, transnational and so on. Transnational feminist, analysis utilizes the operative term "scattered hegemonies" to elicit an image of multiple, overlapping and discrete oppressions in opposition to oppression as hegemonic (Grewal and Kaplan 1994: 17).

Parallel to the shift in depicting sources of power and control as multifaceted, there has been a like transformation in the portrayal of peoples' identities (e.g., Basch et al. 1994; Nagengast and Kearney 1990), and their roles in the production and reproduction of power. More traditional Marxist analysis largely characterizes people as the pawns of capitalist forces, a characterization reflexive and postmodern theorists have criticized as overly structural and

deterministic. Some have pushed for the adoption of a more dialectical approach, one that "brings together the study of structure,
cultural process, and human agency" (Basch et al. 1994: 10).
From a dialectical optic, people play a variety of roles simultaneously; they are both agents and subjects and, as such, they are affected by, challenge, and contribute to the perpetuation of different systems of power. For example, in my own research amidst
Salvadorans who fled civil warfare in their country and sought
refuge in the United States, I now find quite common the following
scenario: A peasant was threatened with death by the United States-
financed Salvadoran army and anti-government guerrillas if he refused to be conscripted. Fearing retribution from either group if
he joined the other, he fled El Salvador for the United States, leaving the rest of his family behind. In the United States he became
an undocumented landscape laborer, working for low wages and
sometimes not being paid at all. When this happened he would
seek assistance from a local immigrants' rights agency where he
joined others and formed an advocacy group. Over several years,
he squeezed out of his earnings enough money to build a new
house in his home town in El Salvador and to buy several acres of
land. He now pays two day workers, known as *mozos*, the minimum
daily wage to work this land and relieve his wife and children of
that burden. The migrant's remittances finance the education of
his children who aspire to become professionals. Meanwhile, the
mozos can barely feed, let alone educate, their children who, in
turn, aspire to emigrate to the land of dollars.

This scenario illustrates the multiple, simultaneous roles people
can play. Is the former peasant exploited, exploiter, both? Can the
meta-narrative of United States hegemony over Latin America explain every level of oppression here? If not, and a multiplicity of
powerful agents and oppressions is acknowledged, shouldn't they
then be distinguished by magnitude of influence and by relationship to other agents? In short, the dualist vision—colonizer and
colonized, core and periphery, First and Third Worlds—is becoming unacceptable, replaced by a more textured and problematized
portrait, but this portrait is nowhere near completion.

Transnational studies are playing a key role in illustrating this multiplicity. Transnational studies research "social, economic, cultural and demographic processes that take place within nations but also transcend them," i.e. globalization. They are different from globalization, however, in that they are "anchored in and transcend one or more nation-states" instead of transpiring in "global space" (Kearney 1995a: 548). This basic definition introduces one fundamental problem besetting "transnationalism"—it is a very slippery concept. One reason for its slipperiness is the outcome of having been used historically in similar yet distinct ways. As early as 1916, authors employed the term (Bourne 1916 cited in Levitt 1996); it became fashionable in the 1970s, as evidenced by the existence of the "Transnational Institute" in Amsterdam and the publication of numerous books and articles bearing "transnational" in their titles, such as *Transnational Relations and World Politics* (Keohane and Nye 1971). The more perplexing problem of the term transnationalism as it is utilized contemporaneously, derives from the fact that it is used to describe a wide array of activities—from social movements to economic relations to mass media to migrants' ties to their homelands. Such breadth is difficult to research and comprehend descriptively, let alone analytically. Consequently, the field has sometimes been delimited into a more manageable size or framework in a number of ways, two of which I will discuss in this paper, drawing on empirical and theoretical research to date, including my own.

Distinguishing Transnationalism "From Above" and "From Below"

This approach is rarely expressed explicitly (Guarnizo 1996b; M.P. Smith 1994) but recurs in numerous texts by transnationalists and focusses on "transnationalism from below," even to the point of leaving readers wondering what exactly is meant by the implied, but not necessarily stated, existence of "transnationalism from above." The basic concept of "transnationalism from above," as I understand it, is that multinational corporations, media, commoditization ("mediascapes," "technoscapes," and "finanscapes" in

Appadurai's terms [1990: 296-99]) and other macro-level structures and processes that transcend two or more states are not produced and projected equally in all areas, but are controlled by
powerful elites who seek, although do not necessarily find, political, economic and social dominance in the world. "In other words,
the resources, range and specialized flexibility of transnational
corporations' activities enable them to present imagery and information on an almost global scale, threatening to swamp the cultural
networks of more local units, including nations and ethnic communities" (A.D. Smith 1990: 174-5).

In contradistinction to the homogenizing and elitist forces of
"transnationalism from above," "transnationalism from below"
generates multiple and counter-hegemonic powers among non-
elites. It is the creation of a new social space—one spanning at least
two nations—that is fundamentally "grounded in the *daily* lives,
activities, and social relationships" of quotidian actors" (Glick
Schiller, Basch and Szanton-Blanc 1992: 5, emphasis added).
Moreover, transnationalism from below describes "the ways that
the *everyday practices of ordinary people*, their feelings and understandings of their conditions of existence, often modify those
very conditions and thereby shape rather than merely reflect new
modes of urban culture" (M.P. Smith 1992: 493-4; emphasis
added). M.P. Smith's vision of transnationalism from below is one
of a "transnational grassroots politics" (1994), wherein coalitions
constituted by a range of social classes exercise power that transcends national boundaries. As such, everyday people can create
change, though this is much less frequently recognized than the
powers enjoyed by macrostructural forces such as capitalist expansion, mass media and patriarchy (what Appadurai [1990] describes
as the "global cultural economy"). For example, people who
think and live transnationally may thwart the forces of assimilation
(Rouse 1992; R. Smith 1995), build ethnic identities that were
problematic if not impossible to sustain within one nation-state
(Nagengast and Kearney 1990), challenge the power of states to
control their movements and interests (Basch et al. 1994; Guarnizo
1994; Nagengast and Kearney 1990; R. Smith 1995; M.P. Smith
1994), and even escape the grasp of global capital accumulation

(Portes 1995). In short, through transnational processes everyday people can generate creole identities and agencies that challenge multiple levels of structural control: local, regional, national, and global. "Transnationalism from below" thus supports and explains, at least partially, the "global ecumene."

As popularly described, "transnationalism from below" or "transnational grassroots politics" is the ethnoscape of migrants, social movements and coalitions. The examples M.P. Smith cites in his 1994 paper are typical: a multinational coalition of transnational refugees from Central America and college students load a caravan full of donations and drive it to El Salvador with the intention of making a political statement along the way; a group of Mixtec Indian migrants to Southern California (citing Nagengast and Kearney 1990) who finance good-will projects in their home towns in Mexico, convene a transnational conference to discuss human rights violations on both sides of the border and exercise more power *vis-à-vis* the Mexican state from California than they could from within Mexico; and a transnational conference is organized by an alliance of women's and immigrants' rights organizations to address human rights abuses suffered by transnational migrant women working in the United States (M.P. Smith 1994: 26-30). Other examples include indigenous rights movements in Latin America (Brysk 1993; Sikkink 1993), the campaign for the rights of "Untouchables" within India launched from Toronto, Canada (*New York Times* October 20, 1996), and transnational feminist alliances (Grewal and Kaplan 1994). They substantiate M.P. Smith's point that people should not be limited by a "think locally, act locally" or "think globally, act globally" politics. Rather, in the world of deterritorialized peoples and mass communications, grassroots political activities do not fit well into this binary perspective. In new, transnational spaces, Smith argues, there is more room for "thinking locally while acting globally," for "thinking transnationally while acting multilocally," and for "thinking and acting simultaneously at multiple scales" (M.P. Smith 1994: 25).

The introduction of radio and television into nearly every corner of the earth facilitates these grassroots politics. Prior to the existence of these mediums, global information was more of an elitist enterprise, limited to those with access to newspapers, books, travel accounts and so on. Many, if not most, people lived a predominantly "local" and perhaps "regional" existence. This raises the question of how easily everyday people could employ a transnational grassroots politics even if they were moderately aware of world geography and events. There are certainly examples of this prior to the past decade or so; the examples of Martin Luther King, Jr.'s utilization of non-violent resistance as adapted from Mohandas K. Gandhi or the anti-Vietnam War movement come to mind immediately. But it seems to me that such practices have become easier in recent years, albeit not universal, with the invention of new technologies such as the facsimile, desktop computer, Internet, and camcorder. These technologies are so widespread that they are virtually impossible to eliminate, and thus control. Moreover, they constitute basic tools of capitalism; to shut them down merely to thwart dissidents, for example, would be very costly. Lastly, they can disperse information so quickly that even if they could be selectively disabled it could not be done in a useful time frame. It should not be surprising then, that these technologies have been central to the transnationalization of protests and social movements, small and large, such as Tiananmen Square, Glasnost and the fall of the Berlin Wall, and Wang Dan's protest of prison conditions in China.

The "transnationalism from below" vision is profoundly democratic and empowering, a balm for those who see the world as hopelessly headed for homogeneity imposed by Western cultural and economic imperialism. Its appeal, however, should not dissuade criticism. In my reading, I see two fundamental problems it presents. First of all, I do not find any definition of "grassroots" outside the references to "every day people" conducting "daily" activities. Kearney (1995a: 559) suggests that this metaphor is somewhat "inappropriate for the organizational challenges facing deterritorialized popular groups attempting to defend themselves in a globalized world." I am more concerned about *who* is deemed grassroots: traditionally disenfranchised groups, anyone who does not represent state or corporate interests, perhaps elites who take counter-hegemonic positions, or even coalitions that include diverse members? Sikkink (1993) raises the issue of membership when discussing the key function that institutional elites often play in social change, such as NGOs' role in defending human rights within nation-states. "The idea of a social movement...with its emphasis on bottom-up citizen protest, fails to portray accurately the range of actors involved in human rights issues, including foundations and international and regional organizations" (1993: 439).

A stickier issue than cross-class coalitions arises with state sponsorship. Can state-sponsored transnational activities be construed as grassroots? For example, as president of Haiti, Jean Bertrand Aristide appealed to Haitians living in the United States to view themselves as members of Haiti's "Tenth Department" and manifest their patriotism (Basch et al. 1994; Richman,1992). Later, as Haiti's deposed president, Aristide once again sought to marshal these migrants' support, only this time as part of a transnational campaign to oust the regime that had overthrown his government. Can either effort be deemed grassroots? This distinction is not petty for there are numerous examples of states reaching across their borders to influence the affairs of citizens who have migrated abroad (Guarnizo 1996a; Nagengast and Kearney 1990; Richman 1992; R. Smith 1995). These efforts can often combine self-interest (i.e. interests of powerful elites) with a concern for migrants' welfare. A good example is when the Salvadoran government began the seemingly preposterous program of assisting its citizens, who were about to lose temporary legal status in the United States, to apply for political asylum in 1994. Nearly 200,000 Salvadorans were at risk of deportation owing to the expiration of Temporary Protected Status at that time. The government stepped in to assist its migrant citizens in the application process, a measure designed to prolong their temporary legal status and delay their return. In essence, however, consular officials aided individuals to claim that they would be persecuted by their government if they returned home! This policy only makes sense when contextualized with respect to the collective power of these migrants' pursestrings. Remittances from them, estimated at $700 million to over $1 billion annually, represent the largest source of hard currency to the country, hundreds of millions of dollars more than export earnings (Funkhouser 1991, 1992; Mahler ,1995b; Siri 1996). El Salvador has not received much international aid to rebuild following its decade-long civil war (1979-92) such that financiers and planners are beholden to transmigrants' remittances. From this angle, the ostensibly altruistic policy of assisting migrants with their applications can thus be reinterpreted. It was implemented to ensure the continued flow of remittances by minimizing the likelihood that large numbers of migrants would return home upon losing their legal status, voluntarily or involuntarily. The government feared this possibility as it would likely destabilize the Salvadoran economy and society as a whole, a society barely emerging from the civil war. The newly minted power of the migrants—only a half generation removed from nearly complete powerlessness in El Salvador as members of the peasant and urban working classes—caught the attention not only of the Salvadoran state but also of opposition leaders such as Ruben Zamora who toured the United States speaking to groups of Salvadoran migrants in an effort to fund his political campaigns. Both examples illustrate attempts by elites to coopt migrants' grassroots power primarily to serve their own interests, albeit shrouded in a veneer of benevolence.

To summarize, "transnationalism from below" requires, at a minimum, a sensitivity to the social constellation of its actors. Should "intellectuals who are at home in the cultures of other peoples as well as their own" (Hannerz 1990: 244) or transnational capitalists such as the "Overseas Chinese" (Ong 1993, 1992) and wealthy South Indian entrepreneurs (Lessinger 1992) be viewed as participants in transnationalism from "above" or "below?" Should they be excluded just because they are elites *vis-à-vis* their societies, even though *vis-à-vis* global social and economic forces they may be inconsequential? Sikkink argues that elites should not be excluded categorically as some transform rather than reproduce "traditional" power relations. Perhaps, then, "transnationalism from below" should be distinguished from "transnationalism from above" on the basis of whether participants' activities reaffirm existing hierarchies of power that favor elites or reconfigure existing hierarchies of power toward empowerment of the "grassroots" (i.e., traditionally excluded populations)? This might "resolve" the problem, except for the fact that actors may participate simultaneously in transnational activities that both challenge *and* contribute to hegemonic processes—such as the case of the Salvadoran landscaper cited above. These questions point to the difficulty and artificiality of distinguishing between transnationalisms for they, indeed, are interrelated.

Through careful research on decentralized loci of power and social change such as "scattered" hegemonic processes and politics "orchestrated through multiple targets, operating at a variety of institutional and geographical scales, [and] mediated by the appropriation of the global means of mass communication by transnational grassroots movements" (M.P. Smith 1994: 31), researchers can avoid reinforcing dualistic, unidirectional paradigms of power, such as "center-periphery."

I still hold a concern about casting transnationalism into a "from below" versus "from above" frame because this may privilege *organized* activities, and does not seem to acknowledge the role that other types of purposive, but not necessarily organized, action can play in transforming power. In another paper (Paul, Mahler and Schwartz, forthcoming), my co-authors and I argue that mass action defined as "purposive action undertaken by a discernibly large segment of the population and marked by resistance (overt or covert) against some prevailing feature of the status quo" (ibid.: 1) transforms social structures in unanticipated ways. We specifically use "mass action" instead of "social movement" or "collective action" to emphasize the inclusion of less organized, more diffuse forms of mass action such as undocumented immigration. And we argue that mass action becomes congealed in social policy in ways that are generally unanticipated (hence not organized in that direction) by participants and go beyond their original purview. Illegal migration is a prime example. Millions of people acting predominantly out of self-interest, and with no collective purpose, walk or fly across a border and precipitate reactive policy making by elites. These policies are how mass actions become congealed and embedded in social structures, influencing decisions and outcomes in subtle ways long after the mass action ceases. Examples are numerous but rarely acknowledged. A case in point is the 1980 Mariel boatlift—the spontaneous mass exodus by small boats of 125,000 Cubans from Cuba and tens of thousands of Haitians fleeing the Duvalier regime whose migration preceded Mariel but peaked during the boatlift—was neither an organized social movement nor a true collective action, yet it precipitated numerous significant changes. The United States public became dismayed by then-president Jimmy Carter's inability to stem the boatlift and this helped cost him re-election. Also, the huge influx of "illegal aliens" into Miami required immediate government attention. Policies and practices were developed and implemented, such as the funding of new schools and health clinics, that old time and traditionally ignored residents such as African Americans could not help but interpret as privileging the newcomers. In the decade after the boatlift these areas erupted several times in protest (see Portes and Stepick 1993).

In conclusion, I recommend that any comprehensive roster of "transnationalism from below" should include mass actions carried out transnationally as well as organized or collective purposive activities. Moreover, since social movements are frequently led by elites, even when their expressed purpose is to subvert established hierarchies of power (Wolf 1969), mass action may provide a more universal medium through which non-elites exercise power (albeit not necessarily toward a reconfiguration of power).

Transnationalism as Transmigration

An alternative means of delimiting the field of transnational studies to a manageable size and focus is to demarcate it as the study of migrants who retain ties to their homeland; i.e., transmigration.[3] This approach has come to dominate transnational discourse, particularly among anthropologists and sociologists. It dates back into the 1980s, when numerous scholars were observing transnational activities practiced by migrant groups that they were studying primarily from the perspective of the "host" country.

They observed activities spanning both "host" and "home"4 countries but lacked a framework to discuss and analyze them systematically. In May 1990, several researchers organized a workshop as an "effort to conceptualize and analyze transnational migration" (Glick Schiller et al. 1992: ix). They invited other scholars to attend, provided them with a series of questions that they felt needed to be addressed and then published the papers in a book. The book's introductory chapter laid out their overall goal of developing transnationalism as "A New Analytic Framework for Understanding Migration." The workshop's organizers, quite astutely I would argue, offered a commodious definition for transnationalism but one limited to migrants' activities:

> We have defined transnationalism as the processes by which immigrants build social fields that link together their country of origin and their country of settlement. Immigrants who build such social fields are designated "transmigrants." Transmigrants develop and maintain multiple relations— familial, economic, social, organizational, religious, and political that span borders. Transmigrants take actions, make decisions, and feel concerns, and develop identities within social networks that connect them to two or more societies simultaneously (Glick Schiller et al. 1992: 1-2).

This definition provides ample space for any number of individual and group activities that span borders to be construed as transnational—from visitation to sending remittances, to making telephone calls. The publication of a definition for transnationalism, and a framework for its investigation leaves the false impression, however, that transnationalism (even if limited to the study of transmigration) is an established field when, in fact, it is a highly contested approach that has yet to form a common agenda for research and analysis. This important conference could be designated the birthplace of transnational migration as a recognized field of inquiry but, I argue, it did not accomplish its goal of laying the foundation for a unified approach. A few weaknesses surface in the definition cited above. For instance, the definition offers little assistance for evaluating the content, intensity and importance of transnational ties, for examining the interests served through these ties and, perhaps most fundamentally, for establishing a typology of transnational actors—individuals, families, households, hometown associations, governments, etc. It is my opinion that these tasks need to be addressed systematically and can be if researchers ask several basic questions that I will posit below.

My aim in this part of my paper is to further the work of the early conference planners and other scholars toward developing a useful research agenda for studying transnational migration. This would assist the comparison of myriad case studies, a task that is currently very difficult, if not impossible. It would also help identify practices unique to groups of migrants; i.e., culturally specific, from those shared by different groups, albeit in varied settings. As my intention is to supplement and not necessarily replace previous efforts in this direction, I will organize my suggestions around three areas: (1) areas that are confusing and need clarification in the existing literature, (2) basic questions that I feel need to be asked consistently in each case study, but have not been, and (3) areas that remain unidentified or insufficiently addressed in the literature to date.

Areas of Confusion in the Transmigration Literature

Absence of an Orthodox Metaphor

A basic, albeit not necessarily critical, problem plaguing researchers is the plethora of metaphors we employ in describing transnationalism. To date, I have identified "transnational social field" (Glick Schiller et al. 1992; 1995), "transnational migrant circuit" (Rouse 1991, 1992; Goldring 1996), "binational society" (Guarnizo 1994), "transnational community" (Georges 1990; Kearney and Nagengast 1989; Portes 1995; R. Smith 1995), "network" (Kearney 1995b: 231), "global ethnoscape" (Appadurai 1991) and "socio-cultural system" (Sutton 1987). Although each has its merits, and no doubt best characterizes its referent group(s), the employ of so many metaphors serves to confuse the field.

I propose the use of the broad metaphor "transnational social field" to skirt this confusion and the terms transnational "processes," "activities," and "ties" to itemize ways in which relations are established and developed within the greater space of the social field. The other metaphors each have difficulties which make them less appropriate. "Transnational circuit" presupposes a degree of mobility that would preclude many if not most migrants; "binational society" precludes ties that span more than two nation-states; "transnational community" carries with it, intentionally or not, the imputed romantic notions of *communitas* when in reality transnational relations may be divisive; "network" is too closely associated with migration and is better conceived of as a constituent feature of a social field; and "global ethnoscape" and "socio-cultural system" are too broad to be of great analytical utility. Transnational "social field" is preferable but not perfect. It gives me an image of a singular, seemless, smooth terrain when, in fact, there is much evidence to suggest that transmigrants, owing at least in small part to regional differences, form multiple, overlapping and even conflictive social fields. Transnational activities change over time as do participants in them, suggesting that the topography of transnational social fields may be more bumpy and discontinuous than the "social field" image represents. Still, I find it the most useful metaphor and the most widely applicable of those proposed to date.

The Centrality of Mobility to Transnational Migration

Although Transnationalism has been defined broadly as the ways in which "transmigrants develop and maintain multiple relations—familial, economic, social, organizational, religious, and political that span borders," (Basch et al. 1994: 7), in my reading of the transnational literature, I find that mobility constitutes a centerpiece of transnationalism. This is particularly true of the literature on Mexican transnationalism (Kearney and Nagengast 1989; Nagengast and Kearney 1990; Rouse 1992), but also of Caribbean transnationalism (Guarnizo 1996b; Basch et al. 1994), and even of some Chinese and other Asian transnationalism (Lessinger 1992; Ong 1992). What these authors refer to is *movement of bodies across space*, the physical translocation of migrants across boundaries dividing two or more nation-states. When people move between places with some regularity, moreover, their identities are shaped by this experience: "The migrants in the study moved so frequently and were seemingly so at home in either New York or Trinidad as well as their societies of origin, that it at times became difficult to identify where they 'belonged'" (Basch et al. 1994: 5). Rouse (1991, 1992) labels this phenomenon "bifocality," the blurring of the distinction between the local and far away, "the capacity to see the world alternatively through quite different kinds of lenses" (1992: 41). Mobile Transmigrants organize their lives "under conditions in which their life-worlds are neither 'here' nor 'there' but at once *both* 'here' and 'there'" (M.P. Smith 1994: 17; emphasis in the original). This latter quote leaves ambiguous, however, the degree to which becoming bifocal is the outcome of frequent physical mobility.

I readily agree with Appadurai's observation that "As groups migrate, regroup in new locations, reconstruct their histories, and reconfigure their ethnic 'projects' the *ethno* in ethnography takes on a slippery, nonlocalized quality" (1991: 191). I also agree that deterritorialization stimulates migrants' memory and imagination, such that they feel betwixt and between. What I ponder is the role of bodily mobility in this conceptualization. Can transmigrants be "bifocal" if they, themselves, do not move between "home" and "host" countries? What about the impact of the flows of *things not bodies*, such as letters, videos, remittances, specialty foods and so on? Do they promote bifocality to the same degree attained by frequent travelers? Are the face-to-face contacts made possible by bodily movement more intense, more important to the development and perpetuation of transnational social fields and bifocal identities than the faceless ties of remittances—the movement of embodied not bodily ties? Also, shouldn't mobility be quantified in some way? Are transnational ties fostered most through monthly, yearly or triannual visits? Or is the number of trips far less important than the time spent with family, friends, etc. in each place? Some of the most frequent travelers are entrepreneurs; a case in point is the Salvadoran couriers I have been studying over several years. Dozens of couriers, men and women with legal status in the United States, travel back and forth between Long Island and eastern El Salvador carrying down letters, remittances, and gift packages, and returning with cheese and other products to sell as

well as a reverse flow of letters. Are the ties they manufacture similar qualitatively to ties formed by workers returning "home" in
the off-season? I am not prepared to answer these questions yet,
but raise them as important areas needing investigation; viz., type,
intensity and mobility of ties.

The courier example also raises another, related, question regarding the degree to which bodily mobility is accessible equally
to all transmigrants. Is mobility the outcome more of privilege
(such as the possession of legal immigration status or sufficient
funds to pay for trips), of personal/familial taste (the desire to return to one's place of origin or not), or of the proximity between
the countries involved? Additionally, the degree of danger travelers
incur may influence actualized mobility. There is a great deal of
evidence that one or more structural factors does, indeed, play a
role in transmigrants' mobility. For example, Hagan (1994) argues
that Guatemalans in Houston have established greater transnational
links homeward *subsequent to* obtaining legal status in the United
States. Similarly, I have found in my own research that legal status
is the *sinequanon* of the Long Island Salvadorans' courier industry.
The price of airfare from New York to San Salvador varies between
$550 and $800 round trip, a sum that discourages working-class
Salvadoran migrants from returning to their homeland unless they
can defray this cost in some fashion. Serving as a courier, whether
on a one-time basis or as a career, provides this hedge. Most Long
Island Salvadorans, however, do not go "home" for three basic
and interrelated reasons: they lack legal status in the United States,
returning illegally is extremely expensive (current pricetag
$3,000), and overland travel is fraught with peril, particularly in
transversing Mexico (Juffer 1988).

Studies of transnationalism need to address whether bodily
mobility is the exception or the rule for different groups of
transmigrants. Is Rouse's "transnational migrant circuit"
metaphor apropos or not? If, as I suspect, it is unusual, except
among groups for whom the cost of regular mobility is not too
high (such as from the East Coast of the United States to the
Caribbean owing to a huge tourist industry, or from Texas and
Southern California to Mexico), then scholars of transmigration

need to focus on mobile information and goods flows and on other transnational ties and processes more than we have to date.

Once we have looked critically at the question of mobility and have examined all the transnational activities and ties people participate in, we will be in a position to analyze the nature of their "lived reality," to determine whether they are "bifocal," "bipolar" (i.e., settled on one side of the transnational social field with a strong local focus but also characterized by occasional transnational activities), or something else. In my case study of Salvadorans on Long Island, a population that, overwhelmingly, migrated once and stayed put, I have documented the creation and perpetuation of transnational ties linking Salvadorans on Long Island to El Salvador, but I have also documented their perception of a disjuncture between life in El Salvador and in the United States (Mahler 1995a). In their words, "people change here." Sister Maria Villatoro, a Catholic nun in El Salvador, drew upon her fond experience of growing up materially poor but rich in social bonds to contrast the egoism she finds in the United States. "Here things are not like over there," she explained. "Over there you eat even if it's only beans with bread. Here you don't. Here whoever has [money] eats and whoever doesn't, can't. You don't know about any groups who will help you or anything. You don't know anything. It's worse living here because here everyone lives for himself." Moreover, and despite this auto-criticism, time and again I encounter Salvadorans who returned to their homeland with intentions of staying and, yet, show up on Long Island less than a year later claiming they could not accustom themselves to life in El Salvador again. I have had similar experiences talking to returnees in El Salvador who wax nostaligic over their lives in the United States and express a deep desire to return. These individuals' stories do not express "bifocality," although they do exhibit a dual frame of reference. Those I have met who most closely resemble the phrase "neither 'here' nor 'there'" are the couriers, and other frequent travelers.

Salvadorans' precarious legal status in the United States, the continued unstable and dangerous conditions of life in El Salvador, and the prohibitive cost of traveling home all contribute to the fact that most of my informants do not live in transnational "circuits," but are settling permanently on Long Island. Noted Salvadoran sociologist Segundo Montes found evidence of settlement almost a decade ago for the wider Salvadoran population (Montes Mozo and Garcia Vasquez 1988). I have observed this process over several years. Individuals I first interviewed between 1989 and 1990 frequently changed residences and jobs, a mark of their instability. When I reinterviewed them five to six years later, I found them in more stable households, with U.S.-born children and only infrequently changing their jobs. Furthermore, few had returned to El Salvador for more than a short, often emergency, visit. Under these conditions, their lived reality is primarily local, punctuated by infrequent transnational events such as sending monthly remittances or watching a video of the local patron saint festival. Maintaining more vigorous transnational ties remains quite formidable for many if not most. This raises the question of whether they will (1) retain transnational links over the coming years and (2) use these links as tools to fashion identities resistant to the forces of acculturation in the United States,[5] a feature of transnationalism that has been suggested by several authors (Kearney and Nagengast 1989; Nagengast and Kearney 1990; Rouse 1992; R. Smith 1995). Salvadoran migration on Long Island is not mature enough to answer these questions with any authority. My evaluation to date is that certain groups of Salvadorans, viz., those that are most mobile and who find opportunities for socioeconomic mobility in transnational space, will maintain active transnational links while the majority of the first generation will live within a transnational social field constructed largely through remittances, letters, and interactions with recently arrived migrants. The U.S.-born children of these migrants are, for the most part, very young, too young to gauge their likely participation in second generation transnationalism.

This extended discussion of the Long Island Salvadoran case study is not meant to challenge other researchers' work, but merely to stimulate careful study of, and reflection on, the heretofore ambiguous and little-questioned area of mobility in transnational studies. It is extremely important to identify what, if anything, is mobile and why. It is also critical to examine the relationship between mobility and identity. Questions such as these need to be raised systematically in transnational research in order to facilitate the comparison of myriad case studies. Moreover, pursuing these questions will facilitate the evaluation of the degree to which transnational space truly offers a more democratic forum for agency, whether it is terrain for the production of new power hierarchies or reproduction of established power hierarchies.

Basic Questions that Need to be Asked Systematically

Disaggregate between Activities Peformed by the Majority and by Smaller Groups

In the past section, I constructed an argument which suggests that most of my Salvadoran informants experience transnational ties through their remittances and through information from letters, couriers and newcomers. Implicit in this discussion is the recommendation that researchers collect information broadly on transnational activities and, then, disaggregate the data along certain recommended lines. Hopefully, these suggestions will encourage researchers to tailor their descriptions to best reflect their empirical findings, while still providing data comparable to other researchers'. To this end, I will suggest a series of basic research questions which help identify patterns in actors and activities. The first step is to cast a wide net and document all the ways individuals, groups, and institutions foster and maintain relations across borders. Naturally, this requires research spanning the entire transnational social field(s), not just on one side of it. Typical activities identified will include remittances, communications (letters, tapes, telephone calls, videos, e-mail), travel "home" for local festivals, business enterprises, home town association projects, cultural exchanges, government initiatives, cultural exchanges and political movements. Then I suggest grouping these activities by participants. Which are performed by most migrants? Which by select individuals or groups? Of the select activities, would non participants like to perform them, and are they precluded by certain constraints (legal, economic, etc.)? Or, do they choose not to participate? These questions will facilitate an understanding of the existence of barriers/aids that structure transnational activities. Perhaps they will shed light on groups' unique cultural preferences and practices as well.

Much of the research to date on transnational social fields yields detailed information on a limited set of activities and practices, not a clear picture of the breadth of the social field, nor of the demography or intensity of players' participation in all the activities people engage in. A prime example is the important treatise, *Nations Unbound*, by Linda Basch, Cristina Szanton Blanc and Nina Glick Schiller (1994). This book begins with a framework for researching transnationalism in a broad sense, but the ethnographic work cited is focused on voluntary associations and political campaigns. The questions that came to my mind when reading this book, and which are not answered therein, are how representative of the entire transnational social field are these activities, and how representative of the entire migrant population are the participants in these activities? I feel that it is important to address these questions, particularly in the quest to research transnational "grassroots" practices.

Key Characteristics to Investigate: Gender, Class, Age/Generation,
Mobility and Regionality

Most scholars of migration provide basic background information on the groups they study—information such as the history of the migration, its quantity, sex, age and residential distributions and economic integration. Transnational researchers should follow this precedent, I feel, but also go further, gathering data on transnational social structures, processes, and identities in particular. I recommend that several key characteristics which are culturally constructed be researched consistently as well. As of this writing I have identified gender, class, generation, mobility, race, ethnicity, and regionality, but I am sure this is not an exhaustive list. To date, only race and ethnicity have received much attention (Basch et al. 1994; Glick Schiller et al. 1992; Popkin 1995) though mostly in the context of identity and its transformation. The other areas deserve careful scrutiny as well, both regarding studies of transmigrants and their activities, as well as regarding broader transnational actions such as social movements. In the following discussion I will focus my comments on the less developed characteristics.

Gender has been raised as an important area of inquiry by several scholars of transnationalism (Georges 1992; Hagan 1994; Sørensen 1996; Sutton 1992), and most notably Goldring (1996); yet, it has often been side-lined (see Mahler 1996 for a discussion). In a review of the transnational literature, I detected several subtle but significant gendered processes. For example, several authors noted that only men were meeting to plan projects for their home town or regional association (Glick Schiller et al. 1992: 2; Kearney 1995b), but never addressed whether men dominate these associations. Goldring (1996) confirms the latter for her research among Mexican migrants. She also found that women and men did not agree on the type of projects that should be funded by home town associations, that "if women played a significant role in deciding how to spend money on community projects, it would most likely be spent somewhat differently" (ibid: 321). There is also an expanding literature from a variety of case studies documenting how male and female migrants differ with regard to their desires to return "home" permanently. Men wish to return home where they can recoup higher status, while women try to settle the family in the "host" country (Hagan 1994; Hondagneu-Sotelo 1994; Goldring 1996; Guarnizo 1996b; Pessar 1986). In short, scholars should examine consistently the degree to which participation in transnational activities and in transnational social fields in general is gendered.

The importance of social class to transnational processes has been another area mentioned but rarely addressed by researchers, with the notable exception of Roger Rouse (1992). He examines how transmigrants can occupy different class positions within their transnational circuits. I feel strongly that social class also be used as an analytical tool in the identification of patterns in transnational activities. Do people of different social classes participate in similar or different transnational activities, and do different classes enjoy similar or different costs and benefits from these ties? I will return to this theme below in the section on whose interests are served. Guarnizo (1996b) is also concerned about class, and supplements Rouse's perspective by introducing the importance of legitimacy for class analysis. Transmigrants may enjoy greater economic success but do they translate that into greater social prestige and acceptance among established elites? Do transmigrants engage in certain transnational activities to further their social acceptance, for example by sponsoring "altruisic" projects in their home towns? I will also return to this topic later with my perspective.

Generation also merits greater attention from researchers. Age is quite straight forward, of course, and some indication should be provided in transnational studies which disaggregates activities by the age of the participant. The question of generation—first, second, third and so on—is obviously related, yet more nuanced. Several questions are repeatedly tossed at transnational scholars; viz., whether transnationalism is really something new and whether or not migrants' children will pursue transnational lives. These questions are not easy to answer. Answers would require, in the first instance, a historical if not archaeological background and, in the second instance, longitudinal studies. Though there are exceptions, most research on migrants provides a snapshot of today with some history of yesterday. Longitudinal studies are rarer, owing to their cost and difficulty. However, some "snapshot" studies do find evidence that at least some children and grandchildren of migrants participate in transnational activities (Basch et al. 1994; R. Smith 1995). Robert C. Smith's (1995) description of the transnational social field constructed between Ticuani, Puebla, Mexico and New York City develops this transgenerational theme most thoroughly.

An examination of the perpetuation of transnational ties among New York Ticuani youth illustrates that the ties are preserved across generation because they articulate self-interests. Smith shows that when they return to their parents' home towns, the youth are inserted at the top of the local hierarchy. In contrast, the same Ticuani youth occupy one of the lowest social strata in New York and, unlike their parents whose identity is rooted in their home country hierarchy, the second generation clearly perceives its position within the United States hierarchy (see also Gibson 1988; Ogbu 1990; Suárez-Orozco 1989). Through the perpetuation and even over-accentuation of their Ticuani identity, Smith argues, they create an alternative niche, one that bulwarks being associated with the negative stereotypes attributed to other poor minorities. "Ticuanense membership and identity provides them with the practices and resources to resist the negative social location, akin to Blacks and Puerto Ricans, they feel the larger society places them in through their common attendance at the same schools, their competition in the labor market, and often their geographical proximity. In this sense, second generation Ticuanense identity is a reactive formation which both defends and benefits the immigrants" (1995: 32).

Smith's study is very interesting and important; it documents transnational ethnogenesis and one that could further problematize the already murky study of ethnicity throughout the globe. Unfortunately, there is little published literature against which his case study can be compared. Is this a general pattern that Smith is identifying, or an extreme measure adopted by a much-maligned group of minority youth? It is impossible to determine at this moment owing to a dearth of comparative information. However, there is at least one comparison that can immediately be made: Deported Salvadoran gang members. Hundreds of Salvadorans have been deported from the United States, principally from Los Angeles and Washington, D.C., back to their country of origin and many have reconstituted gangs there (Jonas 1995; *Washington Post* April 4, 1996; *Los Angeles Times* June 27, 1995. These youth have become part of a transnational social field involuntarily, yet, at least among people I have spoken with in El Salvador, they have a disproportionate influence on many Salvadorans' perceptions of that social field. They also represent an ethnogenesis and a creolization but, unlike for the Ticuani, this second generation identity does not thwart the forces of assimilation; rather it exemplifies a high degree of assimilation, a classic case of "segmented assimilation" (Portes and Zhou 1993). Moreover, the gangs have sparked a new transnational twist—the reappearance of vigilante groups, i.e., death squads, who blame the gangs disproportionately for El Salvador's current crime wave and target them for assassinations (Jonas 1995).

The last two social characteristics I shall stress as meriting close attention during research on transnationalism are mobility and regionality. I have already discussed mobility in some detail earlier, so I will only repeat my main points on this topic. Researchers should determine what is mobile—money, goods, ideas, and/or people—and then make quantitative and qualitative measurements regarding the frequency of mobility for each type and the contribution each makes to the generation and perpetuation of transnational social fields. Lastly, the special case of bodily movement through space needs to be examined *vis-à-vis* identity. What happens to the identity of migrants who are highly mobile versus those who remain quite stationary, and yet retain transnational ties? Do the latter develop a new, hybrid identity to the same degree as the frequent travelers, or will they come to differentiate more between their lived, "local" reality and the world they left behind? So many of today's migrants live under these conditions that this question must be researched.

Finally, regional differences need consistent attention and discussion in the literature. Though transnational studies have tended to focus on one particular migrant group such as Mexicans or Chinese, and this focus is likely to continue to be predominant despite efforts to do comparative research involving several groups simultaneously, regionality always plays a role. By this I mean that most migrant groups are not concentrated in only one area of the "host" country. Some communities are larger and may differ significantly from others along demographic lines; some are older and have more established institutions and so on. Consequently, the transnational linkages these different subpopulations form are also likely to vary. The case I know best is the Salvadoran migrant population, half of whom live in greater Los Angeles and only about 12 percent have made greater New York their adoptive home. There are similarities between these communities but also numerous differences, such as the fact that the Los Angeles Salvadorans are representative of most regions and social classes in

El Salvador whereas the New York Salvadorans come primarily from eastern El Salvador where they were overwhelmingly peasants (Chavez 1994; Chinchilla, Hamilton and Loucky 1993; Hamilton and Chinchilla 1995; Mahler 1995a). Not surprisingly, they vary also with regard to transnational ties and to the development of their transnational social field. Home town associations in Los Angeles are numerous and more highly developed than in the New York area (Popkin 1995); likewise gangs are much more pronounced in California than in New York. These differences suggest a phenomenon that I have not yet seen mentioned in the transnational literature; viz., that there may be multiple, even overlapping, transnational fields that link two or more nation states and that these fields may vary in constituency and topography. Introducing this comparative analysis will yield both a more textured comprehension of transnationalism (i.e., its depth as well as its breadth) and insight into the roles that demographic variables play in the building and reproduction of transnational social fields. At this moment, there may be only a few migrant groups—such as Salvadorans and Mexicans—who have been studied in different regions (in this case of the United States) and, thus, can be compared. In the future, as more transnational work is completed, this important optic is likely to become more readily available. I ask merely that, whenever possible, researchers make the comparisons.

Areas Not Sufficiently Addressed in the Literature to Date

In my quest to strengthen the research agenda for transnational studies of migrants, I have identified several areas that I feel are not sufficiently developed in the literature to date, areas I strongly recommend researchers to consider in the future. They are (1) assessing whose interests are served by engaging in transnational activities, (2) determining whether such activities reaffirm and/or reconfigure "traditional" relations of power and privilege, and (3) the implications of transnationalism, particularly with respect to metanarratives of power. I will now develop these themes individually.

In Whose Interest?

Scholars have long recognized that migrants invest in the construction and reconstruction of homes in their communities of origin as well as in the consumption of luxury goods and other forms of ostentation that communicate their enhanced status *vis-à-vis* non-migrant households (Georges 1990; Gmelch 1980; Mozo and Vasquez 1988; Rhoades 1978; Sider 1992). In other words, some transnational activities are unambiguously self-interested while others, such as the remittance of small sums of money to finance the basic necessities of non-migrant family members, appear more philanthropic. The latter may also represent payments of reciprocity to family members who have provided services to migrants, such as child rearing of migrants' children left in the homeland.

There is growing evidence, however, that the interests served by transnational ties may be more equivocal than they appear at first. A case in point is home town associations. The projects funded by these groups of transmigrants enjoy a veneer of altruism, while serving as a medium through which power relations can be, although not necessarily are, reconfigured. Luin Goldring (1996) and Robert C. Smith (1995) each illustrate how associations which they studied constitute "parallel power structures" (R. Smith 1995: 27) that challenge established modes of local power even though they accomplish this over transnational space. Transmigrants have garnered influence through their pursestrings. They finance local "altruistic" projects such as the construction of potable water facilities and soccer fields, projects which outcompete those sponsored by local authorities whose funds are more limited. Transmigrants can translate their projects' notoriety into real local political power via election to office or selection as honorary patrons. Do transmigrants participate equally in these pursuits? We do not know for sure because, to date, most writing has detailed only the activities, not the actors. In her analysis of home town associations involving Mexican migrants, Luin Goldring (1996), however, found them dominated by men. She argues that the projects they fund are not oriented toward those most needed by the home town, but toward those with the most "symbolic" power. Women she talked to, had they enjoyed the power to decide where monies would be spent, would have favored more utilitarian projects. If her findings are true more generally, they would show that activities, which on one level reconfigure established power relations on another, gendered level, reproduce established power relations. They provide a good example of "scattered hegemonies"—of multiple, overlapping, and intersecting sources of power—as opposed to hegemonic power (Grewal and Kaplan 1994). Without the more nuanced information regarding participation in these transnational activities, readers can be led to believe that home town associations and other transnational activities have universal appeal, democratic structures, and highly altruistic effects when, in fact, this may well not be true.

The power now wielded by transmigrants has not escaped the notice of national governments, many of whom have launched initiatives varying from relatively benign cultural exchanges to full-fledged campaigns designed to institutionalize and control transnational ties. Once again, the overt message of many of the policies developed appears altruistic—such as the passage of laws permitting dual citizenship and protecting dual citizens' property rights in their country of origin (R. Smith 1995; Guarnizo 1996a; Sanchez 1996). Beneath the veneer of benevolence lies the interests of the state and national elites, a point I made previously using the case of the Salvadoran government's involvement in filing political asylum claims for its citizens. Savvy migrants have not consistently capitulated to these efforts to coopt their power and win their allegiance. Rather, there are numerous examples of transmigrants wielding their power *vis-à-vis* the state to demand that it attend to their interests more than it did when they were living within its boundaries (Guarnizo 1996a; Nagengast and Kearney 1990; R. Smith 1995; Richman 1992, Sanchez 1996). To what extent, however, are these groups who advocate for greater power representative of their larger constituencies? Are there select or more universal interests being pursued?

Finally, I will complicate this picture by adding one last dimension. During my most recent trip to El Salvador in the summer of

1996, I discovered a new transnational tie in the process of formation, one initiated by local communities in El Salvador and which links them to communities of migrants from these towns living on Long Island. Formally called "ADESCO" or "Association for the Development of Communities," this is a regional, if not national, attempt at collecting funds from transmigrants in the United States to finance projects in their local communities. According to informants, ADESCO explicitly skirts association with the Salvadoran State, seeking instead to form networks directly between communities. My research reveals, however, that ADESCO is constituted by local elites who cannot obtain the monies they need for major community needs by soliciting them from the centralized national government. These patron-client ties are too weak (a fact that confronted me time and again as local officials sought my assistance, convinced that I had good ties to government agencies— Salvadoran and United States). Snubbed by traditional patrons, local leaders turned to another bankroll, transmigrants, people with whom they can reactivate old patron-client ties and obligations. I gathered evidence that leaders in one town were collecting funds from Long Island Salvadorans through ADESCO to finance needed road repairs, and had even set up a special ADESCO bank account that migrants could wire remittances to. In short, ADESCO reads to me like the mirror image of home town associations; its momentum is spurred by the home town, not the home town association. Both use remittances to gain prestige but, seemingly, in opposition. Of course, transmigrant donors may press for recognition of their efforts, such as through the formation of home town associations, and shift prestige away from the local elites over time.

Reconfigure or Reaffirm?

The discussion regarding "In Whose Interest?" leads directly to a fundamental research question: Do transnational spaces, activities and processes reaffirm or reconfigure established relationships of power and privilege? This question may appear obvious if asked from a transnationalism "from above" versus "from below" perspective. Within this frame, transnationalism "from above" is the province of elites who undoubtedly are engaged in perpetuating their power. Transnationalism "from below," as the terrain of non-elites and multi-class coalitions, could be construed as the space where people work to transform "traditional" power relations, to reconfigure and not reaffirm. Preliminary research, however, reveals that this hypothesis is not so solid. In the Ticuani case study, for instance, transmigrants inserted themselves into established hierarchies of power; they changed the players but did they transform the power structure? I would argue that there is support for both "yes" and "no" answers. The Ticuani transmigrants did not transform their home town hierarchy itself, nor its patriarchy, but they did represent the opening of a new avenue to power. In my own research, I have also documented how the transnational practices of some migrants may both reaffirm and reconfigure traditional gender roles (Mahler 1996). Salvadoran migrant women, for example, remit an equal amount of resources to their kin as men do. Thus, men and women participate equally in the most democratic form of transnationalism practiced by the Long Island Salvadorans. This is extraordinary for several reasons. First, women remit equally and support the same number of dependents in El Salvador as men, despite the fact that they earn less. This suggests that they have become partners in the role of "breadwinner" although in their homeland, at least in the countryside, women were widely excluded from that role. The research I have conducted on male and female couriers, on the other hand, does not support a thesis of reconfigured power relations. Space limitations prohibit a full discussion here, but my findings regarding this industry suggest that women have become couriers largely because this activity is constructed around "traditional" gender roles, not reconfigured ones as might be hypothesized. Quite candidly, many Salvadoran women were preadapted for courier work by following not challenging established gender roles.

The case studies cited above should serve as an admonition to scholars of transnationalism. Much as hegemonies can be "scattered" and multidimensional, so too can be more localized forms of power. Additionally, transnationalism should not be expected to express or produce even, linear or neat patterns. Indeed, it is in the ambiguous and seemingly contradictory findings that scholars are most likely to broaden their understanding of transnationalism. Lastly, we should keep in mind that evaluations of "reaffirm or reconfigure?" need to be made from a historically particularistic perspective. This fundamental advice will assist the comparison of myriad case studies.

What are the Implications of Transnationalism?

To this point I have suggested some of the impacts and implications of transnationalism, but now I wish to raise questions to be investigated regarding transnationalism's implications more generally. Much of what has been written about transnationalism's implications is directly related to identity—ethnic, racial and national identity constructions in particular (Appadurai 1993; Charles 1992; Fouron 1983; Glick Schiller et al. 1992; Glick Schiller 1994; Nagengast and Kearney 1990; Rouse 1995; R. Smith 1995). The findings are too diverse to summarize here, yet point toward the capacity of individuals to hold several different identities simultaneously, i.e., rural Mixtec agriculturalist and urban Chicano machine operator, and the ability to manipulate these identities for different purposes. These investigations are important and should continue to be pursued.

Secondly, and as stated above, I would hope that research will include questions about how transnational processes and ties reproduce or reconfigure established power hierarchies. Much of the literature to date on transnationalism from below paints it as empowering, democratic, and liberating, particularly in light of other global trends toward the concentration of wealth and power. This subaltern image needs to be tested consistently.

Lastly, I wish to discuss the implications of transnational analysis for meta-narratives of power and space. Numerous scholars have criticized much of the literature on migration as being too bipolar (Kearney 1995a; Rouse 1991 1995; R. Smith 1995). "The bipolar model assumes that migration takes place between territorially discriminable communities that retain their essential autonomy even as they grow more closely linked...Settlement is therefore seen as a process in which people inevitably reorient to their new locale, steadily transferring their home base, contextual

focus, and locus of social activity from one place to another"
(Rouse 1992: 42). In other words, the bipolar model is
admonished as too unilinear. I agree with this commentary, but
suggest that unilinearity also rears its head in the transnational
literature, particularly with respect to the implications of
transnationalism. In my reading of this literature, I find a
disproportionate emphasis on the effects of transmigrant activities
vis-à-vis their communities of origin. This emphasis is most evident
in the burgeoning studies of home town associations and the
projects they fund (Glick Schiller et al. 1992: 2; Goldring 1996;
Kearney 1995b; Lungo et al. 1996; Nagengast and Kearney 1990;
Popkin 1995; R. Smith 1995), but it also occurs in the literature on
remittances (both classic as well as more contemporary and
transnational) (Georges 1990; Gmelch 1980; Mozo and Vasquez
1988; Rhoades 1978; Sider 1992). I find myself as guilty as
anyone else on this score (see Mahler 1995b), but this very
culpability has stimulated me to be more critical. I see much less
attention paid in the literature to the role transmigrants play in
transforming those communities that they occupy which are not
their communities of origin. This may be a consequence of the
fact that such a focus has preoccupied the myriad studies of
*im*migrants' impacts on their "host" countries' economies and
service provision systems (e.g, the prolonged debate between Julian
Simon and George Borjas). The rise in xenophobia, nationalism,
and nativism within many nation-states which have received
migrant influxes during the 1980s and 1990s, suggests that these
migrants are playing a broader, and perhaps deeper, role in
transforming these societies than is generally acknowledged.
Saskia Sassen argues that they form a "central object in and a tool
for the renationalizing of political discourse" (1996: 62). That is,
as globalization erodes the power of the nation state, international
migration buttresses this power: "When it comes to immigrants
and refugees,...the nation state claims all its old splendor in
asserting its sovereign right to control its borders (Ibid: 59). At a
minimum, migrants represent a major source of demographic, if
not cultural, change with regard to the United States.
Transmigrants should be researched not only as agents of change

vis-à-vis their communities and countries of origin but also across entire transnational social fields. To not pursue this work vigorously, serves, however inadvertently, to reproduce meta-narratives of space and power such as bipolarity and modernization theory. If, as many transnationalists argue, the global-local duality is based on the false opposition that the global is the site of change and the local is one of stasis, and that change flows from centers of capitalism to the peripheries, then we need to take care not to reaffirm this duality owing to a limited inventory of praxis. I am not fearful of this in the long run but in the short run this limited inventory can be misinterpreted. Being mindful of this will assist researchers in avoiding unidirectional models of change toward more comprehensive and much richer models marked by fundamental disjunctures between "economy, culture and politics which we have only begun to theorize" (Appadurai 1990: 29).

Conclusion

The study of transnationalism holds the promise of shedding new and brilliant light on emerging cultural processes—identity, political, and economic transformations in particular. Through a transnational optic, human agency "from below" comes into focus as well as macrostructural forces "from above." The pathways to creolization become clearer, and the vision of a one-dimensional world marked by cultural and economic homogeneity and hegemony becomes dimmer. Much as transnationalism itself is important, so too is its investigation. Such study warrants more collaborative, comparative research than social scientists, and anthropologists in particular, have traditionally engaged in—such as multi-site projects. At a minimum, we need to work hard to make our case study questions comparable. This is the task I set out for myself in this paper and, hopefully, have accomplished here.

Notes

1. I would like to thank Michael Peter Smith, Luis Guarnizo and Nia Georges for their extremely helpful comments on earlier versions of this paper. I also wish to acknowledge the significance of conversations I have had on this topic with Saskia Sassen.

2. I use the term "growing" to acknowledge the critique of closed corporate societies and other territorialized, isolated cultural representations as not sufficiently portraying cultures' interconnectedness prior to capitalism (Gupta and Ferguson 1992; Wolf 1982).

3. Hereafter, references to transnationalism should be understood as meaning transmigration, unless explicitly stated otherwise.

4. I use such terms reservedly because they promote the bipolar model of migration (e.g., Rouse 1991, 1992; M.P Smith 1994). However, no new terms have been developed and widely disseminated that convey the intended meaning here. Until this occurs, the old terms will be recycled.

5. This process may take on the character of what Alejandro Portes and others have referred to as "segmented assimilation" (Portes and Zhou 1993). That is, the tendency for immigrant groups to assimilate to the predominate population(s) nearby. This model is applied most frequently to urban settings where immigrant children are more exposed to African American, Puerto Rican or Mexican (Chicano) cultures than to "mainstream," white, middle-class culture.

References

Appadurai, Arjun. (1991). "Global Ethnoscapes: Notes and Queries for a Transnational Anthropology." In Richard Fox, (ed.),*Recapturing Anthropology: Working in the Present*. Santa Fe, NM: School of American Research Press. Pp. 191-210.

———. (1990). "Disjuncture and Difference in the Global Cultural Economy." *Theory, Culture and Society* 7: 295-310.

———. (1993). "Patriotism and its Futures." *Public Culture* 5: 411-429.

Basch, Linda, Nina Glick Schiller, and Cristina Szanton Blanc. (1994). *Nations Unbound: Transnational Projects, Postcolonial Predicaments and Deterritorialized Nation-States*. New York: Gordon and Breach Publishers.

Bourne, R. (1993). "Trans-national America." In *The American Intellecutal Tradition: A Source Book*. New York: Oxford University Press. Pp. 153-163. First edition, 1916.

Brysk, Allison. (1993). "From Above and Below: Social Movements, the International System, and Human Rights in Argentina." *Comparative Political Studies* 26: 3: 259-285.

Charles, C. (1992). "Transnationalism in the Construct of Haitian Migrants' Racial Categories of Identity in New York City." In Nina Glick Schiller, Linda Basch, and Cristina Szanton Blanc (eds.), *Transnational Perspective on Migration: Race, Class, Ethnicity, and Nationalism Reconsidered*. New York: Annals of the New York Academy of Sciences 645: 101-123

Chavez, Leo R. (1994). "The Power of the Imagined Community: The Settlement of Undocumented Mexicans and Central Americans in the United States." *American Anthropologist* 96: 1: 52-73.

Chinchilla, Norma, Nora Hamilton, and James Loucky. (1993). "Central Americans in Los Angeles: An Immigrant Community in Transition." In *The Barrios: Latinos and the Underclass Debate*. New York: Russell Sage Foundation. Pp. 51-78.

Featherstone, Michael. (ed.). (1990). Global Culture: Nationalism: Globalization, and Modernity. London: Sage.

Foner, Nancy. (1978). *Jamaica Farewell: Jamaican Migrants in London*. Berkeley, CA: University of California Press.

Fouron, Georges. (1983). "The Black Dilemma in the United States: The Haitian Experience." *Journal of Caribbean Studies* 3: 3: 242-265.

Foster, R.J. (1991). "Making Nationals Cultures in the Global Ecumene." *Annual Review of Anthropology* 20: 235-60.

Funkhouser, Edward. (1991). "Emigration, Remittances, and Labor Market Adjustment: A Comparison of El Salvador and Nicaragua." Paper presented to the 15th Congress of the Latin American Studies Association, Washington, D.C. April 3, 1991.

————. (1992). "Mass Emigration, Remittances, and Economic Adjustment: The Case of El Salvador in the 1980s." In *Immigration and the Work Force*. Chicago: Chicago University Press. Pp. 135-175.

Georges, Eugenia. (1992). "Gender, Class, and Migration in the Dominican Republic: Women's Experiences in a Transnational Community." In Nina Glick Schiller, Linda Basch, and Cristina SzantonBlanc (eds.), *Towards a Transnational Perspective on Migration: Race, Class, Ethnicity, and Nationalism Reconsidered*. New York: Annals of the New York Academy of Sciences 645: 81-99.

————. The Making of a Transnational Community. Migration, Development, and Cultural Change in the Dominican Republic. New York, NY: Columbia University Press.

Gibson, Margaret A. (1988) Accomodation without Assimilation: Sikh Immigrants in an American High School. Ithaca, NY: Cornell University Press.

Glick Schiller, Nina. (1994). "Introducing Identities: Global Studies in Culture and Power." *Identities* 1: 1: 1-6.

Glick Schiller, Nina, Linda Basch, and Cristina Szanton Blanc. (1992). *Towards a Transnational Perspective on Migration: Race, Class, Ethnicity , and Nationalism Reconsidered*. New York: Annals of the New York Academy of Sciences 645.

Gmelch, G. (1980). "Return Migration." *Annual Review of Anthropology* 9: 135--159.

Goldring, Luin. (1996). "Gendered Memory: Constructions of Rurality Among Mexican Transnational Migrants." In *Creating the Countryside: The Politics of Rural and Environmental Discourse*. Philadelphia: Temple University Press. Pp. 303-329.

Grewal, Inderpal, and Caren Kaplan (eds.). (1994). *Scattered Hegemonies: Postmodernity and Transnational Feminist Practices*. Minneapolis, MN: University of Minnesota Press.

Guarnizo, Luis E. (1996a). "The Nation-State and Grassroots Transnationalism: Comparing Mexican and Dominican Transmigration." Paper presented at the 118th Annual American Ethnological Association Meetings. San Juan, Puerto Rico. April 17-21.

————. (1996b). "Transnationalism from Below: Social Transformation and the Mirage of Return Migration Among Dominican Transmigrants." Unpublished manuscript. California: University of California, Davis.

————. (1994). "'Los Dominicanyorks': The Making of a Binational Society." *Annals of the American Academy of Political and Social Sciences* 533: 70-86.

Gupta, Akhil. and James Ferguson. (1992). "Beyond 'Culture': Space, Identity, and the Politics of Difference." *Cultural Anthropology* 7: 1: 6-23.

Hagan, Jacqueline M. (1994). *Deciding to Be Legal: A Maya Community in Houston*. Philadelphia, PA: Temple University Press.

Hamilton, Nora, and Norma S. Chinchilla. (1991). "Central American Migration: A Framework for Analysis." *Latin American Research Review* 26:1: 75-110.

————. (eds.). (1995). "Central Americans in California: Transnational Communities, Economies and Cultures." Monograph Paper, No. 1. University of Southern California: Center for Multiethnic and Transnational Studies.

Hannerz, Ulf. (1990). "Cosmopolitans and Locals in World Culture." In Michael Featherstone (ed.), *Global Culture: Nationalism: Globalization, and Modernity*. London: Sage. Pp. 237-251.

————. (1989). "Notes on the Global Ecumene." *Public Culture* 1: 2: 66-75.

————. (1987). "The World in Creolisation." *Africa* 57: 4: 546-559.

Hondagneu-Sotelo, Pierrette. (1994). *Gendered Transitions: Mexican Experiences of Immigration*. Berkeley, CA: University of California Press.

Jonas, Susanne. (1995). "War and Peace in the Central American Diaspora in California." In *Central Americans in California: Transnational Communities, Economies and Cultures*. Monograph Paper, No. 1: 6-10. University of Southern California: Center for Multiethnic and Transnational Studies.

Juffer, Jane. (1988). "Abuse at the Border: Women Face a Perilous Crossing." *The Progressive* (April): 14-19.

Kearney, Michael. (1995a). "The Local and the Global: The Anthropology of Globalization and Transnationalism." *Annual Review of Anthropology* 24: 547-65.

————. (1995b). "The Effects of Transnational Culture, Economy, and Migration on Mixtec Identity in Oaxacalifornia." In Michael Peter Smith and Joe R. Feagin (eds.), *The Bubbling Cauldron: Race, Ethnicity, and the Urban Crisis*. Minneapolis: University of Minnesota Press. Pp. 226-243.

Kearney, Michael, and Carole Nagengast. (1989). "Anthropological Perspectives on Transnational Communities in Rural California." Working Group on Farm Labor and Rural Poverty, Working Paper, No. 3. California Institute for Rural Studies, Davis, California. February.

Keohane, R. and J. Nye. (eds.). (1971). *Transnational Relations and World Politics*. Cambridge, MA: Harvard University Press.

Kyle, D. (1994). The Transnational Peasant: The Social Structures of Economic Migration from the Ecuadoran Andes. Ph.D. dissertation. Department of Sociology, The Johns Hopkins University.

Lessinger, Johanna. (1992). "Investing or Going Home? A Transnational Strategy Among Indian Immigrants in the United States." In Nina Glick Schiller, Linda Basch, and Cristina Szanton Blanc, *Towards a Transnational Perspective on Migration: Race, Class, Ethnicity, and Nationalism Reconsidered.* New York: Annals of the New York Academy of Sciences 645: 53-80.

Levitt, Peggy. (1996). "Social Remittances: A Conceptual Tool for Understanding the Relationship Between Migration and Local Development." Manuscript. Department of Sociology, Harvard University.

Los Angeles Times. (1995). "The War on 'Disposable People'; Frustrated by Rising Crime, Latin Vigilantes Turn Guns on Gangs, the Poor and the Homeless." June 27.

Lungo, M., Eekhoff, K., and S. Baires. (1996). "Migración Internacional y Desarrollo Local en El Salvador." Occasional Paper, No. 8. San Salvador: Fundación Nacional para el Desarrollo.

Mahler, Sarah J. (1996). "Bringing Gender to a Transnational Focus: Theoretical and Empirical Ideas." Unpublished manuscript, University of Vermont, Department of Anthropology.

———. (1995a). *American Dreaming: Immigrant Life on the Margins.* Princeton, NJ: Princeton University Press.

———. (1995b). "Vested in Migration: Salvadorans Challenge Restrictionist Policies." Paper presented to the conference Transnational Realities and Nation States: Trends in International Migration and Immigration Policy in the Americas at the North-South Center, University of Miami. May 20, 1995.

Montes Mozo, S. and J.G. Vasquez. (1988). "Salvadoran Migration to the United States: An Exploratory Study." Hemispheric Migration Project, Center for Immigration Policy and Refugee Assistance, Georgetown University.

Nagengast, Carole, and Michael Kearney. (1990). "Mixtec Ethnicity: Social Identity, Political Consciousness, and Political Activism." *Latin American Research Review* 25: 2: 61-91.

New York Times. (1996). "Caste May Be India's Moral Achilles' Heel." October 20.

Ogbu, J. (1990). "Minority Status and Literacy in Comparative Perspective." *Daedalus* 119: 141-168.

Ong, Aihwa. (1993). "On the Edge of Empires: Flexible Citizenship among Chinese in Diaspora." *Positions* 1: 3: 745-778.

———. (1992). "Limits to Cultural Accumulation: Chinese Capitalists on the American Pacific Rim." In Nina Glick Schiller, Linda Basch, and Cristina Szanton Blanc, *Towards a Transnational Perspective on Migration: Race, Class, Ethnicity , and Nationalism Reconsidered.* New York: Annals of the New York Academy of Sciences 645: 125-143.

Paul, S., Mahler, S. and Schwartz, M. (Forthcoming). "Mass Action and Social Structure." *Political Power and Social Theory.*

Pessar, Patricia R. (1986). "The Role of Gender in Dominican Settlement in the United States. In *Women and Change in Latin America.* South Hadley, MA: Bergin and Garvey Publishers. Pp. 173-194.

Popkin, E. (1995). "Guatemalan Hometown Associations in Los Angeles." In *Central Americans in California: Transnational Communities, Economies and Cultures.* Monograph Paper, No. 1: 35-39. University of Southern California: Center for Multiethnic and Transnational Studies.

Portes, Alejandro. (1995). "Transnational Communities: Their Emergence and Significance in the Contemporary World System." Keynote address delivered to the 19th Annual Conference on the Political Economy of the World-System. North-South Center at the University of Miami. April 21, 1995.

Portes, Alejandro, and Alex Stepick. (1993). *City on the Edge: the Transformation of Miami.* Berkeley, CA: University of California Press.

Portes, Alejandro, and Min Zhou. (1993). "The New Second Generation: Segmented Assimilation and Its Variants." *Annals of the American Academy of Political and Social Science* 530 (Nov): 74-96.

Richman, Karen. (1992). "A Lavalas at Home/A Lavalas for Home: Inflections of Transnationalism in the Discourse of Haitian President Aristide." In Ninna Glick Schiller, Linda Basch, and Cristina Szanton-Blanc, *Towards a Transnational Perspective on Migration: Race, Class, Ethnicity, and Nationalism Reconsidered.* New York: *Annals of the New York Academy of Sciences* 645: 189-200.

Rhoades, Robert E. (1978). Intra-European Return Migration and Rural Development: Lessons from the Spanish Case. *Human Organization* 37: 2: 136-147.

Rouse, Roger. (1995). Questions of Identity: Personhood and Collectivity in Transnational Migration to the United States. *Critique of Anthropology* 144: 351-380.

———. (1992). Making Sense of Settlement: Class Transformation, Cultural Struggle, and Transnationalism Among Mexican Migrants in the United States. In Ninna Glick Schiller, Linda Basch, and Cristina Szanton-Blanc, *Towards a Transnational Perspective on Migration: Race, Class, Ethnicity, and Nationalism Reconsidered.* New York: *Annals of the New York Academy of Sciences* 645: 25-52.

———. (1991). Mexican Migration and the Social Space of Postmodernism. *Diaspora* 1: 1: 8-23.

Rutland (Vermont) *Herald.* (1996). "Youth Crimes Rises As Political Hostilities Ease." March 17, 1996.

Sanchez, A. (1996) Paper presented at the 118th Annual American Ethnological Association Meetings. San Juan, Puerto Rico. April 17-21, 1996.

Sassen, Saskia. (1996). *Losing Control? Sovereignty in an Age of Globalization.* New York: Columbia University Press.

Sider, G. (1992). "The Contradictions of Transnational Migration: A Discussion." In Nina Glick Schiller, Linda Basch, and Cristina Szanton Blanc, *Towards a Transnational Perspective on Migration: Race, Class, Ethnicity and Nationalism Reconsidered*: 231-240. New York: New York Academy of Sciences.

Sikkink, Kathryn. (1993). "Human Rights, Principled Issue-Networks, and Sovereignty in Latin America." *International Organization* 47: 3: 411-441.

Siri, G. (1996). "Uso Productivo de las Remesas Familiares en El Salvador." Working Document, No. 42, Fundación Salvadoreña para el Desarrollo Económico y Social. San Salvador: El Salvador.

Smith, Anthony D. (1990). "Towards a Global Culture?" In Michael Featherstone (ed.), *Global Culture: Nationalism: Globalization, and Modernity*. London: Sage. Pp. 171-191.

Smith, Michael Peter. (1994). "Can You Imagine? Transnational Migration and the Globalization of Grassroots Politics." *Social Text* 39 : 15-33.

———. (1992). "Postmodernism, Urban Ethnography, and the New Social Space of Ethnic Identity." *Theory and Society* 21: 493-531.

Smith, Robert C. (1995). "Transnational Localities: Community, Technology and the Politics of Membership Within the Context of Mexico-US Migration." Paper presented at the American Sociological Association Meetings, Washington D.C. August.

Sørensen, Ninna N. (1996). "Nueva York is Just Another Dominican Capital— Madrid Es Otro Mundo." Transnational Projects, Project Paper, No. 2.

Suárez-Orozco, Marcelo M. (1989). *Central American Refugees in United States High Schools: A Psychological Study of Motivation and Achievement*. Stanford, CA: Stanford University Press.

Sutton, Constance R. (1992). "Some Thoughts on Gendering and Internationalizing Our Thinking about Transnational Migrations." In Nina Glick Schiller, Linda Basch, and Cristina Szanton Blanc, *Towards a Transnational Perspective on Migration: Race, Class, Ethnicity, and Nationalism Reconsidered*. New York: Annals of the New York Academy of Sciences 645: 241-249.

Washington Post. (1996). "'Peace Summit' Aims to Steer Young Latinos from Gang Violence." April 4, 1996.

Wolf, Eric. (1982). *Europe and the People Without History*. Berkeley: University of California Press.

———. (1969). *Peasant Wars of the Twentieth Century*. New York: Harper and Row.

II

Transnational Economic and Political Agency

4

Transnational Social Networks and Negotiated Identities in Interactions Between Hong Kong and China

Alan Smart
Josephine Smart

The emergence of an export-oriented capitalism in China is one of the pivotal processes of the late twentieth century, combining the influential themes of the collapse of centrally-planned economies and the rise of East Asian capitalism. The emergence of capitalist practices has, since the launch of China's economic reforms in 1978, been consistently in advance of its official recognition and legal codification, and has primarily been associated with the activities of overseas Chinese investors, particularly those from Hong Kong.

In this paper, we explore transnational social networks in action as they are constituted and mobilized for practical (but also solidary) activities. In doing so, we also consider the ways in which others can make claims on such networks and how such claims can be resisted or subverted. In doing so, we deal with issues of identities, as shared identities and claims of exclusion operate in the process of situated ethnicity. However, we are also critical of excessive attention to identity politics at the expense of other influences that the increasing prevalence of transnational social networks are producing.

In the next section, we discuss the nature of transnational social networks and their relationship to concepts of postmodernity. The following section concentrates on cross-border relationships between Hong Kong and China. The third section reviews issues of identity and exclusion among Chinese. The fourth section looks into the dynamics of these issues through the medium of ethnographic accounts of specific situations where identity politics have been involved in transnational networking. The conclusion discusses contributions that ethnographic research can make to the interplay between processes of transnationalism and the mobilization and transformation of identities.

Transnational Social Networks

In the postmodern age of the late twentieth century, national boundaries are becoming less central for social analysis than they were in the past. While this is well known with regard to the practices of transnational corporations, the development and maintenance by individuals of social networks that cross borders are much less known and understood. Changing communication and transportation technologies, international migration, and political changes have been driving these transnational networks, but in few other places have they increased so dramatically and had so much potential for social transformation as in South China.

Transnational flows of investment and people are made possible by and structured through households, family enterprises, "old-boy" networks, cultural understandings and miscommunication. Flows across borders include not only capital and labor, but also gifts, contributions to household expenses, obligations, and cultural influence (Werbner 1990; Hannerz 1992). To describe these transnational practices, we must move beyond political economy to consider "moral economies" or "social economies."[1]

Theories of postmodernism have been influential in producing new forms of analysis of the interaction between the local and the global. Modernity is seen as characterized by homogenizing processes—"cultural imperialism, Americanization and mass consumer culture as a proto-universal culture riding on the back of Western economic and political domination" (Featherstone 1990: 2)—which is now being replaced by a more fragmented but equally global cultural transformation characterized by "the diversity, variety and richness of popular and local discourses, codes and practices which resist...systemicity and order." (Featherstone 1990: 2). Postmodernity has developed through the collapse of faith in the projects of modernity, and through the production of an increasingly multi-centred political economy which cannot be controlled by any single nation-state. Comprehension of these complex processes requires attention to the local situation seen in a translocal context. The challenge is to accomplish this without engaging either in reductionism or ignoring the profound influences of the extralocal upon the local, and to recognize that their interaction will vary over time and space. As Smith (1992: 512) suggests, inquiring into the postmodern condition requires a "provisionality premised on a willingness to cross border zones, consider the cultural improvisations that are part of daily life at the boundaries, and in these sites of intercultural production, critically rework the representations and intellectual constructs through which we have come to know the world." The emergence and heightened activity of transnational social networks has had the result that these border zones are increasingly ethnic spaces (Smith 1992), or "global ethnoscapes" in Appadurai's (1991) term. Such ethnoscapes and transnational networks cannot be dealt with effectively, indeed they can hardly be seen, with the conventional academic division of labor. The global and the local intersect within households, within daily life, within neighbourhoods, and coping with the complex texture and trajectories of these interactions is a challenge which ethnographic perspectives have great "competitive advantages" in addressing.

Ong (1991: 280) found that local situations resulted in "unexpected conjunctures of labor relations and cultural systems, high-tech operations and indigenous values." Social and cultural organization constitutes a set of "resources" which management can use to manipulate labor (e.g., taking advantage of patriarchal systems to recruit "docile" female labor), but which can also be used to resist proletarianization or to contest practices on the shopfloor.

Glick Schiller, Basch and Blanc-Szanton (1992: 1) have defined "transnationalism" as "the processes by which immigrants build social fields that link together their country of origin and their country of settlement." They reject the analytic appropriateness of the term "immigrant" because of the way it "evokes images of permanent rupture," while the reality is that today "immigrants develop networks, activities, patterns of living, and ideologies that span their home and the host society," and they, instead, refer to "transmigrants" (Basch et al. 1994: 3–4). Their definition of transnationalism is too restrictive, since social fields that cross national boundaries can be constructed and maintained without emigration, for example, through Internet participation or tourism, or, more pertinently and significantly, transnational investment. A serious problem with Basch et al.'s approach is that transnational investment and migration are seen as largely distinct processes, despite their recognition of the linkages between transnational flows of capital and labor. The implicit assumption is that migration concerns the flow of labor, while transnational investment involves the flow of capital. Labour flows may be more or less directly a result of the circulation of capital (Sassen 1988; Ong 1992; Bonacich and Cheng 1994), but the processes are generally examined by different scholars with different methods.

In the case of Hong Kong, many entrepreneurs who invest in China have fewer resources than the average Hong Kong migrant to Canada or Australia (Smart and Smart 1991; J. Smart 1995). Thus, rather than transnational flows of capital being only a matter of transnational corporations and the capitalist world-economy, while decisions about immigration involve individuals who are primarily prospective workers, both transnational migration and investment are elements of the opportunity structure of ordinary individuals and households. Decisions in either sphere are related to common processes of decision-making and what Ong (1992) refers to as "strategies of accumulation."

Hong Kong may be an exceptional case, given the ease of border crossing and the existence of dramatic differences in investment costs (hence potential profits),[2] but the trend of development in world capitalism is precisely towards greater ease in transnational investment, and a relative decrease in the average size of economic enterprises that become involved in such practices (Amin and Thrift 1995: 96). With the trend towards freer trade, and the reduced cost and increased access through telecommunications, small companies and self-employed entrepreneurs will be more and more likely to integrate themselves into global or regional, rather than simply local or national, economic structures. Transmigrants are particularly likely to become involved in such activities, since they are usually exposed to barriers to advancement in the country of destination, and their knowledge of the country of origin and their continuing social networks offer them potential competitive advantages. The implication of these factors is that the disjunction between the movements of people and of capital will become less significant, and that the popular view of the "transnational corporation" as a synonym for "giant corporation" will become less and less valid.

Attention to networks in ethnography has derived from a recognition of the reduced salience of groups in certain settings (Hannerz 1980), particularly in urban contexts. Network analysis generally (but not necessarily) begins from a more actor-centric perspective: exploring how individuals are connected with and interact with other individuals, rather than concentrating primarily upon the organization of a group. This perspective does not imply that people are not part of groups, nor that groups no longer have any importance. Rather it begins from a recognition that for most people, there is no single group which encapsulates all of their activities and concerns, so that regardless of how significant membership in a group is, interactions extend beyond that group. Without attending to those extra-group linkages, much that is important about daily experience and problem-solving is likely to be missed.

Despite the origins of network analysis in ethnography, its subsequent development has primarily involved quantitative sociometry: the measuring of quantifiable characteristics of networks. The danger in this development, as illuminating as it can be, is of excessive formalism which "directs attention exclusively to the overall structure of network ties while suppressing consideration of their substantive content" (Emirbayer and Goodwin 1994: 1415). One result has been that network analysis has failed to deal adequately with issues of agency. Networks simultaneously constrain and enable action, but the actions of individuals within these networks are also constrained and enabled by cultural formations (Emirbayer and Goodwin 1994: 1440). The mobilization of a social tie is done within a context of social and cultural expectations, and blatant networking can offend as easily as it can attain one's goals. The formalistic development of network analysis, we suggest, has directed attention away from difficult qualitative issues of *network process*. Ties do not simply exist or not: they are often ambiguous or even contentious. In some cases, their very utility is dependent on their deniability. Networks often have what Anthony Giddens refers to as a 'virtual' quality (see Sewell 1994 for a discussion of the virtuality of structures).

The focus of this article is on network processes rather than the sociometry of network structure, and particularly upon networks-in-action. Through intensive research with informants over a long period of time, we have been able to observe the ways in which social ties are brought into play, maintained, and sometimes disrupted. In doing so, we have followed the anthropological tradition of "situational analysis" (Van Velsen 1967), where events are examined in detail in order to explore the processes of distinct sets of social relations and practices in interaction, with outcomes that are indeterminate for the actors at the time of their action, and which thus captures the flavor of social life more authentically than ex post facto structural analysis.

Social Networks Across the Hong Kong/China Border

Hong Kong investors have drawn on social connections, cultural commonalities, and nationalist sentiments to facilitate their activities in China, and to provide guarantees for them not effectively granted in the legal and political systems (Smart and Smart 1991). In a context where capitalists were seen as the class enemy and the capitalist world economy as fundamentally antagonistic to Chinese socialism, and where accommodations to these threats have been made only reluctantly and for tactical/pragmatic reasons, the capacity of overseas Chinese investors to present themselves as patriotic participants in the building of socialist modernization and loyal supporters of their native places in China was initially of crucial importance in mediating these contradictions. As Helen Siu (1993: 32) points out:

> The regime plays up the assumed connection between cultural identity and political commitment. "Patriotic" overseas investors are pursued as sources of capital, technology, and market.... The claims are based on primordial sentiments and in the name of national unity, territorial bond, and family pride....

The problem with this approach, and thus a potential problem for the central authorities of the People's Republic of China (PRC), is that the claim that is made on the loyalties of the overseas Chinese investor appeals simultaneously to all of these identities of greater and smaller scale, and relies on the belief that the different identities are parallel and mutually supporting rather than potentially in conflict with each other. Feelings of solidarity with locality and kin are thus assumed to be equivalent to solidarity with the nation, and the possibility that loyalty to one's family and native place might be in conflict or competition with patriotism attached to the nation is not considered. Yet this is a serious possibility: a desire to help develop your native place and to provide opportunities for relatives can coexist with strong feelings of distrust and antipathy for the Chinese Communist Party (CCP). Some investors have, for example, been primarily concerned to enhance their family's prestige in their native village, or to prepare for retiring there.

There are multiple Chinas of identification (with the PRC, with 'cultural China,' with the Nationalist Party claims to legitimate rule over the whole of Chinese territory, and so on), and some of them exclude the PRC Government, so that support for one's native place and even for 'China' may be consistent with antipathy to the regime. In reality, investment in China may be undertaken, not to support the CCP's vision of how to develop China, but rather to reduce the reliance of one's relatives and *tong-heung* (fellow natives) on the opportunity structure and hierarchy of power controlled by the official party-state. One of the critical effects of overseas Chinese investment and involvement in the PRC has been to make available to some people routes to social mobility and improved standards of living which are not controlled by the socialist power structure. Indeed, local governments may become reliant on overseas Chinese investment to the extent that they have conflicts of interest with the central authorities which are managed in some cases by token compliance with Party policies while pragmatically acting in contradiction to (orthodox) interpretations of those policies (A. Smart 1995; J. Smart 1993; Fitzgerald 1996).

While loyalties to the nation may be in conflict with local patriotism, it is also the case that even native place is a "malleable construction" whose connotations "may vary by local context, so that what it means to be a *Beijing ren* in Beijing is radically different from its meaning in Shanghai or Wuhan" (Honig 1996: 145). The identities which are invoked are claims, which can be used for different purposes. The ambiguity or multivocality of identity is a central resource in the mediation of some of the conflicts involved in the conduct of capitalist practices in a socialist context.

Non-Chinese capitalism was also utilized in the early years of economic reforms, but the mediation of contradictions was accomplished in ways (primarily through joint ventures and restrictions on the freedom of action of Western managers) that often reduced economic efficiency (Pearson 1991; Mann 1989) and produced considerable barriers to investment. The mobilization of shared identities by overseas Chinese investors made it possible much earlier for them to operate in nearly completely capitalist manners, and in the flexible and rapidly responsive ways characteristic of overseas Chinese capitalism, and which made penetration of Western consumer markets feasible.[3]

The emergence of capitalism within the confines of a Leninist polity is only one of the complex outcomes of the transformation of transnational linkages between Hong Kong and China since 1978. The relatively impermeable border (although the flows of people and materials that did reach Hong Kong from China were of central importance to Hong Kong's "economic miracle") between the two territories that prevailed between 1949 and 1978 was historically unusual, and prior to 1949 Hong Kong was tightly integrated into the Chinese economy and society. Resumption of close ties and heavy flows across the border now brings together entities that diverged during the interregnum: China moved from a divided and ravaged playing field of colonial power politics to become a poor but united socialist society, while Hong Kong transformed itself from a colonial trading post to an affluent colonial manufacturing and financial center. The gulf that yawned between the societies separated by the trickle of the Shenzhen River in 1978 was extremely apparent. Even the contacts which continued emphasized growing separation, as illegal immigrants risked their lives to enter Hong Kong, and Hong Kong carried bundles of used clothes, cooking oil and basic foodstuffs to their relatives. By 1995, the shock of transition that once was felt in passing through the border to China has been replaced by surprise at how Shenzhen is coming to resemble the high-rise congestion and frenetic activity of central Hong Kong.

Earlier appearances of disjunction at the border concealed continuation of strong personal ties resulting from Chinese illegal emigration to Hong Kong, and feelings of a common Cantonese and Chinese identity. Our field experiences in Guangdong contrast very strongly with the following statement by Pickowicz (1994: 83):

> Over the years I have noticed that ordinary people in mainland China have little interest in and experience difficulty understanding the themes of most films made in Taiwan and Hong Kong. If there is interest in this cinema, it is because these films are perceived to be utterly exotic and otherworldly. That is to say, they have little to do with the postsocialist realities of mainland life.

The situations we encountered in Guangdong were very different: there is intense interest in Hong Kong television and popular films (Ikels 1996), and no apparent difficulty in understanding them (although there is less knowledge about the hard realities underlying the glossy exteriors presented in these products of popular culture). Even during our first stay with a family in Guangzhou in 1984, we were struck by how close the patterns of everyday life, interpersonal interaction, and individual priorities we observed were to those found among low-income residents of Hong Kong. The people in Northern China referred to by Pickowicz may be unable to identify with Hong Kong popular culture, but in Guangdong there is relatively little discomfort with the straightforward materialist consumerism that pours across the border in Hong Kong films, television, and popular music. As Friedman (1994) has pointed out, Hong Kong (as well as Taiwan and Singapore) is often seen as representing a possible and desirable future for China, and the popular culture out of Hong Kong and Taiwan can be seen as representing "training films" for the desired future (see also

Guldin 1995). Furthermore, people in Guangdong increasingly see that glossy future as attainable at least for the fortunate few, because that lifestyle is being lived by the new elite around them.

Contacts across the border are more complicated than just a story of Hong Kong's influence on Guangdong, combined with representations of identity that create a 'we' which transgresses the capitalist/socialist divide and excludes northerners. At the same time that Hong Kong people assert inclusive ties that incorporate them into villages and ethnic groups (Johnson 1995), they also assert distinctions between themselves and all mainlanders. There is a kind of colonial mentality that contrasts Hong Kong's achievements with the backwardness, inefficiency and incivility of the People's Republic, and is often tied in with incredible rudeness and exploitation on the part of the Hong Konger in China. In response, there are also extremely negative representations of Hong Kong people and their behaviour in China, particularly from state sector employees with good educational backgrounds. While such opinions may only be vocalized in private and in the absence of the 'other,' these distinctions can also be enacted in non-vocal performances which contain ambiguous elements such as generosity versus paternalism (e.g., the account of the banquet below).

These practices of inclusion and exclusion, reciprocity and criticism, do not occupy distinct social spaces, but interpenetrate, and provide a complex ground of cooperation and distinction. Practices and talk which posit shared identity can almost always be constructed, if not directly then indirectly through shared contacts (*guanxi*), but they can also be subverted and rejected by reference to alternative forms of identity. Cultural identity as an interpersonal relationship, then, is made possible by tactical moves drawing on cultural resources, but such claims are not always accepted, and below we attend to the circumstances which make possible successful claims to shared identity.

Approaches to Cultural Identity in China

Ong (1992) suggests that history has produced a "decentred consciousness" among overseas Chinese, as the focus of their postcolonial and patriotic sentiments appears in a multiplicity of possible objects of identification. Hong Kong people find themselves on the edge of two former empires (Britain and China), and at the center of an emerging transnational diasporic world economy. A sense of cultural allegiance and patriotic solidarity with "China" does not necessarily mean support for the Beijing regime. Beijing is concerned with the threat of the emergence of a strong Hong Kong identity which might be linked politically with Western or Taiwanese capitalist powers (Lee 1995: 130). For many who do not publicly choose sides, solidarity with China involves cultural identification, focus on the compatibility of the pursuit of economic self-interest and the strengthening of China, and emphasis on subnational identities.

Hong Kong people are sometimes referred to as westernized, and mainlanders contrast this with greater cultural purity in China. But Hong Kong Chinese, particularly those without overseas education or in the working class, are not westernized in any deep way (although they are familiar with and interested in many western products, we would hardly say that Anglo-Canadians are orientalized through a similar consumer interest). Their lives and relationships have been transformed by their birth in or incorporation into an industrial (now becoming post-industrial) city ruled by the British in an intensely capitalist way. At the same time, Hong Kong people, many of whom were born in China, are also immediately recognizable as operating within "the net of Chinese culture" which Pasternak (1983: 11) asserts:

> is a loose one. It constrains lightly. Although considerable behavioral variation is evident, we are comfortable that those within this net are Chinese: for the most part a recognizable Chinese inventory of behavioral possibilities is evident. It is not that there are no givens, no relations of necessity: there are. There is a logic to the net's construction, but the net is not unbending or inflexible.

Given the time and space that the Chinese way of life has spread across, it is hardly surprising that it provides ample resources for coping with distinct situations and challenges, while still being able to claim a quintessential "Chineseness" (Nonini and Ong 1996).

Indeed, Guldin (1995: 110) notes that the attraction of the "Hong Kong model" for their counterparts in Guangdong province is in the way that it shows "how to be both Chinese and modern." The influence of this emerging southern Chinese version of modernity is spreading throughout China. Friedman (1994) describes how the dominant nationalist narrative in China has been a Maoist anti-imperialist one in which the CCP saved the nation by "providing the correct leadership that would mobilize patriotic Chinese, push imperialists out of China" and thereby permitted "an independent China to prosper with dignity" (Ibid., 67). This narrative treated the capitalism that China had experienced as "pure imperialism, a total evil made up singularly of 'aggression, plunder, national humiliation,'..." (Ibid., 67). By the 1990s, much of this narrative had been discredited, and one result was a new, southern-oriented imaginary, in which national success was:

> identified with the market-oriented activities of southerners who joined with Chinese capital from disapora Hong Kong, Macao, or Southeast Asia to produce world-competitive products that earned foreign exchange that could be invested in building a prosperous China (Friedman 1994: 79).

Even in the interior provinces Schein (1996: 209) has noted the "shift of attention toward Hong Kong and Taiwan as desirable sites for emulation," and models for how to participate in "the cosmopolitan culture of late capitalist consumption, which itself is dismantling the East-West binary."

These analyses of representations of modernity and being Chinese are fascinating and insightful, but they cannot replace "thick description" of how they actually are drawn upon, negotiated, and reinterpreted in practice. Rouse (1995) suggests that current academic fascination with identity has resulted in tendencies to assume that concern with identity is a universal human experience. He found that in a rural region of Western Mexico, when people made claims on each other, they didn't do so by invoking "common membership in a categorically defined collectivity [identity], but by tracing the string of personal ties that would eventually connect them" (Rouse 1995: 368). This pattern of claims-making through building personal ties is central to Chinese practices of *guanxi* (connections) as well, but the two patterns are not exclusive, because constructing particularistic ties is done partially by asserting commonalities that bring the interactors into an "us." Rouse's skepticism is still relevant, though, since many varieties of common identity are available, and are rarely considered mutually exclusive. Indeed the argument that being part of one "us" precludes being part of another "us" is itself a political move (e.g., rejecting the validity of Taiwanese identity in the Republic of China) which can usually be countered by differently construed claims.

Hong Kong people, like anthropologists, manipulate a combination of insider and outsider identities in engaging in cross-boundary practices, while their mainland counterparts collude, resist and counter-propose definitions of the situation and the sharing or opposing of identities. In pursuit of the new opportunities available in reform China, Hong Kong people regularly engage in identification and self-representation practices that may assert outsider and insider roles simultaneously, just as participant-observation profits from a careful and shifting blend of outsider/observer and insider/participant. Yet, while it is true that Hong Kong people benefit from a skilful blend of the advantages of both insider and outsider roles, it may also be the case that inept performance can result in achieving the disadvantages of both. The Hong Kong capitalist, as an outsider, may be allowed to act in ways that local citizens cannot (and one result is that domestic enterprises frequently establish themselves in Hong Kong shell companies for the tax and other advantages of foreign investment), but equally may be permitted privileges of the insiders which are denied to outsiders, since they are "compatriots" (*tongbao*) rather than foreigners. Inept performance, though, can lead to demands being made on the Hong Kong investor that could not be considered in the case of non-Chinese foreign investors, and this is one reason that many investors avoid establishing important enterprises in their home village. As Granovetter (1990) points out, both undersocialized firms (where everyone is out for their own short-term interests in an opportunistic way) and oversocialized firms (where social obligations may lead to bankruptcy) may be inefficient, and a Hong Kong investor capitalizing on his/her social connections must carefully negotiate the path between the Scylla and Charbydis of insider and outsider status (Smart and Smart 1993). The ideal would be managing to make socially-based claims on the practices of others, while asserting the economic necessity driving one's own actions, but limits to achieving the best of both worlds in such a way are considerable.

The situation is complicated by the existence of multiple insides, some of which include both Hong Kong people and their counterparts across the border, yet exclude other Chinese, for example, Cantonese and *tong heung* (people who share the same native place). The art of *guanxi* does not involve simply the building of a relationship between two individuals, but relies upon constituting an "us" which can encompass both, and within which identity sharing, cooperation and favours are appropriate. Sometimes the inclusive entity invoked in the exchanges and discourse is obvious (e.g., close kin ties), but some basis for a relationship can usually be found, even if only as friends of friends (Yang 1994). Even when there is an obvious relationship to be evoked, multiply-stranded relationships may provide alternative rubrics which may be more advantageous in particular contexts. For example, it may be desirable to downplay kin ties and emphasize shared locality when an investor engages in certain forms of exchange with local political leaders. In another context, it might be desirable to emphasize a broader rather than more specific linkage in order to be able to draw others into the situation. What is explicitly invoked in interchanges between individuals (e.g., shared identity as patriotic Chinese) may not be what the exchange relationship is implicitly about, and all participants and observers may understand the implicit basis for the relationship without anyone making it blatant.

The presentation and negotiation of identity inclusions and exclusions between Hong Kong people and those that they deal with across the border are not simply issues of solidarity and effective performance. Many of the identities that are presented involve very negative assessments of the other side. There is definitely an "ugly Hong Konger" style that resonates uncomfortably with Western colonial interpersonal interactions. This stereotype involves people who see themselves as much more developed and rational than their benighted counterparts who have been degraded and decultured by the socialist experience (or, in a variant, have never risen above peasant ignorance). The ugly Hong Konger emerges in exploitative sex tourism, in labor relations based on coercion and complete lack of respect, in rude treatment of service personnel, in open discussions of the flaws of mainlanders, and so on.

Ethnographic Accounts

Most of the above discussion has been based on ethnographic research by the authors, or on the ethnographic accounts of other researchers. Space limitations make it impossible to provide the evidential bases for the generalizations that have been made (see Smart and Smart 1993 for a particularly detailed account of one enterprise that supports many of the claims). In this section, descriptions of a few particular events and situations will be used to flesh out the dynamics of cross-borders network process.

Say no more, we are ji gei yan (on the same side)

The Cantonese term *ji gei yan* is made up of two parts: *ji gei* means 'I' or 'self' as in 'myself,' and *yan* means 'person' or 'people.' Together the term *ji gei yan* conveys the equivalent of the English terms 'us', 'our own people' or 'we are on the same side.' The antithesis of *ji gei yan* is *ngoi yan*, 'outside people.' Unlike the descriptive kinship terms which specify the inalienable relationship between two individuals based on consanguinity, these terms are highly situational. They are invoked under specific situations to include or exclude others in relation to oneself. Similar to kinship terms, these terms carry specific notions of associated obligation and privilege. For instance, in identifying someone as *ji gei yan*, the actor is placing that person on the same level. Just as outsiders can be incorporated temporarily as a family member or *ji gei yan* kin (especially affinal kin) can be excluded by labelling them as *ngoi yan*. This fluidity of inclusion and exclusion is a central element in the network process.

Robert Chan is a businessman born and raised in Hong Kong, with a mix of Manchurian, Chinese and Portuguese heritage. He received his University education in Canada, returned to Hong Kong and worked for over 10 years before taking up a partnership with an old friend. One of Robert's many lines of trading involves the production and global marketing of ceramics: dining ware, coffee mugs and souvenir items. The company is based in Hong Kong, the production is done in Shenzhen Special Economic Zone in Guangdong province (adjacent to Hong Kong), and the products are sold mostly in North America. In 1995, sales totalled over US$5 million. There are 150-200 workers in the Shenzhen factory and Robert visits the factory regularly to make sure that the products meet with the buyers' specifications. Being a part owner of the factory, Robert is caught in the ever changing but persistent web of bureaucracy and investment-related problems that are common in China. Robert's own description of his experience in China is a good example of the social construction of identities in response to specific contexts and the ongoing negotiations between interacting parties. Specifically Robert identifies several main 'identities' that he assumes under different situations in his business dealings in China: the Manchurian, the overseas Chinese, the Hong Kong Chinese and the dumb foreigner (Robert has Canadian citizenship).

In 1995, during one of Robert's visits to Shenzhen, an official from the local fire department demanded a payment of RMB$7000 (US$1 = RMB$8 in 1995) as a fine for the violation of safety rules at the factory. Robert pretended he did not have that much cash with him and offered to pay him at the fire department office the next day. This official was not happy about that but Robert persisted. The next day he went to see the Chief of the fire department in the company of the Secretary (the highest Party cadre in the unit) from the local administrative unit with whom he and his partner had negotiated their investment contract. Robert played the role of the angry investor, ranted and raved about the harassment he received yesterday from one of the Chief's staff and left RMB$7000 with the Chief as payment of the fine. In this particular scenario, Robert played up his identity as a *lo ngoi*, an 'old' outsider. While he did not outright accuse the Fire Chief and/or his staff of corruption or unnecessary harassment, Robert was able to speak openly about his displeasure without reservation, and the presentation of himself as an outsider, an investor from Hong Kong, lends legitimacy to his complaint.

On the way back to the factory, Robert told the Secretary that the RMB$7000 would come out of the investment contract fees the factory pays to his administrative unit because he considered it the local administrative unit's (the factory's landlord) obligation that all bureaucratic matters be handled properly on behalf of the investors. The same evening, however, Robert invited the Secretary out to dinner, entertained him with lots of cognac, *karaoke* singing and hostesses. All were done to 'make up'—to restore their relationship. This process of reconciliation is a necessary step towards the restoration of the notion of " u s " *(ji gei yan)* between Robert and the Secretary and the reinforcement of the moral claim on the Secretary to look after Robert's investment interest in China.

While the sharing of food and drinks is a common means of cultivating and maintaining guanxi (Yan 1995), the mere offering of a gift in service or kind by itself is insufficient to establish an obligation in the receiver or any guarantee of return of favor (A. Smart 1993). The gift giving merely 'opens a door' as Robert puts it. Yet, this 'opening a door' is a necessary prerequisite to improving the relationship between oneself and one's counterpart which eventually may turn into a relationship of reciprocity that one can call on as a resource to achieve specific ends.

The New Year Banquet

The sharing of food and drinks is a common means to cement social solidarity, but it can also be a means to accentuate the status differential between employers (Hong Kong investors) and employees (Chinese migrant workers or Chinese locals). Mr. and Mrs. Lee began their first investment venture in China in 1994 after months of hard consideration. The Lee's sublet part of a factory complex from a friend who has leased a multi-story factory complex in an industrial district near a holiday resort at the edge of the Shenzhen municipality. By early 1996, the Lee's had their own factory complex and increased their workforce from 10 workers to 35.

The Lee's put on a banquet in 1995 to celebrate the western New Year, partly to entertain their own relatives and friends who had holidays from school or workplace in Hong Kong, and partly to welcome the coming of Chinese New Year (it fell on February 2, 1995) before the workers began their three-week holiday without pay. The banquet was held in the best hotel in the town nearest to their factory. Two rooms were reserved for the Lee's and four tables were set for about 50 guests. All staff (10 workers, one administrative assistant, a factory manager shared with the friend from whom they sublet their factory premise), regardless of rank, were invited to this banquet. The invitation was posted on the notice board outside the factory office. The workers were the first to arrive shortly after 4:30 P.M. They entertained themselves with amateur *karaoke*. The Lee's relatives and friends resorted to *mah jong* (a Chinese game of dominoes) and considerable amounts of money changed hands before the food and drinks were served around 8:00 P.M. The Chinese workers do not usually play *mah jong* with their Hong Kong employers or co-workers because their earnings are too low to afford it.

The seating pattern at the banquet was heavy with symbolism. Mr. Lee and all the *male* VIPs occupied one table: two uniformed representative from the local Public Security Office, the chief of the Public Security Bureau in civilian clothes, several other local men from various administrative units or posts, Mr. Lo (the Hong Kong investor from whom Mr. Lee sublet his factory premise), Mr. Lee's adopted son (Mrs. Lee's brother's son) who is the unofficial heir of the business and Mr. Lee's eldest daughter's boyfriend. This table was the loudest and rudest—they drank, smoked, told dirty and sexist jokes and had endless rounds of a drink-if-you-lose game. Beer, table wine, a bottle of Johnny Walker Black scotch whiskey (courtesy of the visiting anthropologists) and soft drinks were served. Normally, cognac is expected to flow freely at a function like this. The one table at which all the factory workers sat were not served any of the scotch (which was monopolized by the VIP table) or wine; they were served beer and soft drinks only. The other two tables were made up of Mrs. Lee, relatives from Mr. Lee's side, the rest of the Lee children and friends visiting from Hong Kong.

At the end of the banquet, there was a lucky draw for all the workers—prizes included alarm clocks, flashlights and book lights. Before the close of the banquet, Mr. Lee handed out red pockets containing HK$100 (US$1= HK$7.8 in 1995) to each of the workers. Traditionally, red envelopes are handed out during Chinese New Year by married couples and elders to children of their own and those of friends whom they visit. It has become common for employers and senior ranking management staff to do the same for their subordinates.

The total bill for the evening came to HK$3500. The Lee's provided all the soft drinks, wine, beer, hard liquor, and all the gifts in kind and money. While the total cost for the evening of entertainment for close to 50 people at HK$5000 was very cheap by Hong Kong standards (that amount would pay for a modest dinner at a middle-range restaurant for 10–12 people with wine and beer), it was a clear expression of conspicuous consumption in the eyes of the migrant workers and the state sector workers in China (whose monthly salary ranges between HK$300-1000 depending on skill, rank and employment terms). This banquet highlighted the economic and social differential between the Hong Kong investors and their PRC counterparts (employees, government officials, local administrative personnel). At the same time the banquet provides the forum at which the social solidarity or the collective identity of a "us" encompassing both Hong Kong and PRC counterparts is cemented through the sharing of food, drinks, gifts and laughs.

The ethnographic data from these two case studies illustrate the process in which the Hong Kong investors manipulate their identity, sometimes emphasizing their commonality with their Chinese counterparts by constructing an 'us' with shared interests against some implied or explicitly identified 'others' and sometimes taking advantage of their 'outsider' status to serve specific ends.

Conclusion

A sceptical reader might respond to the preceding account by commenting that all the complexities might be rather interesting, but how important is this kind of thing really, given that the real action, the events that count, in the process of transnationalization involves the large transnational corporations, and the handful of powerful nation-states who are still setting the ground rules for transnational trade and production through the financial sector and institutions like the World Trade Organization and the International Monetary Fund (Blim 1996). After all, even transnational movements of immigrants have become subject to more, rather than less, stringent controls by nation-states (Basok 1996). Is not the attention that is being paid to non-corporate transnational networks simply a diversion, another example of social scientists' tendency to pay attention to rather ephemeral and ultimately inconsequential new fashions, rather than concentrating on where the true decisions are made and outcomes produced?

We would agree that there are potential grounds for such a skeptical response. However, it is precisely those kinds of concerns which have led us to emphasize the need to expand the scope from the identity issues usually emphasized under the rubric of transnationalism to a more open set of questions revolving around the increasing prevalence of non-corporate social networks maintained across national boundaries. The time-space compression that has allowed heightened maintenance of contacts between people across national boundaries does indeed have important effects on processes of identification, but these transnational linkages can have many other outcomes as well. Referring to transnational social networks allows us to focus on the phenomenon without reading in preconceptions about what are the important things that are being carried by these media, leaving their impact as an open question to be examined in particular circumstances. Attending to transnational networks, too, immediately forces us to recognize the high degree of individual diversity in these emerging transnational social fields, since the characteristics of one's network and the resources that it makes available will vary considerably and enable and constrain transnational practices in very distinct ways.

Nonini and Ong (1996: 15) suggest that one influence of cultural studies on the study of transnationalism has been to treat it as abstract, dematerialized cultural flows while giving "scant attention either to the concrete 'everyday' changes in people's lives or to the structural reconfigurations that accompany global capitalism." The resulting work on transnational cultural politics has produced a great deal of important work, but has often left out the individual experience, how people's "agencies are implicated in the making of these effects, and the social relationships in which these agencies are embedded" (Nonini and Ong 1996: 15). This criticism can also be extended to analyses that see transnational corporations and powerful nation-states as the only important actors in the contemporary transformation of the world economy.

A critical aspect of what David Harvey (1989) and others have described as a regime of flexible accumulation which is currently emerging alongside a crisis-ridden fordist regime of accumulation is the heightened capacity for smaller enterprises to engage in transnational production and exchange, frequently through the medium of network forms of production integration. Although the production technology used by Hong Kong and other overseas Chinese firms is often unimpressive, the social technology used to collect information, to obtain sourcing contracts from Original Equipment Manufacturers, to break into new markets, and to rapidly expand production without committing to excessive permanent capacity, can be seen as very much in the forefront of the use of flexible strategies to obtain competitive advantages. And a critical element of these overseas Chinese strategies involves the tactical positioning of relatives and other social connections in complementary economies and 'safe haven' polities (Yeung 1995; Oxfeld 1993), as well as the mobilization of existing transnational networks when geographical expansion becomes attractive. This pattern is not something that is found only among the "small fish," but among the largest Hong Kong and other overseas Chinese corporations as well: a good example is the large investments made by Li Ka-shing (whose firms have a market value of an estimated US$22 billion) in Canada, where his son Victor Li has become a permanent resident (Olds 1995). The use of social networks to expand in new markets (as well as the use of expansion to support and construct social networks, since motivations can move in both directions) has a particularly strong impact for large corporations still controlled by their founder, since the founders' social networks may be the primary sources of trusted advice and information, and decisions of family and corporation are often fused (Thrift and Olds 1996). And since the 55 million ethnic Chinese living outside mainland China are estimated to control US$2 trillion in liquid assets alone (Thrift and Olds 1996: 324), the channelling of economic flows through transnational social networks can clearly have considerable impact.

The activities of overseas Chinese business operators is not the only example that could be offered of the significance of transnational social networks for the world economy, but given the contribution that they have made to the 'miraculous' economic expansions of East and Southeast Asia, they would seem to be sufficient to make the point that attention to non-corporate transnational social networks is hardly an insignificant academic preoccupation. But much of the literature on overseas Chinese social networks has concentrated more on trying to assert and estimate their economic importance or on trying to sketch their practical 'sociometry:' who is investing where and with whom. As a result, we still know much less about the *processes* of these transnational networks, the concern of this paper.

Moving from the general to the specific, we have argued in this article that Hong Kong has contributed a great deal to the remarkable advances that China has made since the door was opened to foreign investment in 1978, and that the transnational social networks between Hong Kong and China have played an important role in these outcomes. But network linkages are not all the same, nor is even their existence certain in all cases or occasions. While sociometry reifies network linkages, we have in this paper, instead, emphasized the *process* of constructing and maintaining network linkages. When linkages cross borders between economies as distinct as Hong Kong's and China's, they offer remarkable opportunities for brokerage and arbitrage across that boundary, but the differences also present serious challenges to agents as they deal with the inconsistencies and pitfalls of communication and expectations.

Agents operating in such circumstances require considerable amounts of cultural knowledge, social sensitivity, and tactical 'street smarts.' Not all people have such a desirable combination, and a strategy that worked well for one person may lead to total disaster for another in a comparable situation. The sharpness of the boundary between Hong Kong and China means that, in Goffmanesque terms, Hong Kong investors have to maintain very distinct personae in different settings, and when the curtains dividing these settings are disrupted (for example, an official hearing Hong Kong investors ridiculing mainlanders in a restaurant), the results can be awkward.

For Hong Kong investors, many of whom have worked their way up from the lower middle-class, China presents remarkable opportunities, opportunities which are not available in any other part of the world, given their limited education and lack of English skills. They possess resources such as language skills, cultural knowledge of how things get done in China, symbolic resources of shared Chinese identity, and critical social resources in their social networks. This situation has allowed them to move on from a situation where the low-wage, labor-intensive manufacturing of consumer goods in Hong Kong was increasingly unviable.

Relations across a boundary that separates political economies as distinct as those of Hong Kong and China are fraught with dangers and misunderstandings. On the whole, Hong Kong investors have been successful at acting as brokers across this boundary, and identity claims have certainly been a part of this brokerage, particularly in the early years of the open door. But these successes are often grounded as much in what is not said, as in what is publicly stated, and detailed ethnography is essential if the nature of these cross-border relations are to be adequately understood. In this paper we have only been able to offer some short vignettes of the kinds of network processes that are occurring everyday on this terrain of merging incompatibilities and tactical accommodation,

·but we hope that these brief descriptions will indicate the kinds of contributions that detailed ethnography can offer to a fuller understanding of transnational processes and outcomes.

Notes

1. The burgeoning literature on social economies is too large to summarize here, for overviews (see Granovetter 1990; Mingione 1994; Sayer and Walker 1992). Work on moral economies is less broadly developed, being most commonly applied in social history (Thompson 1968) and in peasant studies (Scott 1976). Within mainstream economics a related expansion of analysis from economic relations in the narrow sense is producing an influential literature on topics such as public choice theory, rent-seeking, human capital, and transaction analysis.

2. One point that should be addressed here is whether Hong Kong/China interactions can reasonably be seen as "transnational," given the imminence of the 1997 transfer of Hong Kong to the sovereignty of the PRC. On a purely technical sense, they are still distinct political entities, despite the colonial status of Hong Kong, and border crossings have the full panoply of official controls, and sharp boundaries between the laws in effect on either side of the border. To a large extent, these disjunctions will persist after 1997, even though Hong Kong will technically be only a Special Administrative Region within China, because of the planned persistence of border controls and the guarantee of the preservation of a separate capitalist system in Hong Kong for fifty years. More important than these technical considerations, however, is the continuing sense of a dramatic change in social system at the border. This disjunction between political economies and social organization is less than it once was, but the sense of transition between different entities is still much stronger than it is in, for example, on crossing the Canadian-United States border, or at the frontiers of nations in the European Union.

3. Incidentally, the encouragement of these patterns of Hong Kong investment by central and local authorities was made easier by the export-oriented nature of most investments, in contrast to the preference of Western multinationals for import-substitution strategies that would allow them to tap the potentially huge Chinese domestic market. Since export-processing produced hard foreign currency, it was easier to present these involvements as strengthening the homeland, whereas production for the domestic market had to rely on sometimes questionable arguments about the absorption of modern technologies.

References

Amin, Ash and Nigel Thrift. (1995). Globalisation, institutional 'thickness' and the local economy. In Patsy Healey et al. (eds.), *Managing Cities: The New Urban Context*: Chichester: John Wiley and Sons. Pp. 91-108.

Appadurai, Arjun. (1991). "Global ethnoscapes: Notes and Queries for a Transnational Anthropology." In R. Fox (ed.). *Recapturing Anthropology*. Santa Fe: School of American Research. Pp. 191-210.

Bailey, F.G. (1991). *The Prevalence of Deceit*. Ithaca: Cornell University Press.

Glick Schiller, Nina, Linda Basch and Cristina Blanc Szanton. (1994). *Nations Unbound: Transnational Projects, Postcolonial Predicaments, and Deterritorialized Nation-states*. New York: Gordon and Breach.

Basok, Tanya. (1996). "Refugee policy: Globalization, Radical challenge, or State Control?" *Studies in Political Economy* 50:1 33-161.

Blim, Michael. (1996). "Cultures and the Problems of Capitalisms." *Critique of Anthropology* 16(1):79.

Emirbayer, Mustafa and Jeff Goodwin. (1994). "Network Analysis, Culture, and the Problem of Agency." *American Journal of Sociology* 99: 6: 1411-1464.

Featherstone, Mike, ed. (1990). *Global Culture*. London: Sage.

Fitzgerald, John. (1996). "Autonomy and Growth in China: County experience in Guangdong." *Journal of Contemporary China* 5: 11: 7-22.

Friedman, Edward. (1994). "Reconstructing China's National Identity: A Southern Alternative to Mao-era Anti-imperialist Nationalism." *Journal of Asian Studies* 53: 1: 67-91.

Glick Schiller, Nina, Linda Basch and Cristina Blanc Szanton. (1992). "Transnationalism: A New Analytic Framework for Understanding Migration." In Glick Schiller et al. (eds.), *Towards a Transnational Perspective on Migration*. New York: New York Academy of Sciences. Pp. 1-24.

Granovetter, Mark. (1990). "The Old and the New Economic Sociology. In R. Friedland and A. Robertson (eds.) *Beyond the Marketplace*. New York: Aldine de Gruyter. Pp. 3-49.

Guldin, Gregory E. (1995). Toward a Greater Guangdong: Hong Kong's Sociocultural Impact on the Pearl River Delta and Beyond. In R. Kwok and A. So (eds.) *The Hong Kong-Guangdong Link*. Armonk: M.E. Sharpe. Pp. 89-118.

Hannerz, Ulf. (1980). *Exploring the City*. New York: Columbia University Press.

———. (1992). *Cultural Complexity: Studies in the Social Organization of Meaning*. New York: Columbia University Press.

Honig, Emily. (1996). "Native Place and the Making of Chinese Ethnicity." In G. Hershatter et al. (eds.) *Remapping China: Fissures in Historical Terrain*. Stanford: Stanford University Press. Pp. 143-155.

Ikels, Charlotte. (1996). *The Return of the God of Wealth: The Transition to a Market Economy in Urban China*. Stanford: Stanford University Press.

Johnson, Graham E. (1995). "Continuity and Transformation in the Pearl River Delta: Hong Kong's Impact on Its Hinterland." In R. Kwok and A. So (eds.), *The Hong Kong-Guangdong Link*. Armonk: M.E. Sharpe. Pp.64-86.

Lee, Ming-kwan. (1995). "Community and Identity in Transition in Hong Kong." In R. Kwok and A. So (eds.), *The Hong Kong-Guangdong Link*. Armonk: M.E. Sharpe. Pp. 119-132.

Mann, Jim. (1989). *Beijing Jeep*. New York: Touchstone.

Mingione, Enzo. (1994). Life Strategies and Social Economies in the Postfordist Age." *International Journal of Urban and Regional Research* 18: 1: 24-45.

Nonini, Donald M. and Aihwa Ong. (1996). "Introduction: Modern Chinese Transnationalism as an Alternative Modernity." In Ong and Nonini (eds.), *Edges of Empire: Culture and Identity in Modern Chinese Transnationalism.* New York: Routledge.

Olds, Aihwa. "Globalization and the Production of New Urban Spaces: Pacific Rim Mega-projects in the Late 20th Century." *Environment and Planning A* 27: 1713-44.

———. (1991). "The Gender and Labor Politics of Postmodernity. *Annual Review of Anthropology* 20: 279-309.

———. (1992). "Limits to Cultural Accumulation: Chinese Capitalists on the American Pacific Rim." In Glick Schiller et al. (eds.), *Towards a Transnational Perspective on Migration.* New York: New York Academy of Science. Pp.125-143.

Ong, Paul, Edna Bonacich, and Lucie Cheng. (1994). "The Political Economy of Capitalist Restructuring and the New Asian Immigration." In *The New Asian Immigration in Los Angeles and Global Restructuring.* Philadelphia: Temple University Press. Pp. 3-35.

Oxfeld, Ellen. (1993). Blood, *Sweat and Mahjong: Family and Enterprise in an Overseas Chinese Community.* Ithaca: Cornell University Press.

Pasternak, Burton. (1983). *Guests in the Dragon: Social Demography of a Chinese District, 1895-1946.* New York: Columbia University Press.

Pearson, Margaret M. (1991). *Joint Ventures in the People's Republic of China.* Princeton: Princeton University Press.

Rouse, Roger. (1995). "Questions of Identity: Personhood and Collectivity in Transnational Migration to the United States." *Critique of Anthropology*

Sassen, Saskia. (1988). *The Mobility of Labor and Capital.* New York: Cambridge University Press.

Sayer, Andrew and Richard Walker. (1992). *The New Social Economy: Reworking the Division of Labor.* Cambridge: Blackwell.

Schein, Louisa. (1996). "The Other Goes to Market: The State, the Nation and Un-ruliness in Contemporary China." *Identities* 2: 3: 197-222.

Scott, James. (1976). *The Moral Economy of the Peasant.* New Haven: Yale University Press.

Sewell, William H. Jr. (1992). "A Theory of Structure: Duality, Agency and Trans-formation." *American Journal of Sociology* 98: 1- 29.

Siu, Helen F. (1993). "Cultural Identity and the Politics of Difference in South China." In Tu (ed.), *China in Transformation.* Cambridge: Harvard University Press. Pp.19-43.

Smart, Alan. (1993). "Gifts, Bribes and Guanxi: A Reconsideration of Bourdieu's Social Capital." *Cultural Anthropology* 8: 3: 388-408.

———. (1995). *Local Capitalisms: Situated Social Support for Capitalist Production in China.* Department of Geography, Chinese University of Hong Kong, Occasional Paper No. 121. Hong Kong: Chinese University of Hong Kong.

Smart, Josephine. (1995). "The Changing Selective Pressure in International Mi-gration: A Case Study of Hong Kong Immigration to Canada before 1997." In J.H.Ong et al. (eds.), *Crossing Borders: Transmigration in Asia Pacific.* New York: Prentice-Hall. Pp.187-208.

————. (1993). "Land Rents and the Rise of a Petty Bourgeoisie in Contemporary China." *The Anthropology of Work Review*, 14: 3-6.

Smart, Josephine and Alan Smart. (1991). "Personal Relations and Divergent Economies: A Case Study of Hong Kong Investment in South China." *International Journal of Urban and Regional Research* 15: 2: 216-233.

————. (1993). "Obligation and Control: Employment of Kin in Capitalist Labor Management in China." *Critique of Anthropology* 13: 1: 7-31.

Smith, Michael P. (1992). "Postmodernism, Urban Ethnography, and the New Social Space of Ethnic Identity." *Theory and Society* 21: 4: 493-531.

Thompson, E.P. (1968). *The Making of the English Working Class*. Middlesex: Harmondsworth.

Thrift, Nigel and Kris Olds (1996). "Refiguring the Economic in Economic Geography." *Progress in Human Geography* 20: 3: 311-337.

Van Velsen, J. (1967). "The Extended-Case Method and Situational Analysis." In A. Epstein (ed.), *The Craft of Social Anthropology*. London: Tavistock.

Werbner, Pnina. (1990). *The Migration Process*. New York: Berg.

Yan, Yunxiang. (1996). *The Flow of Gifts: Reciprocity and Social Networks in a Chinese Village*. Stanford, CA: Stanford University Press.

Yang, Mayfair Mei-hui. (1994). *Gifts, Favors and Banquets: The Art of Social Relationships in China*. Ithaca, NY: Cornell University Press.

Yeung, Henry Wai-chung. (1995). "The Geography of Hong Kong Transnational Corporations in the ASEAN Region. *Area* 27: 4: 318-334.

5

Transnational Lives and National Identities: The Identity Politics of Haitian Immigrants[1]

Nina Glick Schiller
Georges Fouron

In a way it could have been any Saturday evening. Haitians were debating the political situation in Haiti and Haiti's future. The discussion could have been in a barbershop in Brooklyn, a front room of a cement block house in a squatter settlement without streets in Delmas, Port-au-Prince, or a Catholic parish group in Queens. But in this case, as has been the case for the past decade, the location of the discussion was air space and the conversation was transnational. Haitian men and women in New York and in Port-au-Prince were participating in a single discussion about the state of affairs in Haiti. By 1994 the technology had been developed so that callers in Haiti and in the major Haitian settlements abroad such as New York, Miami, California, Boston, and Montreal can participate in the same conversation by calling Radio Tropical, a Haitian owned radio station located in New York and Port-au-Prince. But while people were engaged in the same conversation as they called into the program "Haïti Réalité," in September of 1996, there were differences in what was being said. While in this particular call-in show those who spoke in favor of Jean-Bertrand Aristide were in New York, those against him were in Haiti. The former President is still a significant leader with a large following and an increasingly vocal opposition both among the Haitian immigrant population and those living in Haiti. However the tension lines that emerged in this transnational dialogue exemplify some of the dissonance that exists between diasporic Haitians and those living within the borders of Haiti, even as they participate together in discussions of the future of the country with which they all identify.

For these speakers in New York, the accusations circulating among Haitians about Aristide's recent actions were not cause for despair or even for alarm and the air waves resounded with passionate statements of support: "He fought for us," "He speaks on our behalf," "He stands for the people."

> So what if he became rich, if he became a millionaire and lives in a big new house, with a fancy new wife. These people who criticize him are jealous of him. Even though they say they care for the people, had they been in his position, they would have done the same thing. And whatever he got, he deserves it. He worked for it."

The bonds were more than between a leader and his following. Those in New York who supported Aristide were speaking as members of the Haitian polity and ones that wanted a particular politics for their state. "We are sitting here and waiting for him. He will be our President again in 2001."

Many of those calling from Haiti had a different assessment of Aristide's effectiveness as a leader. Not only hadn't he delivered the good; he had betrayed the nation.

> Go to Site Solèy [the squatter settlement that served as a base for Aristide]. See the conditions in which these people are living. They are still living in squalor. He got rich; they remained poor. In addition, he sold the country to the Americans, he is the main engineer of the second occupation of Haiti. What did he do for Haiti?

In the past decade increasing numbers of governments of states with significant migrating populations from the Philippines to Mexico have been reconceptualizing their polities as transnational (Rios 1995; Guarnizo 1996; Smith 1993). That is to say they are developing both theories and practices that define their emigrating populations as part and parcel of their nation-states. Taking Haiti as a case study, in this paper we shall explore some of the dynamics of this form of nation-state building. We shall look at the transnational processes that unite Haitians living within the territorial boundaries of Haiti with its "diaspora." We shall also look at the ways in which different geographical and social locations of the actors are making more salient and are transforming the contradictions and contestation that divide the Haitian population. The constituents of the transnational nation-state may share social space but the terrain of this emerging political entity has many internal divides. We conclude with some reflections on the way in which the conceptualization and practices of this newly emerging transnational nation-state, as well as its internal contradictions, reflect Haiti's place in the contemporary global capitalist economy.

The insights in this paper emerge from more than two decades of our participation in the process of Haitian immigrant settlement in the New York metropolitan area and of our observations of Haitians' continuing connections to Haiti. Our research included attendance at meetings and informal discussions, and the analysis of Haitian newspapers, radio, and television produced in New York. We have drawn on Georges Fouron's personal experiences as an immigrant from Haiti and his involvement in transnational family networks and Nina Glick Schiller's history of involvement within a range of Haitian immigrant organizations. We also draw on 92 interviews conducted with leaders of Haitian organizations in New York in 1985 and 148 focused interviews conducted in Haiti in 1989, 1991, 1995 and 1996 with government officials, and middle class and poor people in Port-au-Prince, Les Cayes, and several other towns and cities in Haiti.

State and Nation

For the purpose of this paper, we use the word "state" to indicate a sovereign system of government within a particular bounded territory—the state brings "us" together. Premised on identities authenticated by a fictitious or real historicity, the "nation," by contrast, evokes the sense of peoplehood a particular population uses to distinguish itself from other national groups—the nation distinguishes "us" from "them." Often, populations that find it difficult to identify with the state (i.e., the political apparatus of the country) because of its coercive and oppressive nature or its remoteness may consider themselves part of the nation.

Nation-state building is therefore identified as a set of historical and affective processes that link disparate and/or heterogeneous populations together and forge their loyalty to and identity with a central government apparatus and institutional structure. In the course of such a process, the class forces or coalitions who control the state strive to create the conditions in which culturally diverse and class stratified populations identify themselves as a single people. This political process is not restricted or particular to the underdeveloped states; the sense of identification with the nation-state is quite recent for most populations in most countries and nation-state building requires dominant classes to continually reinforce and reiterate the legitimacy of the state. To speak of a nation-state is to imply that populations that share a common identity as a nation also identify with the government of the territory in which they reside, an occurrence that is not common (Gellner 1983; Lemelle and Kelly 1994; Guidieri, Pellizzi, and Tambiah 1988).

Integral to nation-state building is the projection that the people in the state share a common language, history, culture, territory, and set of responsibilities and rights. However, whereas traditional conceptualizations of the nation-state imply fixed and well-delineated boundaries, recently the government officials of a number of states such as Haiti with significant emigrant populations have begun to reconceptualize the nature of the nation-state so that its population is no longer defined as residing solely within the national territory. These emerging transnational nation-states are "deterritorialized" (Basch, Glick Schiller, and Szanton Blanc 1994; Glick Schiller 1995) in the sense that persons who have emigrated and their descendants are defined as continuing to belong to the polity from which they originated. They are seen as having rights and responsibilities in that state even if they have adopted the language and culture of their new country and have become legal citizens in their new home. Leaders of transnational nation-states claim that their governments represent not only the populations of their national territories but populations descended from their national territory, wherever they may reside. In general, nation-state building obfuscates internal differences such as those based on class, region, and gender. The political leaders who engage in transnational nation-state building confront an even more complex task. They must build a unity of identity and a sense of commonality amongst people who share neither territory or emersion in a single society.

The *Lavalas* Movement and the
Construction of Haiti as a Deterritorialized Nation-State

Haiti is an important location in which to study deterritorialized nation-state building and to problematize the projection of national unity that lies within this form and every form of nation-state building. Despite its almost two hundred years of national independence, Haiti is only just now emerging as a nation-state and it is doing so as part of a transnational process within which Haitian leaders are striving to build Haiti as a transnational nation-state. Within the past six years, occurrences both in Haiti and among Haitians settled abroad alternatively have strengthened or weakened the ties that bind various sectors of Haitian society to the transnational nation-state.

Haiti is a polity in which class contradictions have always been a visible aspect of all efforts at unity. The divisions of state, nation, and class in Haiti can be traced to the slave uprising and revolutionary war through which the population in Haiti won their independence from France in 1804. In the course of that upheaval, people of all regions and classes of Haiti came to see Haiti as a black nation that had made its mark on a global stage and had historic responsibilities in relationship to others of African descent. However from the moment of independence Haiti has always been organized and governed as a "Platonic aristocracy" (Lewis 1987) ruled by a clique that has denied the legitimate aspirations of the poor and uneducated peasant majority (Delorme 1870; Nicholls 1979; Lundahl 1979; Trouillot 1990; Hurbon 1979).

Opposition to these classes by the black disempowered majority provided the context within which François Duvalier began his dictatorial regime in 1957. He declared that through his control of the state, the nation "has been reconciled with herself" (1966) but in point of fact the old alliance of dominant classes stayed intact with a growing black technocracy playing an increasing role in affairs of state. The political repression and economic disruption precipitated first by the Duvalier regime itself and then by the penetration of foreign capital in the 1970s and 1980s led hundreds of thousands of Haitians to flee their homeland. At the same time, in the place of state investment in the infrastructure, a myriad of churches, European and United States development agencies, and international philanthropies arrived in Haiti and established non-governmental organization in both country-side and city.

This migration and transnational organizing done by non-government organizations had a profound effect on the political situation in Haiti. A grassroots movement emerged spearhead by *Ti Kominote Legliz* (TKL or Little Church Communities), which organized village groups around liberation theology. The growing *Sektè Demokratik-la* (the Democratic Sector) united around and supported for the presidency in 1990, Jean-Bertrand Aristide, a priest who was a major figure in building the *ti legliz* movement. From the time of his presidential campaign, Aristide put aside his previous critique of capitalism and its use of formal democracy to maintain the exploitation of the people. While not radical in economic theory before his election, Aristide broke with classic definition of the bourgeois democratic nation-state in only one sphere—he redefined the location of the state so it was no longer confined within the territorial borders of Haiti.

Haiti the Deterritorialized Nation-State

In a white paper published during the presidential campaign, Aristide solicited the diaspora's support in his *Pwojè Lavalas* (n.d.) (Lavalas' Project of Government). In this document, the Lavalas Movement underscored the rapprochement it envisioned between Haitians in Haiti and overseas Haitians by declaring:

> The LAVALAS MOUVMAN, which has adopted a good project of government, supposes the participation of all citizens from all social classes. A special place will be reserved for peasants, women, all patriotic movements, and all Haitians in diaspora.

The Lavalas movement began to envision the political power to rule Haiti as emanating from the Haitian people wherever they might reside. As soon as he was inaugurated, Aristide set out to institutionalize the movement's vision by taking a series of steps to redefine Haiti as a nation-state which exists beyond its physical borders. To show his desire to incorporate the immigrants into the fold of the nation-state he also met with representatives of the diaspora in the Presidential palace during his inaugural ceremonies and declared them to be no longer outside of Haiti, although living abroad (Richman 1992; Jean-Pierre 1994). Instead they were the Tenth Department, *Dizyèm Depatman*, an integral part of Haiti whose territory is divided into nine geographical and political departments. In his first New Year message to the Tenth Department (viz. all expatriate Haitians), Aristide welcomed Haitian overseas "communities" anew, as Haiti's prodigal children, in the fold of the "Haitian community" "*under the aegis and the protection of the political power of the Haitian nation-state*" (*Radyo Moman Kreyòl*, WLIB-AM, January 5, 1991).[2] They were no longer a diaspora since they remained a political part of Haiti.

The links between the diaspora and the Haitian government proved to be an important source of funds and personnel. In 1991, to provide the newly elected Aristide government with much needed funds, Haitians in Haiti and throughout the diaspora organized a "marathon of dignity" called VOAM (*Voye Ayiti Monte*, Send Haiti Upward). In less than a week and despite their dire economic conditions, overseas Haitians raised more that $1 million for various projects in Haiti. *La Fanmi Se Lavi*, (Family is Our Life) a benevolent association founded by Aristide to help orphans in Port-au-Prince, received numerous contributions through mini-marathons organized by various overseas Haitian communities. Many organizations such as HEAR (Haitian Enforcement Against Racism)[3] that had been organizing around conditions faced by Haitians in the United States sponsored volunteers who went to Haiti to assist the Haitian poor and teach literacy skills to the masses. Haitian professionals living in diaspora travelled to Haiti to perform volunteer services for the Lavalas government and promised to collaborate with the government through various other programs.

The importance of this constituency became apparent when Aristide was forced into exile in 1991 by a military coup after less than a year in office. The organization of the Tenth Department became a vocal source of support for Aristide's return to the Presidency. During Aristide's three years in the United States he visited many Haitian immigrant settlements and forged stronger ties with immigrant leaders. Overseas Haitians, through their sustained voluntary contributions, helped maintain the upkeep of Haiti's embassies and consulates during Aristide's three year exile. Although in the course of his exile he became increasingly enmeshed with U.S. power politics and refrained from mobilizing Haitian immigrants in public demonstrations of support, both Aristide and the members of his government came to see the immigrants as a constituency. Haitian immigrants more than ever before became part of the political process of Haiti in practice as well as in theory.

In paradoxical ways the coup strengthened the unity between the diaspora and those living in Haiti. The need to support Aristide when he was overthrown united many forces who wanted a democratic Haiti but had serious questions about Aristide or had fears of the grassroots movement that brought Aristide to power. During Aristide's three year sojourn in the United States, many intellectuals and technicians of Haitian origin came to be more directly engaged with or in the Aristide government. Meanwhile, although a U.S. imposed embargo made communication difficult, the familial, religious, and charitable networks that stretch between the diaspora and Haiti became a lifeline.[4] At the same time, most people in Haiti—outside of the bourgeoisie and connected strata—saw the diaspora working in their interest and shared a joint interest in Aristide's return. An 18 year old student, sitting in her small front room surrounded by enormous suitcases in which her families sent goods from the United States, spelled out for us a theme we heard repeated numerous times in the summer of 1996: "They helped Aristide return to power. It was a duty for them to help. Aristide was fighting to return to help the country improve."

Finally, Aristide was returned to power in 1994 in the wake of a U.S. Occupation of Haiti.[5] The United States government as part of its arrangements with Aristide stipulated that he step down from the Presidency at the end of his term, although he had spent most of his tenure in exile. In the short time that he served as President after his return to Haiti, Aristide further institutionalized the links between his government and "the Tenth" and popularized the concept of the Tenth Department. When interviewed in Port-au-Prince in the summer of 1995, ministers of four different ministries of the Aristide government consistently used the term Tenth Department. They interceded in the interview when the term diaspora was used to point out that the diaspora had become the Tenth Department. The third annual meeting of the Tenth Department was held in Haiti in July 1995. Moreover, in the course of public conferences and private consultations, representatives of the Tenth Department developed plans for ways to more closely link Haitian immigrants to political and economic developments in Haiti. In planning for economic development, the organization of the Tenth Department began to work more closely with Haitian hometown associations that have been active in local development in Haiti since the 1980s. In addition, Aristide set up a *Ministère des Haitiens Vivant a l' Etranger* (MHAVE, Ministry of Haitians Living Abroad), within the Haitian Cabinet to work with and protect the interests of the Tenth Department. When interviewed the *Chef de Cabinet* of the Ministry, who himself had lived as an immigrant in Venezuela, indicated that the mission of his office included welcoming Haitian immigrants who travel to Haiti as tourists, as well as those who were seeking to invest their resources or to settle in Haiti. The office strove to serve as a conduit for Haitian investors from abroad, assisting them in navigating the complicated and intertwined Haitian bureaucracy.

Aristide also appointed a *Chef de Mission* attached to the Haitian Consulate in New York City and gave him the task to harness the potentials of the immigrant communities, maintain contacts with the Tenth Department Chapters located in various large cities in diaspora, coordinate the regional organizations' projects and ideas, and support their endeavors inside Haiti (François 1995). When Wilson Desir, the Haitian General Consul in New York, died in September 1995 the effectiveness of the years of institutionalizing the Tenth Department and the constant reiteration of the idea of continuing connections between Haitian immigrants abroad and Haiti assumed a visible presence. Several thousand Haitian immigrants filled the streets of Brooklyn joined by dignitaries from Haiti in what amounted to a state funeral.

The formulation and institutionalization of the Tenth Department provided a public representation of Haitian immigrants as linked to the Haitian state. In the processes of reconceptualizing the Haitian state, Haitian political leaders in Haiti were reevaluating and rehabilitating the way in which they perceived and spoke about Haitian emigrants. Until that point, from Duvalier to Aristide, Haitian leaders had defined Haitians living abroad as no longer a part of the Haitian political process. In excluding emigrants from the jurisdiction of the Haitian state and seeing those who left as abjuring their ties to Haiti, they reiterated a conception of the nation-state common to Western political theory.[6]

The division between the diaspora and the homeland also reflected the contingencies of the Haitian political situation that confronted the Haitian political leadership. As hundreds of thousands of people fled Haiti, including the leadership of the political opposition, the regimes of both François Duvalier and his son Jean Claude (1957-86) tried to sever connections between immigrant populations and Haiti in order to better secure their rule. The Duvaliers insisted that by "choosing" to live abroad, Haitian immigrants had become *kamoken,*[7] suspect and disloyal elements. Worse yet, those Haitians who had adopted other nationalities had become *apatrid*, betrayers of their racial and national legacies.

Many Haitian leaders in the diaspora also embraced a political rhetoric that drew a sharp line between Haitians living abroad and those in Haiti. They separated those in diaspora from those in Haiti portraying the diaspora as political refugees in exile from repression and denouncing those who had remained in Haiti, accusing them of collaborating with the regime (Glick Schiller et al. 1987; Trouillot 1990). At the same time they preached a politics of return which called upon Haitians abroad to first work for the overthrow the Duvalier regime and then return to rebuild Haiti. According to the politics of return, Haitians could realize their loyalty to their homeland only by returning to Haiti. These leaders feared that as Haitian immigrants became incorporated economically and socially in the United States they would abandon the struggle against the Duvalier regime.

Meanwhile sitting in living rooms among a circle of family and friends men of all class backgrounds debated whether it made more sense to plan to return to Haiti or "forget about Haiti." With a few notable exceptions, women were less involved in this debate but participated in churches, schools, and family settings in discussions about the preservation of Haitian culture and the future of the next generation. There was a diversity of views among both men and women about whether they saw themselves as permanent settler in the United States or sojourners who would eventually return to Haiti. However whether the speaker saw herself or himself as an political exile, permanent immigrant, or sojourner, Haiti remained the point of reference among the hundreds of Haitian immigrants we interviewed, spoke to, and observed in New York.

We cannot assume that people who emigrate either continue automatically to look back to the country of their ancestry or readily cut their home ties. In the case of Haitian migrants, cultural assumptions about family obligations and the personal motivations of using home town connections as a way of obtaining or maintaining cultural capital are strengthened by the racial discrimination they confront when they settle in the United States and Canada.

Family ties bind in both directions: those left behind in Haiti depend on money sent from abroad and on food and goods brought on return visits; those who live the precarious life of immigrants in societies that function and revolve around nefarious racial and ethnic ideologies look to Haiti to provide periodic solace to their often harsh living conditions and secure for them a home base in case they are unable to continue to live in their immigrant milieu. Thus, family ties have remained at the base of Haitian transnational connections. As Edner, a 59 year old house painter, explained in an interview in Haiti in 1989, "There are those who have and those who have nothing. It is a collaboration among these people that give you the diaspora."

The experience of racism and the scapegoating of Haiti as part of broad attack on immigrants of color has made Haitians feel that no matter how long they stayed they would never be accepted fully as "Americans" or "Canadians." In the United States in particular, Haitians find that although there are strong pressures on immigrants to assimilate and abjure loyalties to other nation-states, these pressures are filtered through a racial lens (Portes and Zhou 1993). United States nation-state building processes have defined a mainstream culture of whiteness (Omi and Winant 1986; Takaki 1989). Black immigrants find that the assimilation they are allowed is structured to a racial ordering that defines them as either a distinctive black ethnicity or as African Americans positioned at the bottom of the society. Consequently many Haitians, including a prominent section of those born in the United States, maintain ties with Haiti, even though they remain settled in the United States.

From Ethnic To Transnational

Ties are one thing; public identities are something else. Immigrant identities are multiple and situational. To understand the cultural politics of immigrant leaders and "communities," we need to assess the forces that contribute to the articulation of public racial, ethnic, and national identities among immigrants. The U.S. racial order was not the only force at work within the United States which shaped the political identities of Haitian immigrants. The various locations in which Haitians settled, the New York metropolitan area, Miami and South Florida, Chicago, and Boston, differed in ways that proved significant to the formation of their political identities.[8]

In New York, Haitian immigrants find themselves settling in a city that allocates to immigrants distinctive "ethnic identities." Most Haitian immigrants begin to labor in the most subordinated sections of the working class, but their identification is not as undifferentiated labor. As they are disciplined in shop floor or service industry routines, they are perceived, discussed, and stratified in terms of their race and ethnicity (Kasinitz 1992). Both immigrants who live and work in New York City and scholars who study immigration in New York soon learn to speak about New York City as if it were an ethnic mosaic, made up of distinctive groups, each with its own distinctive identity, culture, and way of life.

Until the 1960s, European immigrant groupings in New York were commonly known as "nationalities," and were distinguished from black migrants who, whether they were from the United States. South or from the Caribbean, were considered to be a single and racially distinct population. In the 1960s, nationalities came to be called ethnic groups under a rubric of cultural pluralism as nationally, scholars, the media, and public institutions put aside a rhetoric of assimilation and adopted the New York city model of competing ethnicities (Glazer and Moynihan [1963]1970). During this period, as the civil rights movement of the 1960s turned into demands for black empowerment, black urban populations and other groups who had been seen as racially distinct from whites were publicly equated with immigrants and constructed as ethnic groups. The ideology of ethnic cultural pluralism did not acknowledge persisting racial barriers but presented the United States as a salad bowl—a single tasty dish made up of multiple distinctive and discrete flavors. In a confusing elision of U.S. racial classifications and national distinctions, people of color were classified into units of varying degrees of specificity. Blacks, Haitians, Caribbeans, Asians, Chinese, Puerto-Ricans, Latinos were referred to as separate and distinct ethnic groups.[9] For the first time in New York there was a political space for the expression of various black ethnicities. And it was during this period that, in response to the changes wrought by new levels and forms of capital penetration in decolonizing states, increasing numbers of black immigrants including Haitians began to arrive in the United States (Foner 1987; Portes and Rumbaut 1990).[10]

As they arrived and settled in New York, Haitian immigrants were told that the road to economic and political success lay in identifying themselves publicly as members of "an ethnic group" (Glick Schiller 1975, 1977). The word was communicated through political speeches, patronage, ethnic festivals, invitations to City Hall, and in the case of Haitian organizations, funding from city, state, federal, and philanthropic agencies. Haitian immigrants were invited to join the Mayor's Commission on Ethnic Affairs. They were also encouraged to organize support groups for mayoral candidates and to cast their votes for politicians who spoke to the Caribbean immigrant experience. This encouragement towards a form of ethnic organizing directly linked to participation in U.S.

political system found a receptive audience among the Haitian population in New York which included a significant strata of professionals, intellectuals, and persons aspiring to political leadership.

In contrast, other areas of dense Haitian settlement in the United States such as Miami, Chicago, Boston, Washington, and California had their own distinct combination of persons from different class backgrounds in Haiti and local level of cultural politics in the United States. Each developed its own styles of being Haitian and its own version of a Haitian identity in the United States. For example, while Haitian organizations in Boston by the 1980s also had developed a form of ethnic politics with links to the local power structure, the situation in Miami evolved somewhat differently.

First of all, the composition of the Haitian population in Miami has been different from the other areas of Haitian settlement in ways that have effected the incorporation of Haitians in South Florida into the United States. An important sector of the Haitian economic and political elite always have maintained homes and business interests in that region of the United States. They were joined in the 1970s and 1980s by a large number of poor people who arrived by small boats and who were identified as "Haitian refugees," and stigmatized as boat people.[11] However, it is important not to see the Haitian population in Miami as totally distinct from that of the Northeast United States because there has been an ongoing secondary migration of Haitians from the Northern states into South Florida.

Those who settled in Miami entered a political terrain in which the salient political players were not multiple ethnic groups; the landscape was dominated by contestation between Cubans, whites, and African Americans, with African Americans the least powerful group (Portes and Stepick 1993).[12] The result has been that many Haitian immigrants in South Florida, though incorporated to a certain extent into the United States through employment, schooling, and religious institutions, have had less of a sense of Haitians as a part of the United States ethnic mosaic than Haitians settling in New York or Boston. To some degree, they defined themselves, even before the development of a Haitian transnational nation-state, as still a part of Haiti by naming the main Haitian business district in Miami "Little Haiti."

The differential construction of a Haitian ethnic identity within the United States political process reflected only one aspect of the social field and political affinities of these immigrants. At the very same time that Haitian immigrants were becoming incorporated in the United States—making up a growing proportion of the New York work force, becoming important in neighborhoods, beginning businesses, and serving as members of school and community boards—they were also building and maintaining ties to home. Many were living their lives across borders, becoming "transmigrants" who were simultaneously incorporated in two or more societies (Glick Schiller, Basch, and Szanton-Blanc 1992: 1). For a number of years these practices were sustained largely through family and personal networks and for a long time this transnationalism had no public face. Instead, Haitian immigrants in the United States framed their discussion about their political identities and destinies within what they thought to be two contradictory possibilities. Building the nation back home was distinguished from racial or ethnic politics within the United States. Ethnic identities stopped at the United States border; yet Haitian immigrants became increasingly involved with political processes "back home" that also shaped their public identities.

It was only after the 1990 election of Jean-Bertrand Aristide as President of Haiti on a wave of political organizing that was transnational in scope, that Haitian immigrant leaders begin to develop an identity politics that reflected their transnational ties and years of transnational political organizing. While Haitian candidates for elective political office in Haiti began campaigning in the United States as early as 1986, by the 1990s transnational politicking took a novel turn. Candidates for political office in the United States campaigned before Haitian audiences in New York claiming that Haitians could assist Haiti by becoming U.S. citizens and voting in U.S. elections. Moreover the Haitian Consulate went on record as supporting Haitians gaining U.S. citizenship as a way to strengthen the Haitian state. At the same time Haitians who were long term residents and even citizens of the United States or other countries held positions in the Aristide government or ran for po-litical office in Haiti.

Two points should be noted about Aristide's impact and his concept of the Tenth Department in contributing to these devel-opments. On the one hand, political leaders such as Aristide are playing a central role in the construction of the concepts of the transnational nation-state. In order to construct a theory about the current significance of nation-states within global processes and examine the links between contemporary cultural politics within these states and transnational migration, the role of aspiring politi-cal leaders and of intellectuals must be examined. It is these actors who organize a politics of identity which seeks to define the nature of the ties that bind immigrants to the political processes of their homelands.[13]

On the other hand, the emergence of the transnational nation-state cannot be reduced to a top down imposition of an ambitious leadership. In important ways immigrants outside this leadership strata are reading from the same text, and are at home with the new rhetoric of the transnational nation-state. There is of course a vari-ety of opinions among Haitian immigrants of different classes about how much energy to invest in various types of organiza-tional activities and identities. Here the role of the second and third generations is particularly noteworthy. A large section of persons of Haitian descent identify themselves in some contexts as African-Americans and maintain fewer transnational family-based activities than first generation immigrants. However, our observations lead us to conclude that a vocal and influential sector of this population participates in organized activities that link them with the home country and its national identity. For example, in October 1996, a group of Haitians in their twenties, many of the second generation began to organize a "Haitian National Community Network" with the following slogan: "A strong Haitian community equals a strong Haiti; a strong Haiti equals a strong Haitian community." Haitians of various generations of settlement increasingly now do not see participating in U.S. ethnic politics and in activities organized to build identification to countries from which they or their ancestors originated as evoking opposing loyalties or contradictory interests.

Equally significant has been the growing presence of women transmigrants as both participants and leaders in organized transnational activities and public assertions of identity with the nation-state. From the beginning of the immigration to the United States, while men had been the major holders of public leadership roles and had been the main participants in political discussions in private spaces such as living rooms, women had attended public meetings and demonstrations in almost equal numbers and followed the political debates on Haitian radio programs. They had been the majority in the congregations of Catholic parishes which had priests engaged in Liberation theology and linked to the growth of the Lavalas movement in Haiti. As this movement grew in strength, women emerged as political activists, sometimes holding leadership positions. In 1986, after the Duvalier regime had fallen 30,000 women in a broad coalition of women from different classes took to the streets in Port-Au-Prince to demand justice and social and economic transformation (Anglade 1986; Charles, n.d.). Many of the women who led this movement were from the diaspora and had gained a commitment to building the Haitian nation-state while living abroad. Moreover, in the next decade many of these women remained linked to political activities in both the United States, Haiti, and Canada. They formed an important base for Aristide, in both his years in power and in exile. When Aristide developed a whole new Ministry of the Feminine Condition, many among the leadership and activists of this Ministry, including the Minister were women who had gained their experience in politics in the transnational space of the Haitian diaspora. Many of the leaders of the second generation efforts to build transnational organizations that participated both in U.S. political and social movements and in the Haitian body politic are women, with women playing a prominent role in the efforts to build a Haitian National Community Network.

Disjunctures Within the National Terrain

In their efforts to move from ideological statements by the Haitian political leadership about the unity of the Haitian people to actual participation in the political process of Haiti, Haitian transmigrants whether they remain abroad or return to Haiti face a series of obstacles. If there is interconnection, there is also a history of simultaneous disjuncture and hostility between Haitians settled abroad and those who remained in Haiti. Aristide's reappropriation and redefinition of the term "diaspora" as a positive force in the rebuilding of Haiti as well as his articulation of the concept of the Tenth Department plastered over deep divides. These fissures in the body politic reflected significant differences within various sectors of the Haitian population. Competition erupted between those vying for political leadership, tensions emerged among those defending different class interests, and the competing perspectives that continue to divide those in the diaspora from those who live in the territory of Haiti resurfaced.

Contradictions that had always existed in the efforts of the Haitian government to institutionalize the Tenth Department came to the fore. From the beginning, the attempt to create a political leadership for the Tenth Department was fraught with difficulties. It was one thing for Aristide to make the ideological statement that Haitians everywhere were part of Haiti. It was quite another to develop mechanisms by which those included in the Tenth Department could develop decision making processes, choose leaders, and organize activities. Early on, many pertinent questions were raised by some of the constituents. For example, who could vote and hold office? Who could control funds? What were the mechanisms to insure that the leadership would be responsible to those they claimed to represent? Moreover, the boundary lines of what constituted the population of each chapter were not well-defined and the population of Haitian immigrants could readily disassociate themselves from their local.

Critics raised two kinds of questions. First of all, did the officials of the Tenth actually speak for the Haitian diaspora? And second of all, who was represented in the Tenth Department? Were people of Haitian descent in areas of settlement such as the Dominican Republic and the Bahamas considered valued members of the Tenth Department. Underneath these questions were differences in class. It was true that these yearly conferences of the Tenth Department included people from many areas of significant Haitian settlement including the Dominican Republic, the Bahamas, and Cuba. Their presence served to legitimize the claims that all people of Haitian descent outside the territorial boundaries of Haiti were members of the Tenth Department. Yet the entire project was dominated by those areas of settlement such as the United States and Canada where people had more wealth and education. In addition, in the United States and Canada, the more impoverished and less educated immigrants did not participate in, nor did they feel represented by those who claimed to lead the Tenth Department.

In the election of 1995 to replace Aristide, the Lavalas movement splintered and although Aristide's designated candidate René Préval won the Presidency, soon after the election, Préval began to distance himself from Aristide on many important points, including the use of the term the Tenth Department. The policy of building Haiti as a transnational nation-state continued but there were organizational changes in the way in which this policy was institutionalized. The Ministry of Haitians Living Abroad was retained and it affirmed that it:

> se veut le lieu de la "Coopération Inter-Haïtienne" coherente et systematique, c'est-à-dire, le lieu de participation ou de contribution des Haïtiens de l'étranger à la vie nationale et au developpment politique, social et économique d'Haïti (MHAVE, n.d.) (wishes to be the location of coherent and systematic "Inter-Haitian Cooperation", that is to say, the place of the participation or of the contributions of Haitians living abroad to the national life and to the political, social, and economic development of Haiti).

In addition, the Haitian government continues to see as legitimate its participation in activities conducted by Haitian immigrants who are incorporated in other nation-states. The ministry declared its intention "to help and to participate in the structuring and in the consolidation of the associations, organizations, and the communities of Haitians living abroad" (MHAVE n.d.). Paul Déjean, Préval's new MHAVE Minister who had lived in Canada from

1969 to 1986 repudiated the use of the term "Tenth Department." Instead he embraced the extended meaning of the word diaspora so that it referred to Haitians who were still a part of Haitian nation-state although permanently living abroad.

Moreover, Déjean made it clear to us that the Ministry was organizationally distinct from and could not speak for the Tenth Department, the organization claiming to speak for all Haitians living outside the territory of Haiti. The Tenth Department emerged as only a voluntary organization with chapters in various locales of Haitian settlement such as New York, Miami, Boston, Montreal, and the Bahamas. In addition, "in no case will the Ministry of Haitians Living Abroad execute or manage funds of projects" coming from abroad (MHAVE, n.d.).

Some of this readjustment probably reflected efforts on the part of the Préval government to find its own political base in the diaspora, different from that of Aristide who announced in the fall of 1996 that he was a candidate for the Presidency in 2001. At the same time, these political differences sustained and reinforced differences that continued to exist between Haitians living abroad and those in Haiti. The multiple familial, social, economic, and political ties that transmigrants maintain with Haiti contain many areas of dissonance and conflict as well as interconnection. The years of political rhetoric that defined the diaspora as traitors to the nation spoke to a duality of connection and social distance. This duality continues to exist. There are at least three major areas of disjuncture between Haitians living in the diaspora and those living in Haiti.

(1) Families economically dependent on those in the diaspora often resent their apparently more prosperous relatives and feel that the support sent is inadequate. Many of those living in Haiti have developed an ideology of obligation. In 1996, in interviews conducted in Les Cayes in an impoverished neighborhood settled by families with relatives abroad, we were told repeatedly "yo oblije ede fanmi-yo, yo oblije ede peyi-yo" (they are obliged to help their family, they are obliged to help their country). As one interviewee put it to us: "In the case of someone who leaves Haiti and does not help his family left behind, I would send him to a

doctor to see if he is not sick...he is not normal. That person should get a check up."

On the other hand, those in the diaspora find themselves overwhelmed by financial responsibilities they have to shoulder in both the country of settlement and Haiti. Transmigrants rarely find among those they support in Haiti a person who understands the dilemmas and stresses that they face because many in Haiti believe that Haitians of the diaspora are rich. And since Haiti is a country where one's social standing is very important, few transmigrants try to dispel this myth. At the same time, they feel overburdened with responsibilities to attend simultaneously to the needs of their family abroad and in Haiti. A woman described her frustration with the demands place on her both places:

> Since I was a young girl, I supported my whole family, you hear? Now that I have come to New York, it's worse. I have bills here and there to pay.... If I quit my job now, what would I do for the bills here and in Haiti? ...Well I can tell you, if I leave my job, my whole family would die, because I'm the one who keeps them afloat (Kerner 1991: 4).

(2) Those who stayed behind in Haiti and have jobs that require special training or are employed by the government feel threatened by members of the diaspora who return with more credentials and connections. In 1996 we asked respondents whether or not persons should be able to return from the diaspora to occupy good jobs or high positions in Haiti. People such as Alexandre, a struggling thirty year old mechanic, were opposed to this type of role for the diaspora. Alexandre who labors in an open air garage located in a run down section of Port-au-Prince to support his nuclear family and relatives left in his provincial home-town declared to us:

> I don't believe that neither those who are in the diaspora, nor those who returned have something positive for Haiti. All they think about is to come, take, and leave. They all come to enrich themselves. They take the money and they go away.

In Haiti, the people who return from the diaspora are perceived by many as nothing but opportunists bent on continuing the tradition of pilfering state wealth and resources. Haitian teledyòl (words of mouth) refers to them as the gran majè (big eaters) who devour everything in their passage.

The traditional bourgeoisie sees the transmigrants and their social, political, and economic capital as threatening to the established social order. As a merchant in an well known mulatto family in Port-au-Prince stated in an interview in 1995:

> These people they call the Diaspora know nothing about Haiti. They come back thinking they understand everytuing and they understand nothing. They are no longer Haitian in their thinking. All their ideas are imported and don't fit the reality of Haiti.

On their part, many among those who return may not have had the opportunity to accumulate significant material wealth in diaspora, encumbered as they were by family responsibilities in both Haiti and the society of settlement. Therefore they may be unable to display great material wealth, may be made to feel that the decision to leave Haiti did not benefit them, and may even lose their past social standing (Carolle Charles personal communication). Yet, migration, as many respondents told us in 1996, is perceived as a means to change class and improve on one's social image. In addition, they may find that some of the strata of educated professionals and technicians who stayed in Haiti or returned over a decade ago have acquired significant social and economic positions in Haiti. Unable to compete, they therefore turn to government functions, and use their position to pilfer, a practice followed by generations of public officials, but not one that people expected from U.S. educated diaspora.

(3) There is a divisions within the Haitian population both in Haiti and abroad about the plans to privatize the public utilities such as the telephone and electricity system. Some technicians and professionals in the diaspora believe that the enlargement of the private sector will mean good jobs for them in Haiti, at a time when immigrants, especially immigrants of color are under attack in the United States. Their support for privatization is echoed by families living in Haiti who receive money from relatives abroad. Many of these families believe that privatization will provide them with more access to phones and electricity, better service, and will make it easier to maintain communications with relatives living abroad.

Typical of this sector was Julienne Andre, age 33 who depends on her husband in Florida to pay the rent and her every day living expenses. Because you have to be wealthy and have political contacts to get phone service from the state monopoly, she has no phone although she could pay for one. Her lack of a phone impedes her efforts to keep in constant touch with her husband and brother in the United States. Sitting in her well kept front room near her television, VCR, and cd player, she told us that she was for privatization.

> If the white man comes, he will stabilize the price (and)...people won't be able to steal. For example, now I have my meter (meaning that she pays the state owned electricity company for her electricity). At least four people are taking electricity from my meter and I end up paying for their electricity.... There will be better services too.

But many of the poor who have no family in the diaspora, told us that privatization means that their already impoverished lives will become even more difficult. They will not be able to help themselves to electricity through illegal connections. They will not be able to afford any improvement in service.

A 23 year old young man who lives in near Port-au-Prince supported by a brother who scrapes together a living by doing tailoring at home could only get the electricity that powered his brother's sewing machine by taking "priz," that is by using an illegal connection. For him privatization

> is not good.... I don't have a meter. If they privatize I won't be able to take priz anymore. If they privatize I will have to use a meter and I can't afford one. I have been living for five years in a house without a meter.... I have no telephone and I don't have the means to get it.

Implications of Transnationalism
For the Concept of the Nation-State

We began this paper with excerpts from a transnational conversation in which Haitians living in the United States propounded a different point of view than those living in Haiti. The divisions between those living abroad and those living within the territory of Haiti are lines of discord that compound the many profound cleavages among people who define themselves as "Haitian." In order for us to make sense of both the Haitian transnational discourse as well as the many similar discussions that link transmigrants in immigrant receiving societies to the nation-states from which they migrated, we must understand both the processes that generate disjunctures between immigrants and their homelands, and the processes by which continuing identities to homeland are sustained and reinforced.

The paradox of our times, and one that must be central to our understanding of the identities and dilemmas of current day immigrants, is that the "age of transnationalism" is a time of continuing and even heightening nation-state building processes. In the current heightening of nationalist sentiment in a globalized economy, transnational migration is playing a complex, significant, yet little noted role (Miles 1993). It lies as a silent subtext that contributes to the actions, motivations, and sensibilities of key players within the political processes and debates of both states that have histories of population dispersal and states that have primarily been and continue to be recipients of population flows.

While the concept of independent nation-states arose in conjunction with the rise of a global capitalist economy, it can be argued that until the last few decades, most states developed arenas of national autonomy. Their organization of the economy, national currency, control of national borders, and social and cultural institutions provided a material basis for political leaders to assert, and for the general population to believe that their government was a sovereign state, able to institute its policies within its territory, and act in the world of states as an independent country. As national institutions have become eroded by transnational processes of the restructured global economy, it is less possible to maintain the old national myths. Transnational immigrants and their multiple connections furnish the political leadership of both countries that send migrants and countries in the United States and Western Europe that receive migrants with new possibilities of maintaining discourses of nationalism.

The ideology of the transnational nation-state allows dominant sectors of immigrant-sending countries to develop a new rhetoric of national independence. Immediately after independence the classes that dominated post-colonial states invested in the cultural, political, or economic domains of the state in order to construct a sense of national sovereignty. Currently such nation-state building processes are being savaged as the World Bank and the International Monetary Fund dictate policies that impose privatization and forbid investment in schools, health care, housing, and public services by global capital. Many countries can be said to have been "recolonized" rather than post-colonial (Fouron and Glick Schiller 1996). The word "recolonization" is being used to emphasize that the contemporary penetration of what are considered independent states closely resembled the indirect rule through which the British governed Africa, using indigenous local institutions as the instruments of control.

However the leadership of these states are developing a reconstituted discourse of independence that both acknowledges global processes and yet denies the dominion of global capitalist institutions. The multiple transnational social relations of immigrants are providing a new type of space from these leadership project the sense and sensibilities of national sovereignty and autonomy. The rhetoric and institutions of the deterritorialized nation-state serve to obscure the totality of the penetration of many post-colonial nation-states such as Haiti.

Even as Haitians engaged in this discourse speak of national reconstruction, the current situation differentially benefits different classes, maintaining and deepening the class divisions that have since early in Haitian history disempowered most of the Haitian people. The recolonization of Haiti serves some Haitian professionals well because capitalist globalization and penetration create small pockets of opportunities for professional expatriates and entrepreneurs in their native societies while they live in the core economies. During the tenure of the military junta, many Haitian immigrant professionals and investors aligned themselves with the various *de facto* governments and the Haitian bourgeoisie and took lucrative advantages of the political and economic spoils of the coup. After Aristide's return to Haiti, most embraced the United States backed privatization programs and the U.S. rhetoric that described the United States shaping of Haitian national politics as "the restoration of democracy in Haiti."

The conceptualization of the Haitians deterritorialized nation-state has encouraged even those professionals who staunchly opposed the Haitian military to abate their criticism of the United States domination of Haiti. For example, during a program on Radio Tropicale that was broadcast on the eve of the United States occupation of Haiti, one of the speakers quickly dismissed inquiries by those who called the radio station to voice their suspicions concerning the real motives that pushed the Americans to become involved in the Haitian morass. Angrily one of the guests shouted: *Depi desanzan nap pale, nap kritike, ki sa nou janm realize? Anyen. Nou jwen-n etranje ki vle ede nou. Kou nou ye-a, se pou nou bliye tout pale anpil, se pou nou mete men nou ala pat pou fè peyi-a mache* (During the past two hundred years we have been criticizing others, what have we accomplished? Nothing. Now we have foreigners who want to help us. The time to philosophize is over, we must participate in this new attempt to make the country work). Similar statements continue to be made despite the accumulating evidence that the United States occupation has not led to positive change in Haiti. Such pronouncements are directly connected with the economic and social prospects capitalist penetration grants to Haitians educated or even born elsewhere. For, besides extending to Haitians living abroad the possibilities to return to Haiti for short or long periods of time to participate in the administration of Haiti, it also provides them with social and economic privileges that endow them with the sense of purpose and worth they unsuccessfully covet in the core economies.

This mind-set has narrowed down considerably the ideological and political space for critical discourse. It has also abated resistance to outside domination of Haiti and facilitated the willingness of nationalists to participate in and collaborate with foreign penetration, domination, and control of Haiti. Moreover, the acrimonious ideological polarization, the perilous political atmosphere, and the fear of being denounced as a Duvalierist and a makout are cowering many and preventing them from initiating new perspectives to probe the country's realities.

Yet the process of conceptualizing Haiti as a transnational nation-state does not encompass fully the complexity and multiple identities which constitute the lives of transmigrants. There is something within the experience of being a transmigrants that does transgress borders and boundaries both of the state and of the conceptual terrain mapped by states. To be forced to migrate from your home with the dream of a better life, to confront difficult economic conditions and racism instead of a world of prosperity and security, and to map out transnational connections as a strategy of personal and cultural survival is to enter a realm not totally penetrated by dominant ideas and practices. Transmigrants through their lived realities provide us with insights about the need to think beyond the cultural politics that the hegemonic institutions of states use in their efforts to shape national cultures. Scholars of transnational migration have a role to play in linking the transnational experiences of immigrants to the sense of displacement that is shared by people throughout the world who have been stranded with no identity that can voice their subordination to global capitalism. We must confront the contradictions that are unfolding from the policies of structural adjustment, privatization, deindustrialization in the core and export-processing in the margins, all mediated by global financial markets. Scholars of transnational migration can help to articulate the nature of the system that confronts the global work force. We can be part of a transgressive movement that builds opposition to the forces that continue to structure our imaginations while they exploit our labor.

Notes

1. An earlier version of this paper was prepared for the American Sociological Association conference, Monday August 19, 1996 organized by Luis Guarnizo and Douglas Kinkaid. Portions of this paper appear in Caribbean Circuits, Patricia Pessar ed., published by the Center for Migration Studies, Staten Island, New York 1996. This paper builds on work on transnational migration done by Linda Basch, Nina Glick Schiller and Cristina Szanton Blanc and research on the building of Haitian identities in New York conducted by the authors together with Josh DeWind, Carolle Charles, Marie Lucie Brutus, and Antoine Thomas (NICHD Grant #281-40-1145). Funding for research in Haiti was provided by the UNH Center for the Humanities, Office of the Dean of Liberal Arts, and the Wenner Gren Foundation.

2. *Moman Kreyòl* is a widely popular Haitian radio program that is aired on WLIB-AM every Sunday from 10:00 AM to 4:00 PM. WLIB-AM is a minority medium owned and operated by Percy Sutton, a prominent African-American business and political leader with roots in the Caribbean community in New York.

3. In 1990 this loosely organized student coalition was able to spark a protest march of tens of thousands of Haitians in New York against the continuing designation of the U.S. Food and Drug Administration that Haitians were an "at risk" group for AIDS and could not give blood. (Fouron 1995.)

4. To force the hands of the Haitian military to accept Aristide's return to power, the United States and the Aristide government agreed to impose a total embargo on the country. While the embargo was meant to return the country to democratic rule, it ran roughshod over the most vulnerable sectors of the Haitian populations, namely the poor and the peasants. The elite took advantage of the embargo to amass scandalous fortunes. Meanwhile, the United States proved unwilling to enforce the embargo against the elite who made fortunes by smuggling goods through Haiti's shared border with the Dominican Republic. The United States even directly violated the embargo by creating loopholes to allow industries to continue to produce goods such as softballs for U.S. military contracts.

5. During the three years Aristide spent in exile, attempts made by the international community to negotiate his return with the military regime that had led the coup were unsuccessful. To regain power, he agreed with the United States on the terms of a formal invasion of the country, which occurred on October 15, 1994.

6. A division between an immigrant population and its country of origin is legitimated by classic political theories of the nation-state (Hobsbawm 1990, 1992; Calhoun 1994; Weber 1976; Fukuyama 1995).

7. The word Kamoken was derived from Camoquin, a quinine based and very bitter anti-malarial pill dispensed to Haitian peasants and urban poor throughout the 1960s by representatives of the World Health Organization (WHO). It regularly caused great discomfort to those who ingested it but since it was necessary to check the spread of the disease, the Haitians consented to take it as a necessary evil. The word Kamoken was originally utilized by Haitian peasants and the urban poor to convey the message that those who opposed Duvalier constituted the radical antidote needed to rid Haiti of Duvalier and his cohorts. Later on, however, Duvalier used the terminology to terrorize and severely punish those who professed to oppose his regime. Once one was accused of being a Kamoken, the price, under the Duvalier regime, was instant death without any due process or trial.

8. The New York metropolitan area was the first region of dense Haitian settlement and according to the Immigration and Naturalization Service in 1993 more than one-third of the newly-arrived Haitian immigrants continued to settle there (United States Immigration and Naturalization Service 1994). From the 1970s, Miami began to receive large numbers of Haitian immigrants. By 1993 another third of newly arrived immigrants were settling in either Miami or other cities and towns in South Florida. Other locations of

dense Haitian settlement are Boston, Massachusetts; Newark, New Jersey; Bridgeport, Connecticut; Orlando, Florida, and Washington, D.C. However, there are also Haitian cities in California and Illinois. (For the Canadian situation, see Déjean 1978, 1990.)

9. In the multi-culturalism of the 1990s, the continuing imposition of barriers of "racial" difference is simultaneously signaled, reinforced, and obscured by categorizing people who migrated from different countries as distinct ethnic groups and yet "racializing" them under a single descriptor. People from Puerto Rico, Cuba, the Dominican Republic, are both referred to as ethnic groups and yet racialized together with immigrants from Mexico, Central and South America as Hispanics. Immigrants from the various countries in Asia are also treated as both ethnics—for example, "the Chinese"—and as a separate racially distinct group of "Asians."

10. There are no reliable figures on the number of Haitian immigrants and people of Haitian descent in the United States. According to the Immigration and Naturalization Service, only 5,544 Haitians entered the United States as immigrants from 1932-1950. After 1950 Haitian immigration to the United States accelerated but the large numbers only began to come after 1959. In the years from 1959 to 1993, 302,458 Haitians entered the United States with permanent resident visas and 1,381,240 others arrived, most with tourist visas. Because it was relatively easy until the 1980s for those with tourist visas to regularize their status, many of these "tourists" latter became permanent residents. It is likely that one fifth of Haiti's six million people live outside of Haiti, with the largest concentration settled in the United States.

11. Between 1977 and 1981 more than 60,000 Haitians arrived in South Florida by small wooden sailboats (Portes and Stepick 1993: 51).

12. It is difficult to assess the relative significance of the various Haitian settlements in the emerging construction of Haiti as a transnational nation-state. During Aristide's exile in the United States, his government in exile developed links with Haitians in various sections of the United States and in Canada and Haitians who had settled in all areas became part of his government. There are also family networks that stretch among the settlements and there has been a significant amount of secondary migration within the various locations, including between Montreal, Canada and the United States. However, New York, until recently, has been seen as the most vocal of the Haitian settlements.

13. In the 19th and early 20th centuries, immigrant leaders in the United States among populations that ranged from the Irish (Higham and Brooks, 1978) to the Hungarians (Vassady 1982) made such connections in a nationalist rhetoric that highlighted struggles to liberate homelands and set up independent states with their own territory to which exiled or dispersed population could return.

References

Anglade, Mireille. (1986). *L'Autre Moitié du Développement: á Propos du Travail des Femmes en Haïti*. Pétion-Ville, Haiti: Éditions des Alizés.

Basch, Linda, Nina Glick Schiller, and Cristina Szanton Blanc. (1994). *Nations Unbound: Transnational Projects, Postcolonial Predicaments and the Deterritorialized Nation-State*. New York: Gordon and Breach.

Calhoun, Craig. (1994). "Social theory and the Politics of Identity." In Craig Calhoun (ed.), *Social theory and the Politics of Identity*. Cambridge: Blackwell.

Charles, C. (n.d.). "The Women's Movement in Haiti." Unpublished paper.

Déjean, Paul. (1990). *D'Haïti au Québec*. Montréal: CIDIHCA.

-----. (1978). *Les Haïtiens au Québec*. Montréal: Les Presses de L'Université du Québec.

Delorme, Demesvar. (1870). *Les théoriciens au pouvoir*. Paris: Plon.

Duvalier, François. (1966). *Oeuvres essentielles*, Vols. 1 and 2. Port-au-Prince: Presses Nationales d' Haiti.

Foner, Nancy. (1987). "The Jamaicans: Race and Ethnicity among Migrants in New York City." In Nancy Foner (ed.), *New immigrants in New York City: Race and Ethnicity among Migrants in New York City*. New York: Columbia University Press. Pp. 195-217.

Fouron, Georges. (1995). "Head in the Diaspora, Heart in Haiti: The Great AIDS March." Paper delivered at a conference of the University of District of Columbia, Washington D.C.

Fouron, Georges, and Nina Glick Schiller. (1996). "Haitian Identities at the Disjuncture between Diaspora and Homeland." In Patricia R. Pessar (ed.), *Caribbean Circuits*. Staten Island: Center for Migration Studies.

François, M-M. (1995). Interview on *Kontrovès/Controversy*, Radyo Moman Kreyòl, WLIB-AM. November 26.

Fukuyama, Francis. (1995). *Trust: The Social Virtues and the Creation of Prosperity*. New York: Free Press.

Gellner, Ernest. (1983). *Nation and nationalism*. Oxford: Blackwell.

Glazer, Nathan. and Patrick Moynihan. ([1963] 1970). *Beyond the Melting Pot: The Negroes, Puerto Ricans, Jews, Italians, and Irish of New York City*. Cambridge: MIT Press.

Glick Schiller, Nina. (1995). "The Implications of Haitian Transnationalism for United States-Haitian Relations: Contradictions of the Deterritorialized Nation-state." *Journal of Haitian Studies* 1: 1: 111-123.

———. (1977). "Ethnic Groups Are Made, Not Born." In George L. Hicks and Philip E. Leis (eds.), *Ethnic Encounters: Identities and Contexts*. North Scituate, MA: Duxbury Press. Pp. 23-35.

———. (1975). *The Formation of a Haitian Ethnic Group*. Ph.D. dissertation. Department of Anthropology, Columbia University.

Glick Schiller, Nina, Linda Basch, and Cristina Blanc Szanton. (1992). *Towards a Transnational Perspective of Migration: Race, Class, Ethnicity, and Nationalism Reconsidered*. New York, NY: The New York Academy of Sciences 645.

Glick Schiller, Nina, J.DeWind, M.L. Brutus, C. Charles, G. Fouron, and A. Thomas. (1987). "Exile, Ethnic, Refugee: Changing Organizational Identities among Haitian Immigrants." *Migration Today* 15: 7-11.

Guarnizo, Luis E. (1996). "The Nation-State and Grassroots Transnationalism: Comparing Mexican and Dominican Transmigration." Paper presented at American Ethnological Society Annual Meeting. San Juan, Puerto Rico. April 17-21.

Guidieri, Remo, Francesco Pellizzi, and Stanley J. Tambiah. (1988). *Ethnicity and Nations: Processes of Interethnic Relations in Latin America, Southeast Asia, and the Pacific.* Austin: University of Texas Press.

Higham, John, and C. Brooks. (1978). *Ethnic Leadership in America.* Baltimore: Johns Hopkins University Press.

Hobsbawm, Eric J. (1992). "Ethnicity and Nationalism in Europe Today." *Anthropology Today* 8: 1: 3-8.

———. (1990). *Nations and Nationalism since 1780.* Cambridge: Cambridge University Press.

Hurbon, Laennec. (1979). *Culture et Dictature en Haïti: l'Imaginaire sous Control.* Paris: L'Harmattan.

Jean-Pierre, J. (1994). "The Tenth Department." In James Ridgeway (ed.), *The Haiti Files: Decoding the Crisis.* Washington, D.C.: Essential Books/Azul Edition. Pp. 56-63.

Kasinitz, Philip. (1992). *Caribbean New York: Black Immigrants and the Politics of Race.* Ithaca, NY: Cornell University Press.

Kerner, J. (1991). "Focus Group Notes: Women's General Health Issues." Sloan-Kettering. Unpublished document.

Lemelle, Sidney, and Robin D. G. Kelly. (1994). *Imagining Home: Class, Culture, and Nationalism in the African Diaspora.* New York: Verso.

Lewis, Gordon. K. (1987). *Main Currents in Caribbean Thought.* Baltimore: The Johns Hopkins University Press.

Lundahl, Mats. (1979). *Peasants and Poverty: A Study of Haiti.* New York: St. Martin's Press.

MHAVE (n.d.). *Ministère des Häitiens Vivant à l'Etranger.* Port-au-Prince: PubliGestion, H. Deschamps.

Miles, Robert. (1993). *Racism after "Race Relations."* London: Routledge.

Moman Kreyòl. (1991). Radyo WLIB-AM, February 10, and January 5.

Nicholls, David. (1979). *From Dessalines to Duvalier: Race, Colour, and National Independence in Haiti.* Cambridge: Cambridge University Press.

Omi, Michael. and Howard Winant. (1986). *Racial Formation in the United States.* New York: Routledge.

Portes, Alejandro, and Ruben G. Rumbaut. (1990). *Immigrant America: A Portrait.* Berkeley: University of California Press.

Portes, Alejandro. and Alex Stepick. (1993). *City on the Edge: the Transformation of Miami.* Berkeley: University of California Press.

Portes, Alejandro and Min Zhou. (1993). "The Second Generation: Segmented Assimilation and its Variants." *The Annals of the American Academy of Political and Social Science* 530: 74-96.

Pwojè Lavalas (n.d.). *"Pwojè Lavalas ak Batay Nasyon-an pou Demokrasy."*

Richman, Karen. (1992). "A Lavalas at Home-A Lavalas for Home: Inflections of Transnationalism in the Discourse of Haitian President Aristide." In Nina Glick Schiller, Linda Basch, and Cristina Blanc-Szanton (eds.), *Towards a Transnational Perspective of Migration: Race, Class, Ethnicity, and Nationalism Reconsidered.* New York, NY: The New York Academy of Sciences.

Rios, Palmyra. (1995). "International Migration, Citizenship, and the Emergence of Transnational Public Policies." Paper presented at the American Ethnological Society Annual Meeting. San Juan, Puerto Rico. April 18-21, 1996.

Smith, Robert C. (1993). "De-territorialized Nation Building: Transnational Migrants and the Re-imagination of Political Community by Sending States." Paper delivered at the Seminar Migration and the State. Center for Latin American and Caribbean Studies, New York University.

Takaki, Ronald. (1989). *Strangers from a Different Shore: A History of Asian Americans.* New York: Penguin Books.

Trouillot, Michel-Rolph. (1990). *Haiti: State against Nation. The Origin and Legacy of Duvalierism.* New York: Monthly Review Press.

United States Immigration and Naturalization Service. (1994). *Statistical Yearbook of the Immigration and Naturalization Service.* Washington, D.C.: United States Government Printing Office.

Vassady, Bela. (1982). "The Homeland Cause" as a Stimulant to Ethnic Unity: The Hungarian-American Response to Karolyi's 1914 Tour. *Journal of American Ethnic History* 2: 1: 39-64.

Weber, Eugen J. (1976). *Peasants into Frenchmen: The Modernization of Rural France, 1870-1914.* Stanford, CA: Stanford University Press.

III

Constructing
Transnational Localities

6

The Power of Status in Transnational Social Fields[1]

Luin Goldring

Transnational social spaces or fields and the practices of trans-migrants[2] have emerged as an important topic among social theorists. Analyzing these social spaces, and the social actors associated with them, is attractive for several reasons. First, they offer an arena in which to investigate the agency of collectivities that M.P. Smith (1994: 16) describes as "unbound" by national borders, without loosing sight of the structural processes that contribute to their formation (Goldring 1992a, Ch. 2). Second, focusing on transnational social fields contributes to rethinking territory- or nation-bound concepts like *community, assimilation, citizenship*, and *immigrant* (Kearney and Nagengast 1989; Platt 1991; Rouse 1991; Goldring 1992a, 1996b; R. Smith 1995; Alarcón 1995a), and research strategies associated with them, e.g., community studies (M.P. Smith 1994). Processes such as settlement can also be reconsidered (Alarcón 1995b; Goldring 1992a). Third, this focus draws attention to hybridization in cultural domains (García Canclini 1990). Fourth, the political dimension of transnational political practices can be recognized and analyzed (Goldring 1992b; M.P. Smith 1994; R. Smith 1995). This is yielding rich analyses of the construction of racial and ethnic categories and their intersection with class formation in ongoing processes of nation building in extraterritorialized states[3] and countries of immigration (Basch et al. 1994; R. Smith 1994). In this way the state, and in particular state responses to transmigrant practices, has entered the research agenda (Basch et al. 1994; Goldring and Smith 1993; Goldring 1994, 1996c; Smith 1995).

This essay addresses the question of why (im)migrants[4] or transmigrants from Mexico construct and maintain transnational social fields. The question is part of a broader concern with the citizenship practices of people who orient their lives around more than one nation state, and state responses to them. The issues that concern me here can be rephrased in terms of the following types of questions: Why do transmigrants maintain ties to their place of

165

origin? Why do so many continue to send and spend money there, even after appearing to have "settled" in the United States? Why do they become involved in home-town or home-state associations, and the community development projects that many of these organizations support? What does the place of origin mean to them, especially in comparison to the social spaces they inhabit in the United States?

Research on transnational migration has highlighted several factors that contribute to the creation and maintenance of transnational communities or social fields (Rouse 1991; Goldring 1992b, 1996b; Basch et al. 1994; R. Smith 1995; Alarcón 1995a). Some, such as cheaper and more accessible travel and communications and reliable money transfer businesses, are *means* that facilitate transnationalism. They are contributing mechanisms, rather than *reasons* or *motivations* for it. Other factors, such as kinship and social networks and norms concerning social obligations, are means and reasons at the same time. This essay focuses on reasons behind transnational communities or social fields and associated identities.

The scope of concern is further narrowed because I am particularly interested in reasons for transnationalism from the perspective of transmigrants as members of social networks and transnational communities. This is not to minimize the importance of structural processes in shaping cross-border population movements and transnationalism. However, there is already a large body of work on macro-structural factors and policies that contribute to transnational labor flows, and Mexico-United States migration in particular.[5] This allows me to leave aside a discussion of the role of, for example, Mexico's position in the world-system, economic restructuring in the United States and Mexico, the role of U.S. employers' demand for cheap and/or unorganized labor, labor market segmentation and split-labor markets, U.S. immigration policy and its implementation, and agriculture, trade, and industrialization policies in Mexico, in structuring the migrations that have led to the development of transnationalized societies and communities. Instead, this essay is part of an effort to analyze migration by focusing on the interaction between social actors and institutions that surround them (Cf. Giddens 1979; Pedraza 1990; Goldring 1992a, 1992b, 1996b; R. Smith 1995).

I argue that Mexicans tend to continue to orient their lives in part around their place of origin, maintaining transnational spaces and multiple identities, based on the following line of reasoning. 1) The locality of origin provides a unique social and spatial context within transnational communities for making claims to and valorizing social status. 2) In making and valorizing such claims, transmigrants and other members of transnational communities may reorient regimes of stratification. There may be several dimensions to this reorientation: individuals and families may change their own status, alter definitions of how status is achieved, and perhaps help to shift the position of the community in relation to regional or state-level authorities. 3) Transnational communities may also offer organizational resources that permit the development of alternative power hierarchies. Becoming active in any of the preceding processes gives transmigrants an opportunity to participate in the modification of their social landscape, that is, to alter the social, economic, and political geography and role of their place of origin.

In other words, transnational social fields, and localities of origin in particular, provide a special context in which people can improve their social position and perhaps their power, make claims about their changing status and have it appropriately valorized, and also participate in changing their place of origin so that it becomes more consistent with their changing expectations and statuses. This is because of the communicative dimension of community: transnational social communities are also communities of meaning in which status claims are interpreted based on shared histories and understandings of practices, rituals, goods, and other status markers. Furthermore, transnational social organization can be a significant resource in the formation of social and political capital for community "leaders" who use transnational spaces to generate power/status hierarchies which may provide an alternative arena of interaction with Mexican authorities in Mexico and the United States, and sometimes with American authorities and Chicano/Latino organizations in the United States. This exploration of reasons behind the maintenance of transnational social fields points to a need to broaden existing conceptions of citizenship, so that practices that express social, cultural, political, and civic claims/rights are examined in a transnational context. Examining why people bother to maintain transnational spaces, relationships, and identities is a step in that direction.

The remainder of this essay is divided into three parts. The first reviews reasons for transnationalism and their applicability to the Mexico-United States case, and makes an argument for analyzing status in transnational migration. In the next part I discuss practices related to the claiming and valorization of status in transnational social fields with reference to individuals, families, communities, and relations between the Mexican state and transmigrant organizations. The last part presents concluding comments. Most of the information comes from research conducted between 1988 and 1990 in Las Animas, a village in southern Zacatecas, and parts of California where Animeños live and work (Goldring 1992a), and from follow-up visits with Animeños in Mexico and California over the last five years. Interviews conducted with Mexican Consulate staff in Los Angeles and officials in Mexico (intermittently, since 1993), and with leaders of Mexican home-state organizations in Los Angeles (June, October, and November, 1996) as part of a related project (Goldring 1996c) are also used.

Reasons for Transnationalism

In their analysis of transnational migration from Haiti, St. Vincent, Granada, and the Philippines to the United States, Basch et al. (1994) identify the following reasons behind the creation and maintenance of transnational social fields and identities: (1) family reproduction in the face of economic and/or political insecurity, (2) social exclusion in countries of origin—especially for some transmigrant groups, and (3) racialized exclusion in the United States. They argue that maintaining transnational ties and the various class, national, and racialized identities that accompany them, helps transmigrants improve or maintain their economic situation, reinforce or raise their social standing, and validate their self-esteem.

Active relations between extraterritorialized home states and transmigrants can be a fourth reason for transnationalism— whether transmigrants are supporting an opposition party or movement from afar, returning to participate in a newly formed government, or whether states are attempting to gain legitimacy and support from a diaspora (Basch et al. 1994; R. Smith 1995). Basch et al. (1994) note that while political and economic crises often act as catalysts of migration, they may also motivate people to maintain ties and return home. Haiti after Duvalier and the Philippines after Marcos are examples of such crises. In both cases, transmigrants played important roles in the transformations surrounding regime changes.

Each of these processes is important for understanding Mexico-United States migration and transnationalism, although recent political struggles in Mexico have not involved significant regime changes and have been, on the whole, less transnationalized than the cases analyzed by Basch and her colleagues.[6] There has certainly been no shortage of events contributing to the uncertainty and marginalization experienced by many households. These include the Mexican revolution (1910-17); droughts; changes in the structure of agricultural production; successive periods of xenophobia in the United States associated with repatriations and more recently, anti-immigrant legislation; and the series of economic (and political) crises that have taken place since the early 1980s, making social reproduction increasingly problematic for lower-and even middle-class families. As Jones (1992) argues, migration to the United States offers Mexicans a means of maintaining or improving their standard of living. Kin relations have usually provided the basis for transnational migration, and as migration becomes a cumulative process, it in turn contributes to the expansion of family and extended kin relations across space (Mines 1981; Massey et al. 1987; Goldring 1996a, 1996b). Social networks also reinforce transnationalism to the extent that Mexicans in the United States continue to orient part of their lives around their community of origin in one way or another, for example, by keeping in touch with family and friends in Mexico, sending money back, returning there, and maintaining versions of rituals and practices rooted in the home region.

Mexicans also face exclusion and marginality in the United States, where they encounter a process of racial formation (Omi and Winant 1994) that locates them towards the bottom of a racialized hierarchy: below Americans of European origin, above African-Americans and Puerto Ricans on the east coast (R. Smith 1994), and in a variable and sometimes competitive position in relation to other Latinos, Asian-Americans, and African-Americans in other parts of the country. As R. Smith (1994) argues, this leads to "double bounded" solidarity and incorporation for Mexicans in New York. They are doubly bounded by attempts to distance themselves from African-Americans and Puerto Ricans, thereby defining themselves as *not black*, and by being defined by the dominant society as *not white*. Mexicans in California also distance themselves from the bottom of the racialized hierarchy (Goldring 1994). The experience of migrating to a country where hegemonic racial constructions locate them in a disadvantaged position certainly contributes to people retaining ties and identities associated with their home countries and communities, as these offer a refuge from U.S. racialization.[7]

Mexican state policies also help to explain transnationalism. Since the administration of Salinas de Gortari (1988-94), the Mexican government has established an active program to develop and maintain relations with Mexicans abroad (R. Smith 1995). The Program for Mexican Communities Abroad, or PCME (Programa para Comunidades Mexicanas en el Extranjero), is designed to reach Mexicans from various social groups including rural campesinos and urban migrants, workers and business owners, the poor and the rich. The program is part of a division of the Ministry of Foreign Relations, and is directed by Ministry staff who also work with personnel at the Consulates and Mexican Cultural Institutes.[8] One of the PCME's main goals is to encourage Mexicans and people of Mexican origin to maintain ties with Mexico. It is organized around the following program areas: education, culture, sports, business, and communities. The companion *Programa Paisano* was designed to improve conditions for

Mexicans who return home for visits. Under this program, returning paisanos can report abuses by authorities (e.g., customs and immigration agents, and federal police) to a toll-free number. The Federal Attorney general's office is then responsible for investigating and charging offenders. That the PCME was developed, at least in part, as a response to Cuahutémoc Cárdenas' opposition party campaign in the United States prior to the 1988 presidential elections, supports understanding the PCME as part of the hegemonic nation building practices of an extraterritorial state.[9]

The PCME attempts to build or reinforce national identity among migrants whose home-town, regional or provincial identities may have been stronger than their national identity when they first began to migrate. For example, the education program provides Mexican government text books for literacy training. These books also teach Mexican history and reinforce national symbols and identity. The culture program includes sponsoring tours of Mexican artists, singers, and musicians who show their work or perform for Mexicans in the United States. The community program promotes the creation of home-town clubs and state-level associations. These organizations often work on community development projects in Mexico, and promote the maintenance of social and economic ties with their sending regions. More recently, the program has encouraged municipal presidents to travel to the United States to visit with their constituents who reside abroad (Interviews). Under certain circumstances, they may also provide a base for organizing. For example, home-town clubs and state-level associations in Los Angeles and Chicago contributed time, money, and/or organizational resources to the campaign against Proposition 187 (Interviews; Zabin 1995). The rise in hometown clubs, the emergence of state level umbrella organizations registered with Mexican consulates since the early 1990s,[10] and stepped up consular activity all reflect the state's growing relationship with transmigrants.

Changing patterns of social reproduction among family groups, responses to socioeconomic marginality in Mexico and racialization in the United States, and the state's extraterritorial practices are crucial for understanding the general development of Mexico-United States transnational social fields. However, the research agenda on transnationalism is quite open, as many questions remain. The above cited processes should also be analyzed in relation to other variables, such as the history and prevalence of migration (Massey, Goldring and Durand 1994), the presence and concentration of ethnoracial groups, and employment opportunities or constraints, in the multiple sites of specific migrant circuits in order to gain a better understanding of how and why particular localities and regions become transnationalized. As Mahler (1966) points out, it is also important to analyze the role, gender, geographic mobility, range of activities, and changing socioeconomic position, of different members of transnational social fields (e.g., couriers, entrepreneurs, women and others involved in social reproduction, non-migrants etc.).

Status in Transnational Social Fields

I wish to contribute to the analysis of transnational social fields by directing attention to the power of social status and what I argue is a related issue, the meaning of community among transmigrants. Focusing on these issues can complement current analyses of transnationalism. This can help explain why some individuals and families continue to orient their lives around two countries, investing time and money in Mexico even though they seem to have settled in the United States, and also contribute to the "un-binding" of nation-bound concepts such as social citizenship and civic participation. Social actors may claim status as individuals *and* as members of families, communities, and other collectivities (Turner 1988: 2-8). Thus, one's status may vary depending on personal accomplishment, education, occupation, and/or wealth; family reputation, connections, and resources; and the status groups to which one claims membership (e.g., those based on ethnicity, religion, property rights or land tenure, occupation, sports, nationality, or place of origin).

Status claims based on membership in transnational collectivities and their associated northernized[11] home-localities are particularly important. As Robert Smith (1995) persuasively argues, and as I have tried to suggest elsewhere (Goldring 1992b, 1996b), political negotiations surrounding community projects organized by U.S.

based transmigrants (with varying degrees of participation by people in the locality of origin) are crucial to the making and reinforcing of Mexico-United States transnational social fields. Conflict over which projects a home-town organization will support, who will carry out and manage the project, who will get credit for it, and how money is accounted for, are central to ongoing processes of claiming community membership and altering the services and infrastructure—and accompanying status—of the home-community one claims membership to (Smith 1995; Goldring 1992a, 1992b). These projects and accompanying negotiations may also lead to changes in the regional power structure, giving people from the community more leverage *vis-á-vis* local and regional authorities.

I argue that people engage in these transnational negotiations, creating and/or maintaining transnational social fields, because transnational social spaces and the locality of origin in particular, offer a special context for claiming and valorizing status. This argument is informed by a conception of transnational community discussed elsewhere (Goldring 1992a, 1996b), which I outline here. *Community* involves a sense of shared history and identity, and mutually intelligible meanings. I am particularly interested in meanings that allow status claims to be understood through the interpretation of practices, rituals, goods and artifacts in the context of transnational communities and broader transnational social fields (Goldring 1992a, 1996b). Community is therefore related to status because transnational communities and social fields offer a unique context for interpreting individual and collective status claims.

For migrants embedded in broad social networks or community traditions of migration (Mines 1981), which usually means those from rural areas,[12] the place of origin represents a unique context for valorizing status and social capital for transmigrants—as individuals and as members of families and communities. This is precisely because people interpret status claims in a historical and community context, where certain practices, rituals, goods, and artifacts have mutually intelligible meanings to community members. Home-town men and women, and families, can be understood as having done well in relation to what they were by others who have seen them change and who understand the meaning of their driving a particular vehicle, making additions to their home, and so forth (Rhoades 1978; Platt 1991; Goldring 1992a). Even if transmigrants claim membership in U.S.-based communities (e.g., churches, community groups, sports teams, etc.), and even if they experience little marginality in the United States, having one's status valorized among peers who share claims to community membership provides an important context for expressing statuses and identities that has not been readily available in the United States.

A conception of community that emphasizes shared meanings does not assume consensus over all areas of meaning, only general agreement (Platt 1991; Goldring 1992a). For meaning to be contested, there must be some degree of intelligibility within which to struggle over meaning. Migration itself leads to disagreements over meanings, and the creation of new meanings and practices. For example, women who have migrated to the United States may dress, behave, or speak in ways that do not necessarily make "sense" to other women or men in the village. Their practices may be contested directly by family members, or indirectly through gossip. Over time, non-migrant women may adopt some of the "new" practices.

This approach to community also assumes the existence of social divisions, differentiation, and exclusion. There is little question that transnational labor migration can accentuate or engender new bases of social differentiation[13] depending on variables such as type of U.S. employment, wages and benefits, knowledge of English, legal status, and ownership of or access to land or other resources in Mexico or the United States. There are other examples of divisions drawn from my fieldwork in Las Animas. When the norteños[14] are back, young women who have not migrated complain about how norteñas often speak English among themselves, excluding them from the conversation. Young norteños bring back spending money, which they spread around, inviting friends to drink and eat and paying for musicians, but they also spend among themselves, going into the municipal seat in a group for a night on the town, which non-migrants cannot afford.[15] These seemingly minor practices contribute to norteño status and identity construction, a process which is also gendered (Mahler 1996).

In spite of social divisions, common geographic origin, regional history, kinship, friendship, and other processes of identity formation including those associated with migration itself (crossing the border without documents as a *mojado*, legalizing one's status, or being stuck in low-wage jobs), create and reinforce social ties between people, often across different strata. These linking processes <u>and</u> those leading to differentiation produce and reproduce zones of sociocultural intelligibility which contribute to the construction of commonality and shared meanings at the level of a migrant circuit. It is in this medium or social field that social networks are activated and that cultural, social, political and money capital are deployed and interpreted. These practices, in turn, contribute to the maintenance or expansion of transnational social fields. Thus, the transnationalized community is not only a source but a also a key *context* in which forms of capital can be deployed as status claims (and perhaps increased power), and translated into status through appropriate valorization by a community who speaks the same language of stratification.[16]

The scope of these status claims is not necessarily limited to the community of origin. If transmigrants are able to participate in altering the look and feel of their communities, and raise the status of their communities, their power in relation to Mexican authorities in Mexico and the United States may begin to change.[17] The extent to which transnational social fields can offer increased autonomy in relation to local or state authorities in Mexico remains to be investigated through further comparative work (Goldring 1992b; Goldring and Smith 1993; Goldring 1996c; Smith 1995).

Claiming and Valorizing Status and Power in Transnational Contexts

In what follows I outline the importance of status claims and valorization in transnational spaces at the levels of individuals and families, communities, and transmigrant organizations. The first part of the discussion begins with four vignettes intended to illustrate transnationalism and the importance of the place of origin among individuals and families.

Cases of Everyday Transnationalism

Case 1. Licha[18] is raising her two sons in Las Animas, while her husband Pepe works in San Jose for eight to ten months of the year. She lived with him in the United States for a couple of years when they were recently married, but she says he did not want her to continue there. He argued that it would be a bad influence on the children, and they wouldn't save money as quickly. When Licha first returned to Mexico, she and the children lived with her husband's parents and unmarried older sister and brother. They now live in a modern two bedroom brick home with an ample kitchen, dining room, livingroom, and indoor bathroom with a shower. The house is not large, but her husband has also bought farmland. The purchase of materials for the house began with bricks that Licha began to buy after returning with money she saved from her husband's remittances, and from doing embroidery in her "spare" time. Licha almost seemed resigned to living apart from her husband, as many women do in Las Animas. She was not happy about living apart from her husband for so many months, but she did not see how she could join him if he was against it. And with the construction of the house, she seems far happier than when I first met her while she lived with her in-laws. When Pepe returns, he drives a large pick-up and, like other norteños, brings clothes, electronic goods, perhaps an appliance, toys or other gifts for his wife and children. He is happy to see them and the rest of his family, and seems glad that the house has made Licha more content with their arrangement—although he does not spend much time in it except to sleep and eat. In addition to occasional visits to his land, Pepe spends a great deal of time socializing with other migrant and non-migrant friends, some of whom were in San Jose with him and others whom he has not seen in months. He and the other migrants are expected to buy rounds of drinks for their non-migrant buddies, and to pay for musicians. Pepe usually times his return in order to be in town for the *fiesta* (patron saint's day celebration). The fiesta includes a dance and a rodeo-like event (*coleadera*). He also pays for tickets to the dance and usually brings Licha a new dress to wear to it. Although he is not much of a rider he has kept a horse—which is expensive— and pays to participate in the coleadera, in which riders display their skill by grabbing a bull's tail and making it fall (Goldring 1992a, 1996b).

Case 2. Olivia and her husband, Fernando, both from Las Animas, have been in the United States for over 30 years together. Before his wife joined him there shortly after their marriage, Fernando had been working in the San Francisco Bay Area for 15 years. When they married, he was 36, she was 20 years old. He was among the first men of his generation to "bring" his wife with him to the United States so soon. They had six children, all born in the United States. The children occasionally return to Mexico, especially on trips with their cousins, as Olivia has three brothers who live nearby. Fernando has retired from a well-paying job in a foundry, and Olivia continues to work in a local factory. They own a house in the United States, and they also built a home in Mexico many years ago. It is not a large or particularly showy house, but it is very comfortable and has an indoor toilet and shower, which is not very common. They return to Mexico nearly every year, especially now that the children are grown. Sometimes they go for the patron saint's day, sometimes during the summer. Fernando never was an avid participant in the coleadera, and now he is too old for it. However, the walls of his den in his San Francisco home are covered with posters from the last 18 years which advertise the coleadera and the bands playing at the dance. While Fernando harbours the desire to return to Las Animas to live, Olivia is happy to visit, but has no interest in returning there permanently. Her children lead their lives in the United States, and she has no interest in the village lifestyle (Cf. Goldring 1996a). None of their married children got married there. Yet when the conversation turns to whether they will go again the following year, they are both enthusiastic, and a couple of the children are usually eager to go.

Case 3. Mario, a young man of 24, just had his first child a year ago. He and his wife, Lydia, who is from the municipal seat near Las Animas, live in Riverside county where he works in construction. Lydia finished high school and went to secretarial school in Mexico, but for now she is home taking care of the baby. Each of Mario's four brothers live in the area, one of his sisters got married recently and is in the Bay Area, but his parents and three other sisters are in Mexico. He and his siblings got married in the church in Las Animas, with various relatives and other townspeople as *padrinos*[19] for the wedding, and with their mother's excellent version of the local wedding *mole*. Mario is starting a family in the United States, unlike his father, who migrated and left his wife and growing family in Mexico until the sons were old enough to join him. Mario and his wife want the family to be together, and criticize the older generation of men who left their wives behind. Although they are planning to live in the United States and are saving for a down-payment on a house, they still return to Mexico on a regular basis and are making plans to build a house there as well. Lydia says these returns are important for two reasons: so that their daughter should know where she is from, and to visit their families. Before Mario was married, he would return and spend part of his savings on the coleadera and give part to his parents. Their stove, two sewing machines, washing machine, refrigerator, two trucks, farm land, and cattle were bought with money that his father, and later he and his brothers, earned in the United States. He no longer contributes much to his parents' budget, and spends less on the coleadera. But it means a great deal to him to return. What better place to show his horsemanship, for which he is quite well known.

Case 4. Julia is in her mid-30s, just had her second daughter, and lives near Riverside with Luis, her husband of four years. They are both from Las Animas. Luis is five years older than Julia. He asked her to marry him on one of his visits back for the coleadera. Julia has a younger brother in Watsonville, and two unmarried sisters in Las Animas. Their parents are both dead. When I first met Julia it seemed she would remain an old-maid in Las Animas because she was past the age when most women marry. But she began her courtship with Luis when she was 32, and married soon after. She speaks with her sisters in Las Animas every week-end, now that their cousins, who live next door, had a phone installed. She speaks with her brother about once a month. The recent installation of

telephone lines in Las Animas has dramatically improved communication and made it cheaper. Before, people travelled to the
county seat to place calls to, or receive them from, relatives in the
United States. Now that Julia's legal status has been regularized,
she and Luis plan to travel to Las Animas every year, at fiesta time
if possible. Next year they will introduce their new daughter to
their relatives—those who live there in Las Animas and those who
will be visiting from other parts of California and Las Vegas. It is
probable that her younger sister will get married during the next
fiesta to a young man who also lives near Riverside. They are
likely to follow the emerging pattern among younger Animeños
and both live in the United States together, even though she will be
undocumented. When that happens, only one sister will remain in
Mexico, but several uncles and cousins will also be there. Julia and
Luis almost have enough money saved for a downpayment on a
house in the United States, which will improve their living situation.
They have been living with one of his brothers and his wife, a
woman from Jalisco with whom Julia does not get along. When
they return to Mexico, they stay in Julia's family home. They are
not talking about building a home there, at least not while they
have a place where they can stay.

Individual and Family Status

The importance of kinship and friendship networks in international migration has been well documented. We know that networks encourage further migration, providing the social bases for
an ongoing process of migration (Mines 1981; Massey et al.
1987). They can also provide recent arrivals with everything from
employment information and housing, to baby-sitting and contexts
for socializing. These networks often represent extended families
that are spread out over several locations in the United States and
Mexico. Because the prevailing historical pattern has been that
men are the first to migrate from their communities, with women
joining them later on (Massey, Goldring and Durand 1994: 1516),
many of these bi-national or translocal kin groups link women and
children or parents in Mexico to their husbands or children and
other kin in the United States. For these families, and also for those

that migrate as entire families, transnational migration often provides much more than an increased income. It also offers an opportunity to claim a higher social status and a context in which those claims can be appropriately interpreted.

As indicated in the vignettes presented above, these claims are generally made by acquiring various goods, improving or building a home, and/or investing in property, cattle, or a business. The order and choice of means depends, among other things, on the prior standard of living, disposable U.S. income, having U.S. born and raised children, the local or regional opportunity structure in Mexico, and internal family negotiations. Most migrants from Las Animas try to improve their housing by buying, building, or improving a house, but not all invest in a parabolic antenna. Depending on what they had before migrating, they may turn an adobe structure into a brick home, add indoor plumbing, large appliances, or a parabolic antenna. As in many communities, a change in construction materials also implies a new architectural design more consistent with North American designs. For example, an improved house is likely to have an open fence through which the house can be admired rather than being completely enclosed. In some cases, expenditures may be highly contested: for example, a father's decision to invest in Mexico may be challenged by a wife or children who would rather see that money spent in the United States, because that is where they spend more time (Goldring 1992a).

Jones (1992) identifies a preferred order of consumption with U.S. earnings based on data collected in the pueblos surrounding the municipal seat of Villanueva, Zacatecas. He found that the spending of U.S. earnings begins with purchases of clothing and appliances (a television and sewing machine), and expenditures for medical and education expenses. Then, as "more money is accumulated, the family invests in agricultural inputs or in house improvements.... Finally, larger appliances such as a refrigerator or a stove may be purchased" (1992: 505). If local farmland is available and there is a strong farming or cattle-raising tradition, migrants may also invest in land and/or cattle (Mines 1981; Goldring 1992a). If not, investment in housing may be more elaborate

(Goldring 1992b).[20] Business investment is often focused on small grocery and liquor stores, pharmacies, and restaurants, especially in rural areas with low agricultural productivity. Transmigrants with enough capital to invest in larger ventures generally do so in the United States (Cf. Guarnizo 1996).

In addition to spending U.S. earnings on consumer goods, homes, vehicles, land, cattle, or productive activities, transmigrants engage in other practices which reinforce their claims to community membership and allow them to make status claims. For example, when Pepe, Mario, or Julia return with gifts for their family, extended and fictive kin, and friends, they are asserting and maintaining their community membership. When they recognize and greet godparents appropriately they are also doing this. They may have kept in touch with people while they were gone, but these practices fulfill social obligations, help to affirm or reinstate their social roles, and can also raise their social status. At the same time that community membership is claimed, transmigrants also distinguish themselves as norteños through various practices. Mario's sharp attire and expenditures on the coleadera prior to his marriage, Pepe's drinking practices, and transmigrants' use of English in Mexico are examples of this.

Rituals such as weddings, *quinceañeras*,[21] baptisms, and funerals offer an ideal context in which to reaffirm community membership, display spending power, claim status, and have it valorized. These are often occasions marked by large concentrations of fellow townspeople, people with whom one shares a history and language for valorizing and interpreting status claims. This is true whether Animeños marry or hold other life-cycle celebrations in the United States or their home town. When they do so in Las Animas, the invocation of community membership is more firmly rooted in the social landscape of their childhood and/or their parents' childhood. Moreover, non-migrant members of the community can also participate in the festivities, which is important, as these events provide migrants and non-migrants additional opportunity to meet, interact and court each other in approved settings.

For Animeños, the fiesta is one of the most important contexts for claiming and valorizing individual and family status claims

(Goldring 1992b; Platt 1991). Ball games held in the United States also gather large numbers of Animeños, let them affirm community membership, and give them an opportunity to see how others are doing, but people usually have to go back to work the next day. In contrast, when Animeños return for the fiesta they generally take at least a week if not more time off. They are on vacation and in a festive spirit, having left their United States work routine and minority status behind. Returning men can affirm their masculinity and home-town identity and make status claims by participating in the coleadera, through their use of public space, wearing clean clothes not marked by work, driving a fancy truck, and through spending practices associated with drinking and hiring musicians. Returning women can display status through clothing, distinctive presentation of self (which may range from elaborate hair and make-up to "un-feminine" attire such as pants), giving gifts, and having leisure time instead of chores to do. Parents can also claim status through their children by having them dress well, play with imported toys, and so forth.

Migrants and non-migrants also claim and deploy claims to membership and status in the arrangements surrounding the fiesta.[22] These practices also reflect the gendered quality of transnational practices, as most of the organizing is done by men, at least in this case (Goldring 1992a; Cf. Mahler 1996). Various individuals and committees take care of acquiring cattle for the coleadera, booking the band, organizing the liquor and food sold at the dance and the coleadera, and managing the proceeds from the fiesta which have been spent on various community projects over the years. Few people want to serve in these positions because those who do are sometimes accused of mishandling funds. At the same time, potential candidates need to have a certain degree of power and trustworthiness in order to be chosen.

Jones (1992) argues that migrant earnings offer a broad base of formerly poor families the opportunity to increase their purchasing power, and to translate this into membership in a new "migrant elite" whose strength is derived from "wage labor earnings rather than from land, commerce, social status, and political pull." Mines (1981) also argued that U.S. earnings were generating a new migrant elite, although in his case the elite was a land- and cattle-owning elite because migrants could afford to buy land and cattle while others generally could not. Regardless of how members of a migrant elite spend their money, they not only raise their status, but also help to reorient the local regime of stratification by setting trends. This is a fairly dynamic process because the ease of entry into a migrant elite appears to be more open than entry into non-migrant elite circles (Cf. Guarnizo 1994).

Spending practices and other status claims made in the context of transnationalized localities offer individuals and families an opportunity for social mobility within a local stratification scheme, and at the same time help to alter the prevailing stratification scheme by introducing new elements into the status lexicon. Home improvement patterns and clothing styles change, consumer goods that few people could afford in the past become part of the bare minimum of any household, English words are introduced into the local vernacular, and so forth. In doing so, they are helping to change the social landscape of their place of origin, and this may also alter the status of their locality in the regional context.

Community Status

A transnationalized locality's status and perhaps regional position can change in a at least two ways. One is through the aggregate effect of individual and household spending on consumer goods, home improvements or construction, private wells, businesses, telephones, etc. A second is through community-level service and infrastructure projects e.g., road pavement, community drinking-water wells and potable water systems, building schools, and so forth. These processes alter the look and feel of a place, stimulate the local economy (Jones 1992; Durand et al. 1996), make people feel that the place they come from has a certain social stature, and that they contributed to it having that position. That is, they alter the material landscape and services available, and contribute to changing social status and shifting identities for transmigrants. Participating in these changes also increases people's feeling of having a stake in the community, which again reaffirms community membership.

Many localities with a high prevalence of migration bear signs of these processes in Mexico. Migrant houses are clearly distinguishable, and community projects of one kind or another are tangible markers of the transmigrant presence, even during their absence. Although these patterns are more noticeable in smaller places, comparative data documenting their scope are not available. In Las Animas, transmigrants and former migrants have played a key role in organizing the investment of proceeds from the annual fiesta and *coleadera*, collecting contributions in various sites, and organizing the work involved in a number of community projects. Over the years these have included improvements to the cemetery and church, a base-ball field, a pump and clothes washing area, school buildings, a community hall, paving the road to the county seat, fixing a bridge on that road, building a clinic, and the potable water system (Goldring 1992a, 1992b, 1996b). Each of the Animeños introduced in the vignettes above contributed to these projects, as do most people who were born there and even some of their U.S.-born children. Although Animeños acknowledge the difficulty of carrying out community projects, they speak proudly of their accomplishments and of their improved community. In the county seat, Animeños have developed a reputation for getting things done for their town, without much need of local authorities. Thus the place of origin is both an important context for claiming status, and an element of collective status and identity.

Transnational Organization, Power, and the State

A transnationalized locality's status and regional position may also improve because of the upward mobility, wealth and emerging power of its transmigrant and non-migrant members, acting as individuals or as part of an organized group. Individuals who have done well in U.S. business ventures may "do something for their community," like the transmigrant who built a rodeo ring (*lienzo charro*) in the county seat near Las Animas. "Migradollars," or migrant dollars (Durand et al. 1996), and their spending power can also give a group of transmigrants the pull they need to attract additional funds from local or state authorities, as Animeños were able to do for their road paving project. A transmigrant group's power is enhanced if members have connections that help direct resources towards the community. But these connections may be easier to establish for people who present themselves as community leaders of transmigrant organizations, leaders capable of mobilizing people and money.[23] In turn, leaders who present themselves as having useful connections tend to have their positions strengthened because their legitimacy increases.

In this sense, transnational social fields and the formal or informal organizations they may generate can be an important source of social capital for people interested in "doing something for the community." While the extent of these leaders' altruism may vary, transmigrant organizations offer them an opportunity to develop an alternative hierarchy of power in relation to Mexican authorities. I say "alternative" because although leaders may sometimes follow clientelist or corporatist patterns of interaction that prevail in Mexico, their source of support is outside the customary forms of regulation of the Mexican state and local government, and because it may be oriented towards doing things for members in Mexico *and* the United States.

Transmigrant organizations are also a source of potential social capital and legitimacy to an increasingly extraterritorialized state facing serious economic and political challenges. The ruling party has identified first-generation Mexicans as relevant actors *vis-á-vis* Mexico (Cf. González Gutiérrez 1993), particularly those who are organized in transmigrant or immigrant associations. Their importance is articulated more or less explicitly at several levels: as sources of dollar remittances, potential supporters of Mexico-friendly policies in the United states, and, now that Mexicans may be able to vote for President from the United States (García 1996), as potential party loyalists. Leaders of transmigrant groups stand to benefit from the state's interest in these organizations. The state's interest makes them important brokers of social and political capital. This in turn may accrue benefits to them as individuals, if their social (and economic) capital increases through improved contact with state representatives. It may also benefit their constituencies depending on whether and how resources or benefits are channelled towards them. The next section discusses the Federation of Zacatecanos in Los Angeles to illustrate these processes.

The Federation of Zacatecanos. One of the largest and most organized home-state associations in the United States is the Federation of Zacatecan Clubs of Southern California, based in Los Angeles. The Federation is an umbrella organization that includes just over 40 dues-paying home-town clubs, each with three elected representatives that have a vote in the Federation. For the last few years, the Federation has organized the Day of the Zacatecan, when someone, usually a businessman, is honored with the title of Zacatecan of the Year. The day usually coincides with the visit of the Governor of Zacatecas. The festivities also include the coronation of the Miss Zacatecas Queen, with most of the clubs entering a candidate for the contest. Home-town clubs from various parts of Zacatecas are active in community development projects similar to the ones that have taken place in Las Animas. The clubs organize dances, raffles, and other events to raise money for these projects.

Zacatecanos have been active in home-town clubs and broader organizations for several decades. Before 1985, when the current Federation was established, they were the major force behind several coalitions of Mexican immigrant associations that existed since the early 1970s. In fact, the Federation is one of the few state-level organizations that pre-dates the establishment of the Mexican government's PCME, which has been an active promoter of home-town clubs and state-level federations.

Membership, as they say, has its privileges. Federation members pay less than the standard price for access to a Mexican health plan administered by the Ministry of Social Security (IMSS) which provides coverage for individuals or families, in Mexico. Money raised by the organization is used to sponsor student exchanges, scholarships, and a base-ball league. Perhaps most importantly, the Federation of Zacatecanos acts as an intermediary, lobbying and obtaining funds from the state and federal governments for community projects, scholarships, and Federation programs. Only registered clubs are supposed to have access to Federation bokered funds under the so-called "two-for-one" program. The Federation claims responsibility for starting the "two-for-one" program, in which the state of Zacatecas and federal government each put in a dollar for every dollar raised by a home-town club for a community project. The program was an important element of the PCME from 1993-1995, when the program was run by the Ministry of Foreign Relations and the Ministry of Social Development's (SEDESOL) International Solidarity program.

Total expenditures for the two-for-one program include the shares put in by clubs, the state government, and the federal government. Total expenditures were NP$6,497,446 in 1993, NP$10,544,518 the following year, and NP$9,798,000 in 1995 (Consulado de México 1996: 16; SEDESOL n.d.). Since the program began in 1993, six states have participated in the two-for-one program, including Zacatecas. However, Zacatecas has clearly been one of the most important players: in 1993 the Zacatecas expenditures accounted for 36 percent of total program expenditures, and in 1994 this figure rose to 46 percent (SEDESOL n.d.). According to the community affairs director of the PCME, in 1995, organizations from Zacatecas "had committed up to $600,000 for 56 projects in 34 Mexican towns." With matching funds from the state and federal governments, their money was tripled to $1.8 million dollars (Gurza 1996).

Zacatecanos may be a model for other clubs and federations, but they are not alone. In Los Angeles there are presently 10 state-level federations or associations of Mexican home-town clubs, although there are clubs from 21 states in Mexico. In March of 1995 there were nearly 150 home-town clubs in Los Angeles, 10 state-level associations, and three Mexican organizations not based on a common place of origin (González Gutiérrez 1995: 90-191). By the end of 1995 there were over two hundred clubs (Consulado de México 1996: 16). Clubs and associations also exist or are being formed in other cities with active consular PCME outreach, such as Chicago, Houston, New York, Dallas, and Atlanta (Gurza 1986). Establishing relations with transmigrants and helping them to organize is clearly a high priority for the Mexican state.

Part of the Zacatecanos' success is due to their relationship with state governors. Starting in 1986, the then governor Borrego established fairly close ties with the Federation in a series of meeting with Zacatecanos in the United States, especially those in Los Angeles, by being resposive to their interests. This relationship has continued under the present governor through an office responsible for migrant affairs. Federation leaders meet with governors when these visit the United States, and they also travel to Mexico. This kind of interaction has led to obtaining funds for community projects and other benefits as outlined earlier. More recently, the PCME has begun to encourage municipal presidents to travel to the United States and meet with their "constituents" there (Interviews; Gurza 1996). The Federation and club leaders meet and negotiate with them as well. In most cases, these politicians are meeting with people they never would have dealt with in Mexico.

People who would have had little or no "pull" in Mexico now have an alternative source of social capital and power as representatives of transmigrant organizations. Whether or not this alternative will offer increased power in the long run remains to be seen. R. Smith (1994a) identifies a very strong transmigrant organization in New York from the state of Puebla that has important decision-making power *vis-á-vis* events in Ticuani, Puebla. However, this case may be at one end of a continnum compared to other home-town associations, and with the Animeños' located somewhere in the middle (Goldring 1992a).

State level or ethnic organizations, like those of the Zacatecanos or Mixtec transmigrants (Nagengast and Kearney 1990) may offer more possibilities for social and other dimensions of citizenship, with citizenship no longer being contingent on territorial residence. There will undoubtedly be considerable variation among cases, as leaders and organization members promote their agendas, while PCME staff pursue other, more hegemonic, interests. Their aims may overlap in enough cases to encourage careful analysis of transmigrant organizations and state responses to them, rather than assuming a zero-sum scenario, with an all powerful state, or fairly autonomous organizations.

Conclusion

Recent work on transnationalism proposes several factors behind the maintenance of transnational social fields. These include family reproduction practices which are adapted to a transnational context, social exclusion in countries of origin, racialized exclusion in "host" countries, and nation-building practices of extraterritorial states (Basch et al. 1994). I argue that in order to adequately respond to question about why transmigrants from Mexico construct and maintain transnational social fields, why they support community projects, or why they participate in more or less formal transmigrant organizations, it is important to investigate the claiming and valorization of social status.

Transnational social fields, and places of origin in particular, represent a unique context in which transmigrants can make claims to social status and have their status and social capital valorized. This is because the transnational community, like other communities, is a community with a shared version of history and mutually intelligible meanings, particularly concerning status. Individuals and families can improve their houses, wear U.S. clothing styles, drive imported vehicles, buy rounds of drinks, travel to Mexico to get married, return for the patron saint's day, or engage in other practices and know that these claims to mobility, some of which are also claims to community membership, will be properly interpreted. In doing so, they may also reorient the regime of stratification, changing definitions of wealth and poverty, and setting trends in consumption or housing styles.

These practices and community improvement projects generally alter the look and feel, and status, of the locality of origin. Coming from a "better" place, one with paved roads, more services and other amenities, and having helped to improve it, also enhances one's status and may reinforce one's identity as a member of the community. Migrant earnings and their deployment in transnationalized localities can allow people to shift from being marginal campesinos, to being transnational wage workers with improved homes, consumer goods, and new services and infrastructure. In some cases, the transnationalized locality's relations with local authorities may also change as migradollars raise the profile of the community. Transnational social fields also represent an organizational resource, or form of social capital, for transmigrant organization leaders. Leaders who can manage community projects successfully, or mobilize government funds to add to those raised by the organization generally find their leadership reinforced. This offers an opportunity for them to develop an alternative power hierarchy outside the Mexican political hierarchy. This has become particularly important since the Salinas de Gortari administration, when the Mexican state began to pay closer attention to its diaspora in the United States. The extent to which these alternative power and status hierarchies represent semiautonomous spaces remains to be seen. Future research can analyze the orientation and implications of transmigrant organizations' activities, and changing forms of state regulation by both the Mexican and United States.

Notes

1. This is a revised version of a paper published in German in *Soziale Welt*. I am grateful to Ludger Pries, Michael Peter Smith, Robert Smith, Peter Vandergeest, and anonymous reviewers for their comments.
2. Basch et al. use the term "transmigrants" to describe immigrants who build and maintain multiple relationships and social fields that span borders (1994: 7). For additional discussions of the emerging focus on "transnationalism" also see Kearney (1989), Rouse (1991), Goldring (1992, 1996), M.P. Smith (1994), R. Smith (1995), and Mahler (1996).
3. Basch et al. (1994) use the term "deterritorialized states" to draw attention to nation-building activities conducted beyond a nation's territorial boundaries, e.g., actively maintaining ties with diasporic populations. I prefer the term "extraterritorialized states," because it more aptly describes the processes analyzed by Basch et. al (1994). These states are indeed decoupling membership in the national imagined community (Cf. Anderson 1991) from residence in the national territory. But rather than diminishing the significance of national territory, state strategies often invoke transmigrants' relationship to their nation and *place* of origin--to their geographic as well as sociocultural terrain of origin. In attempting to extend their relationship to "members" living beyond their borders, these states may be recognizing the changing meaning of borders and membership, but they are also proposing a seemingly new relationship with transmigrants, and not jettisoning the nation's historical association with a territory.
4. See Goldring (1992a: 33) for a discussion of the use of *(im)migrants*.

5. See Portes and Bach (1985) and Sassen (1988) for discussions of macro-structural determinants of international labor flows. To locate this in the broader context of the international migration literature, consult Massey et al.'s (1993) useful review article. For an excellent introduction to Mexico-U.S. migration, including theoretical discussions, general history, and case studies, see Massey et al. (1987).

6. Examples of transnationalized politics do exist in the case of Mexican. Contemporary examples include Cuahutémoc Cárdenas' campaigning in the United States prior to the 1988 election; trinational NGO alliances against NAFTA; binational organizing by Mixtec indigenous people in the United States and Mexico; Subcomandante Marcos' effective engagement with foreign media, activists, and scholars; and the Mexican government's PCME program (see below). However, I would not equate these with the situation of Haiti or the Philippines.

7. Mixtec indigenous people, who often experience negative racialization in Mexico, have developed strong transnational ethnic associations which, among other things, reject and attempt to counter their subordinate position in both Mexico and the United States (Nagengast and Kearney 1990).

8. The PCME has also worked with the Ministry of Social Development's program for "International Solidarity" (see the section on "The Federation of Zacatecanos" below).

9. It is worth noting that the Program builds on existing transmigrant and immigrant organizations that took the form of mutual benefit associations based on common national, regional, or home-town identity. Many of these first arose with the purpose of covering funeral costs, including transportation to Mexico, and perhaps money for the family of the deceased.

10. Most states with high rates of U.S. migration also have home-state associations. However, in spite of its importance as a labor exporting state, Michoacán has few home-town organizations in Los Angeles or elsewhere (Interviews; González Gutiérrez 1995; Imaz 1995).

11. See Alarcón (1992) for a discussion of *norteñización*, a term he uses to describe the process whereby migration becomes self-perpetuating.

12. Research on Mexico-U.S. migration has examined small towns, municipalities, and relatively small cities. I am not aware of case studies of migration from large Mexican cities. Whether social networks operate in a similar manner in these settings or not is a question for future research.

13. Mines (1981) discussed the emergence of a migrant elite whose wealth was based on better U.S. jobs and the purchase and control of land and cattle in Las Animas.

14. Migrants are called *norteños*, or northerners.

15. Divisions may also surface when norteños are not in town. For example, several families, some without migrants and others with migrants in relatively low-paying U.S. jobs, complained that several (norteño) families who had installed toilets in their houses thought they were so much better than other people, but that in fact, they were polluting the river more than people without toilets because their sewage ended up in the river.

16. As in the case of ethnic enclaves, the extent to which Mexican transmigrants can carve out a niche that insulates them from low-status assignment, discrimination, and other negative experiences in the U.S. may be related to their interest in creating and maintaining transnational communities (Cf. Portes and Sensenbrenner 1993; Guarnizo 1994).

17. Examining the role of transmigrant organizations in relation to local and state authorities and community organizations in the U.S. and Mexico is a logical direction for further inquiry (Goldring and Smith 1993; Smith 1995; Goldring 1996c; Zabin 1995).

18. These are pseudonyms.

19. In addition to overall godparents of the wedding, a couple will ask people to be godparents for different parts of the wedding, e.g., rings, veil, flowers, and bouquets. They are responsible for paying for these.

20. Goldring (1991, 1992b) identified distinct migrant investment strategies in a town in Michoacán, where land was more difficult to acquire and the migrant elite constructed very elaborate houses, compared to Las Animas, where migrants continued to invest in land through the late 1980s.

21. The celebration of a young woman's fifteenth birthday.

22. See Mahler (1966) on the importance of including non-migrants in discussions of transnational social fields.

23. My initial research, and that of Carol Zabin, Luis Guarnizo, and Robert Smith, indicates that these leaders are self-employed businessmen (the majority are men), or have jobs that permit them the flexibility to spend unpaid time on organization activities.

References

Alarcón, Rafael. (1992). "Norteñización: Self-perpetuating Migration from a Mexican Town." In Jorge Bustamante, Clark Reynolds, and Raúl Hinojosa (eds.), *United States-Mexico Relations: Labor Market Interdependence*: Stanford: Stanford University Press. Pp. 302-318.

———. (1995a). "Transnational Communities, Regional Development, and the Future of Mexican Immigration." *Berkeley Planning Journal* 10: 36-54.

———. (1995b). *Immigrants or Transnational Workers? The Settlement Process Among Mexicans in Rural California*. Davis: California Institute for Rural Studies. (October).

Anderson, Benedict. (1991). *Imagined Communities: Reflections on the Origin and Spread of Nationalism*. London: Verso. First edition , 1983.

Basch, Linda, Nina Glick Schiller and Cristina Szanton Blanc. (1994). *Nations Unbound: Transnational Projects, Postcolonial Predicaments, and Deterritorialized Nation-States*. New York: Gordon and Breach.

Consulado General de México. (1996). *Informe de Actividades, 1995*. Los Angeles: Consulado General de México.

Durand, Jorge, Emilio Parrado and Douglas Massey. (1996). "Migradollars and Development: A Reconsideration of the Mexican Case." *International Migration Review* 30: 20: 423-444.

García Canclini, Nestor. (1990). *Culturas Híbridas: Estrategias Para Entrar y Salir de la Modernidad*. Mexico, D.F.: Grijalbo.

García, Guillermo X. (1996). "Mexican election-law proposal may bring candidates to Orange County. *"Orange County Register*. Page. 1. June 24.

Giddens, Anthony. (1979). *Central Problems in Social Theory: Action, Structure and Contradiction in Social Analysis*. Berkeley and Los Angeles: University of California Press.

González Gutierrez, Carlos. (1993). "The Mexican Diaspora in California: The Limits and Possibilities of the Mexican Government." In Abraham Lowenthal and Katrina Burgess (eds.), *The California-Mexico Connection.*. Stanford: Stanford University Press. Pp. 221-235.

———. (1995). "La organización de los inmigrantes mexicanos en Los Angeles: la lealtad de los oriundos." *Revista Mexicana de Política Exterior* 46 (primavera):59-101.

Goldring, Luin. (1991). "Migration and Development?: A Comparative Analysis of Two Mexican Migrant Circuits." In S. Díaz-Briquets and S. Weintraub (eds.), *The Effects of Receiving Country Policies on Migration Flows*. Series on Development and International Migration in Mexico, Central America, and the Caribbean Basin. Vol. VI. Boulder, Co.: Westview Press. Pp. 137-174.

———. (1992a). *Diversity and Community in Transnational Migration: A Comparative Study of two Mexico-United States Migrant Circuits*. Ph.D dissertation, Department of Rural Sociology. Cornell University.

———. (1992b). "La Migración México-EUA y la Transnationalización del Espacio Político y Social: Perspectivas desde el México Rural." *Estudios Sociológicos* 10: 29: 315-340.

———. (1994). "Transnational Communities, Citizenship, and Nation States." Presented to the Department of Sociology, York University, North York, Canada. May 4, 1994.

———. (1996a). "Gendered Memory: Reconstructions of the Village by Mexican Transnational Migrants." In Melanie DuPuis and Peter Vandergeest (eds.), *Creating the Countryside*: Philadelphia: Temple University Press. Pp. 303-309.

———. (1996b). "Blurring Borders: Constructing Transnational Community in the Process of Mexico-United States Migration." In Dan Chekki (ed.), *Research in Community Sociology* 6: 69-104.

———. (1996c). "Membership and Rights in the Context of Mexico-United States Transnational Migration: Changes in State Claims and Transmigrant Membership Practices. " Proposal to the International Migration Program of the Social Science Research Council.

Goldring, Luin and Robert C. Smith. (1993). "Substantive Citizenship and Transnational Communities: Sociolegal Dimensions of Mexico-United States Transnational Migration. " Manuscript. January.

Guarnizo, Luis E. (1996). "The Mexican Ethnic Economy in Los Angeles: Capitalist "Accumulation, Class Restructuring, and the Transnationalization of Migration. Manuscript, University of California, Davis.

———. (1994). "'Los Dominicanyorks': The Making of a Binational Society." *Annals of the American Academy of Political and Social Science* 533:70-86.

Gurza, Agustín. (1996). "Counting on the "home" advantage. *Orange County Register*." Page 1. June 23.

Imaz, Cecilia. (1995). Las Organizaciones por Lugar de Origen de los Mexicanos en Estados Unidos (California, Illinois y Nueva York)." Presented at the XX Congreso de la Asociación Latinoamericana de Sociología. Mexico City, October 1-5.

Interviews. Author's interviews with leaders of Mexican home-state organizations and Mexican Consulate staff in Los Angeles, PCME staff in Mexico city, and state governors' offices for migrant affairs in four Mexican states (June 1993, 1994; July 1995; June, July, September, October, and November 1996).

Jones, Richard C. (1992). United States Migration: An Alternative Economic Mobility Ladder for Rural Central Mexico. *Social Science Quarterly* 73: 3: 496-510.

Kearney, Michael and Carole Nagengast. (1989). Anthropological Perspectives on Transnational Communities in Rural California. Davis, Ca.: California Institute for Rural Studies, Working Group on Farm Labor and Rural Poverty, Working Paper, No.3 February.

Mahler, Sarah J. (1996). "Bringing Gender to a Transnational Focus: Theoretical and Empirical Ideas." Manuscript. Department of Anthropology, University of Vermont.

Massey, Douglas, Rafael Alarcón, Jorge Durand, Humberto González. (1987). *Return to Aztlán: The Social Process Of International Migration from Western Mexico*. Berkeley: University of California Press.

Massey, Douglas, Joaquín Arango, Graeme Hugo, Ali Kouaouci, Adela Pellegrino, and J. Edward Taylor. (1993). "Theories of International Migration: A Review and Appraisal." *Population and Development Review* 19: 3: 431-46.

Massey, Douglas, Luin Goldring and Jorge Durand. (1994). "Continuities in Transnational Migration: An Analysis of Nineteen Mexican Communities." *American Journal of Sociology* 99: 6:1492-1533.

Mines, Richard. (1981). *Developing a Community Tradition of Migration: A Field Study in Rural Zacatecas, Mexico and California Settlement Areas.* Monographs in United States-Mexican Studies, No. 3. La Jolla, CA: Program in United States Mexican Studies, University of California at San Diego.

Nagengast, Carole and Michael Kearney. (1990). "Mixtec Ethnicity: Social Identity, Political Consciousness, and Political Activism." *Latin American Research Review* 25: 2:61-91.

Omi, Michael and Howard Winnant. (1994). *Racial Formation in the United States*. New York: Routledge. Second edition.

Pedraza, Silvia. (1990). "Immigration Research: A Conceptual Map." *Social Science History* 14: 1: 43-67.

Platt, Katherine. (1991). "Ritual and the Symbolic Geography of Community." In Leroy S. Rouner (ed.), *On Community*. Notre Dame, Indiana: University of Notre Dame Press. Pp. 105-116.

Portes, Alejandro and Robert Bach. (1985). *Latin Journey: Cuban and Mexican Immigrants in the United States*. Berkeley: University of California Press.

Portes, Alejandro and Julia Sensenbrenner. (1993). "Embeddedness and Immigration: Notes on the Social Determinants of Economic Action." *American Journal of Sociology* 98: 6: 1320-50.

Rhoades, Robert. (1978). "Intra-European Return Migration and Rural Development: Lessons from the Spanish Case." *Human Organization* 37: 2: 136-147.

Rouse, Roger. (1991). "Mexican Migration and the Social Space of Postmodernism."*Diaspora* 1: 1: 8-23.

Sassen, Saskia. (1988). *The Mobility of Labor and Capital.* Cambridge and New York: Cambridge University Press.

Secretaría de Desarrollo Social (SEDESOL). (n.d.). "Solidaridad Internacional entre Mexicanos." Mexico City: SEDESOL. [1994 or 1995.] .

Smith, Michael Peter. (1994). "Transnational Migration and the Globalization of Grassroots Politics." *Social Text* : 38: 15-33.

Smith, Robert C. (1995). *Los Ausentes Siempre Presentes: The Imagining, Making and Politics of a Transnational Community between New York and Ticuani, Puebla.* Ph.D Dissertation, Department of Political Science. Columbia University.

————. (1994). "Doubly Bounded Solidarity: Race and Social Location in the Incorporation of Mexicans into New York City." Presented at the Conference of Fellows: Research on the Urban Underclass. University of Michigan, Ann Arbor . June.

Turner, Bryan S. (1988). *Status.* Minneapolis: University of Minnesota Press.

Zabin, Carol. (1995). "Immigrant Responses to Proposition 187: The Role of Mexican Hometown Associations." Proposal to the Aspen Foundation, Non-Profit Sector Research Fund. Manuscript, UCLA.

7

Transnational Localities: Community, Technology and the Politics of Membership within the Context of Mexico and U.S. Migration[1]

Robert C. Smith

"The tubes for the water project have come in!" Don Ramon and the other members of Ticuani's Potable Water Committee tell me with excitement. As it has done for the last 22 years, the Committee is gathering funds for public works in its home town of Ticuani, a small *municipio* (county) of less than 2,500 people in southern Puebla, in one of the poorest regions of Mexico, the Mixteca Sur, in southern Mexico. Some of the Committee members are going to discuss the installation of the project with Ticuani's municipal authorities and the contractor. Happily, the Committee members tell me yet again the benefit of the project: The old one-inch tubing cannot handle the increased water flow in the municipio, so they are installing three-inch tubes that will allow the water to flow smoothly for showering, watering plants, cooking, or anything else at any hour of the day. It will make life better in Ticuani, says one Committee member.

At first glance, this scene describes an ordinary civic project by concerned Ticuanenses. However, consider the following: the Committee members and I are not standing in Ticuani, Mexico, but rather on a busy street corner in Brooklyn. Moreover, the Committee members are not just going to the outskirts of the municipio, but rather, to JFK airport for a Friday afternoon flight to Mexico City, from which they will travel the five hours over land to Ticuani, consult with the municipal authorities and contractors, and return by Monday to their jobs in New York. Moreover, the potable water project is the biggest project they have done yet— bigger than the two schools, church repair, and others—and the Committee will ultimately gather more than $100,000 for it from Ticuanenses in New York in donations of $300 or less. Finally, they have created a seal which they stamp on all official corre- spondence, mostly with the municipio. It has the words "Por El Progreso de Ticuani: Los Ausentes Siempre Presentes—Ticuani y

196

Nueva York, 1970-1992 (For the Progress of Ticuani: The Absent Ones Always Present") arranged in a circle around a church bell, within it a picture of a handshake, superimposed over a drawing of a book with a picture of a corn stalk—Ticuani's official symbol— on one of the pages. Considering these facts, the installment of the water pipes is an essential act in constituting a transnational Ticuani community between Brooklyn, New York and Ticuani, Puebla.

Immigration, Migration and Political Community

The very notion of transnational community differs from our paradigmatic models of political community, immigration and migration, and has important implications for our thinking about them. We are accustomed to equating membership in a political community with citizenship, or membership in a nation-state; to treating immigration as a unilinear, stage-like process of incorporation or assimilation; and to treating migration as a structural phenomenon through which migrants passively respond to "push" and "pull" forces. These images have captured the imaginations of scholars precisely because they correspond to important realities: most of us *do* live our lives as citizens in nation-states; immigration *is* a process of incorporation; and migration *is* induced by structural causes. However, these conceptualizations also lead us to develop what Veblen called "trained incapacity": the inability to see what is there because of how we have been trained to look (cited in Hirschman 1970: 17). In short, these approaches do not tell the whole story, and the part of the story they miss is increasingly interesting and important.

In this article, I attempt to overcome such trained incapacity in telling the story of the transnationalization of Ticuanense social and political life and the creation of community by Ticuanenses over the course of more than fifty years of migration to New York City. The article focuses on analyzing the social construction of community (Suttles 1968) and identity within a transnational context, giving theoretical weight to both its historical and contemporary contexts, including the changing relations with different levels of the Mexican (especially) and American states, and with ethnic, racial and gender hierarchies. I argue that migrants can and do create meaningful communities within a transnational context, and that a central process by which they do so is through negotiating settlements on the limits to membership, and by creating institutions and practices that manifest that membership, and foster the imagination of a communal identity. Moreover, I make three other claims: first, that technology, especially telephones, airplanes and video tapes have facilitated and catalyzed these processes;[2] second, that the state—at its various local, regional and national levels—plays an essential part in creating and maintaining transnational life, including transnational localities, and other forms, such as diasporas; and third, that membership in such a transnational community is usually defined in relation to migrants' other and simultaneous memberships in their multiple local, ethnic and national or other communities (Calhoun 1994). Empirically, the main focus is on Ticuani, but where relevant other communities and the Program for Mexican Communties Abroad are considered. Analyzing these stories provides a first pass at addressing the question posed by Appadurai (1991:196): "What is the nature of locality, as a lived experience, in a globalized, deterritorialized world?".

These practices are examples of "globalized grassroots politics" (M.P. Smith 1994) and have implications for the standard ways of looking at community membership, migration and immigration, reviewed below. This article draws on ethnographic and survey research done over the course of eight years, beginning first as I did work in the neighboring town of El Ganado in 1988, and then with more intensive involvement with the Ticuanenses in 1991-93 in Mexico and in New York for my dissertation research, and intermitently since then. The most recent fieldwork was done in summer 1996, when the Ticuani municipal President visited Ticuanenses in New York for the first time.

Immigration and Political Community within the Citizenship and Post-National Models of Membership

The first standard way of looking is the citizenship model of membership in a political community, which has been challenged by the post-national model. In the citizenship model, membership in a nation state and in the national political community are seen to be coterminous and exclusive; one can be a member of only one state and nation at a time (Brubaker 1989: 3). There is a necessary link between territory and community (Walzer 1969), forged as the modern national state emerged as the developer of the modern, national economy (Habermas 1981). Moreover, national identity is more central and salient than local identity under the citizenship model (Walker and Mendlovitz 1991; Grew 1989; Bendix 1964). Given this definition of membership in a community, immigration necessarily involves an "uprooting" (Handlin 1951) and "clean break" with the country of origin. This clean break is the obverse of the process of "Americanization", theorized in a harder version as traditional assimilation to Anglo Saxon mores (Warner and Srole 1945), and in a softer version of ethnic pluralism wherein immigrants become ethnics over time (Nelli 1983; Portes and Rumbaut 1990). In both versions, immigrants are seen to experience an incorporation into a state of full membership over time, despite the discrimination often directed at the first or second generation. Hence, failure to achieve such full membership must then lie with the group itself, regardless of racial, ethnic, or gender discrimination (Basch, et al. 1994; Smith 1995).

The post-national model is an explicit attack on the citizenship model. Treating the same issues of territoriality and identity salience as well as others, post-national models argue that immigrants and the state or social structures protecting them have transcended the individual nation state, thus, escaping its hegemony. Kearney (1991), for example, argues that Mixtec migrants have escaped the ability of the nation state to "inscribe" a national identity upon them (Rodriguez 1996). In a very different context, Soysal (1994) argues that international immigrant, refugee, and human rights conventions signed by states have codified an international system based not on the sovereignty of the state, as is the state system, but rather in the inviolability of the rights inherent in the "modern person."

The problems with the classical model for understanding immigration and transnational life lie with their two assumptions regarding the clean break and full and exclusive membership. As analyzed by Brubaker (1989), Bosniak (1988, 1994), Schuck (1984) and others, immigrants often have second class status in their countries of destination, holding a status Brubaker calls "Membership without Residence." Secondly, increasing numbers of migrants are maintaining and deepening long-term links with their communities and countries of origin and holding identities from these places, *and* the governments and local authorities of their countries of origin are also cultivating these links and identities. Similarly, while the post-national view captures something essential and new, at least in degree, it neglects the continued and even increased importance of the home state—in its local, state, and national incarnations—in creating transnational forms of political and social life, and in maintaining local, ethnic and national identities linked to the home country.

The Migration Paradigm

Theories of migration provide a second standard way of looking, and offer both insights and problems for understanding transnational life. The equilibrium model of migration, or "push-pull" model, identifies which factors or changes in them push migrants out or pull them in, and can flexibly accomodate levels of analysis from individual to national or beyond. The structural historical model of migration begins with the same questions regarding the causes of migration, but answers them by situating migration within its larger context, including labor market segmentation in advanced economies and dependent development in sending countries (Castells 1975; Castles and Kosack 1973; Portes and Walton 1981; Piore 1979, 1986). Moreover, structural-historical work often takes account of social networks, the "micro-structures" (Portes and Walton 1981) of migration, and can treat migration as a social process evolving over time to have its own internal, social logic (Massey et al. 1987).

The problem with these approaches lies with the underlying conception of community and ontological assumptions about causality. Even in historical structural work that is expressly "transnational," as in Sassen's (1988) "global" analysis of the causes of migration, Soysal's (1994) analysis of immigrant rights within a "world" system of rights, and Zolberg's analysis of a "transnational system" (1981) of migration created by states, migrants are conceived of mainly as passive subjects, coerced by states and marginalized by markets. Rarely are they seen as active agents who can significantly shape their destiny, even within circumscribed limits. Because migrants and their actions are conceived of as being, above all, the products of forces beyond their control, these approaches cannot adequately apprehend the processes through which migrants can create meaningful transnational political and social life spanning two societies, sovereign territories and political systems, even if they do so within determinative constraints (Glick Schiller et al. 1993; Basch et al. 1994).

The tendency of migration research to depend on community surveys also causes problems. Because surveys locate causality in the individual, they tend not to be ontologically, epistemologically or methodologically up to the task of asking the question of how transnational communities might emerge, in examining the dynamics of transnational political and social life or how systems of meaning and membership spanning borders can be created. Massey et al. (1987) do an impressive job of analyzing the social process of transnational migration, but their primary reliance on surveys moves them away from posing the question of transnational communities, despite analyzing transnational processes that underlie them.

Transnationalization, the State and the Problem of Community

The concept of community has been treated in conflicting ways in literature on transnational migration. It has been ably critiqued by Rouse (1989, 1991) for implying a "functionalist dream" of equality and harmony within a Redfieldian "little community" (Redfield 1955). Rouse proposes "migrant circuits" as an alternative to community, because he feels this concept can better handle the often conflicting class, gender, generational and other positions and identities held by migrants, their relatives and their children. Glick Schiller and her colleagues (1992, 1994) do not give the term any theoretical attention in their pioneering books, and Glick Schiller (1994) calls it a "bounded concept," a focus which obscures processes of nation building, racial hierarchization, and global capitalism, which help create and organize transnational social fields. Others treat transnational communities as separate and autonmous from the state, and/or simply assume that such entities exist (Goldring 1996). For example, Nestor Rodriguez (1996) argues for a concept of "autonomous migration" as "state-free migration," focusing on the sphere wherein the migrants and their communities create and use institutions, including local governmental ones, while paying "little heed to the nation-state divide" (1996: 25).

While these positions have merit, it is not necessary to either abandon the concept of community altogether, nor accept it as an unproblematic given. To use the concept of "community" is not to thoughtlessly embrace *gemeinschaft*. Indeed, neither Rouse's critique, nor Glick Schiller et al.'s elision preclude an analysis of transnational community that takes into account the historical specificities within which that community is being formed, including its being situated within and structured by racial, gender, capitalist, and nationalist hierarchies. This paper attempts to analyze the social construction of one transnational community and multiple identities of its members within specific regional, local, and historical contexts.

Another complicating aspect of the concept of community in analyzing transnational life is its relationship to "the state." In the above example, Rodriguez (1996) correctly argues that most transnational migration takes place in violation of laws and boundaries of nation-states. However, the central government or federal state is not the only incarnation of the state. Local governments are also "the state", as are the intermediate-level governments (e.g., provinces or states in a federal union), and these more localized forms of the state are essential parts of most processes of community formation within a transnational context. This is reflected in the Mexican word *oriundo*, an affective word that describes someone from a particular place that can be the locality or even the state, but never the nation, of origin. I argue that some level of engagement with the state is a crucial aspect of transnational life (Hagan 1995; Graham 1995), from transnational localities to the attempts of sending states to form diasporas (R. Smith 1996, 1993). Moreover, this engagement with the state of origin helps migrants create the conditions for transnational life in a variety of ways. It provides a place for migrants and their children to register demands (which they often feel they do not have in the United States) and receive recognition; and, it creates a public sphere within which to create an alternative identities to the stigmatized ones the dominant society often assigns them (Smith 1995, 1996; Calhoun 1994). Moreover, the legalization of so many formerly undocumented immigrants by the American state greatly boosted the quantity and quality of transnational activity by making border crossing cheaper and easier (Smith 1995; Hagan 1995).

At least part of the reason for the absence of community from the work of Glick Schiller, Basch, and Szanton (1992, 1994) may be due to empirical differences between the cases they studied (Haiti, the Philippines, St. Vincent and Grenada) and the Mexican case. First, the relatively smaller populations and more dependent, less sovereign states of Glick Schiller et al.'s cases[3] may have made the immigrants connections, with the federal state more important than in the Mexican case. That Mexico is less of an economically peripheral, post-colonial state, and more a post-revolutionary state with a (very) asymmetrical partnership with the United States, but with more leverage in dealing with it, may also make a difference in the relative importance of the locality in organizing transnational migrant life. More importantly, for most of Mexican migration history, the local state (the municipal authorities) and to a lesser extent the regional state (provinces or states) have been the most involved in the everyday life of the migrants, while the federal state's attention to them has waxed (sometimes) and waned (mostly). Moreover, in many places, localities have been historically important structures for the organization of politics and society, through such structures as the *ejido* (Zendejas 1994), or through closed corporate peasant communities (Wolf 1957). Moreover, even in localities without an ejido or a corporate tradition, the very fact of Mexican political life, and then migrant political life, being so much organized and administered at the local level makes it important. The meaning-creating function of the migration as a common journey has usually been organized at the local level as well (Anderson 1983; Smith 1992 and 1995; Goldring 1996). Research also shows community-level differences in labor market incorporation, collective spending and other strategies, which influence the kind of transnational activities and status-regimes that result (Mines 1981; Durand and Massey 1992; Goldring 1992). Hence, to leave out the locality, the community, as an important analytical concept would be to pull transnational life out of its historical context.

The contestation over the meaning of membership is a central process in forming a community. Focusing on the local level, including attempts to form community, can offer a fine-grained approach to understanding the kind of "betweeness" (M.P. Smith 1994: 20) that transmigrants experience, also captured nicely in Guarnizo's (1993) analysis of the condition of "los Dominicanyorks" who create lives in New York and the Dominican Republic, but are considered native to neither place. Ontologically and epistemologically, this focus on contestation can accomdate social causality at individual, structural and group (communal) levels, but argues that we must recognize that meanings, boundaries and identities are in a fundamental sense socially constructed (Suttles 1968), and within particular contexts (Zendejas 1994), though these identities need not be mutually exclusive (Calhoun 1994). Hence attention should be directed towards the creation of shared meanings and shared practices (Smith 1995, 1993; Goldring 1992, 1996), *and* on the bewildering tensions that can result from the differing class positions, cultural orientations, and role expectations that often form within transnational migrant circuits (Rouse 1989, 1991). Emphasis on negotiation treats community-formation as a fundamentally political process, focusing on "the boundaries that people draw and redraw for themselves" as they make lives balanced between and still active in both their "old" and "new" worlds (M.P. Smith 1994: 18; R. Smith 1995). Such a focus enables linkages with other levels of analysis or concepts, such as the ways in which micro-level transnational practices embody Clifford's notion of diasporas as people "dwelling differently" within their "host" countries, retaining identities or lived experience linked to the "home" country. Such is the case with the Mexican government's attempt to institutionalize a diaspora of Mexicans and Mexican Americans in the United States, as further discussed below. Intense focus on local level phenomenan can also offer insight into the same processes at higher levels, such as globalization (Guarnizo 1995; Portes and Guarnizo 1991; Portes 1995; Kyle 1995) or gender (Levitt 1994; Goldring 1995). Finally, technology plays an important role in providing the means for this contestation to take place, even while migrants live in different places (Smith 1995; Portes 1995).

The Creation of a Transnational Locality: Ticuanenses in New York and Brooklyn

How is it that a Committee of Ticuanenses living permanently in New York have come to gather the bulk of the funds for the largest public works project in Ticuani's history? By what processes has a context developed where it makes sense for Ticuanenses living in New York to return to Ticuani to negotiate with the municipal authorities there and inspect a public works project? The development of a transnational community in the case of Ticuanense migration can be most clearly seen in the changes over time in the way that the New York Committee relates to the Ticuani municipal authorities. They approached them in 1970 as humble expatriates simply wishing to do something from New York for their hometown—they put bricks in the *zocalo* (town square) so feet would not get muddy during the feast of the Patron Saint. Today, they negotiate powerfully with the municipio regarding the conditions for the release of funds. Their language in discussing these two times reflects the differences. Whereas at the beginning they discuss asking only for a chance to "participate" and "to do— thanks to our people—what was possible," they now speak of being co-equal with the municipal authorities. In response to a question regarding the relations between the Committee and the Municipal Palace (*Presidencia*) in Ticuani, one member said of the Committee in New York: "Economically, this *is* the *Presidencia*!"

How did this change happen and what does it mean? Part of the answer to these questions lies in the social, economic, and demographic changes that Ticuani has experienced since Don Pedro Simon, the first Ticuanense migrant, went to New York more than 50 years ago, crossing the border on July 6, 1943.[4] The fact of massive outmigration from the municipio and the region is one compelling part of the answer. In the 50 plus years of migration from Ticuani, it has come to pervade every aspect of life in the town. For example, several of the highest migration municipios in the region collectively experienced a population loss of 8.6 percent during the 1980s. For Ticuani, 41 percent of Ticuanense live in New York City, while 48 percent live in Ticuani. More than half (51 percent) of the town's residents live in households that depend for 90 percent of their income on remittances from New York. Dollars as well as pesos, and even travellers' checks, are accepted in Ticuani's market and stores—and this in a small, rural town of less than 2,500 people, three hours from the nearest large city and located thousands of miles from the United States border in southern Mexico. Moreover, those in New York constitute the bulk of Ticauni's working population; those remaining behind are mainly the elderly, young children and their mothers. For example, 33.6 percent of the population in Ticuani are children between the ages of 1-14, while only 4.5 percent of the Ticuanenses in New York are between 1-14 years of age. Similarly, 45 percent of the Ticuanenses in New York are between 15-40 years of age, while only 19.5 percent of those in Ticauni fall into this age group. Moreover, there are more men than women in the Ticuani population in New York (63.1 percent and 36.9 percent, respectively), and more women than men in Ticuani (52.3 percent and 47.7 percent respectively). Ticuani has become a "nursing home and nursery" (Cornelius 1990). Hence, one reason why the New York Committee has raised this money, instead of the Mexican state (in the form of the municipio) is that the Ticuanenses with money do not reside in Ticuani most of the year, but rather in New York. This gives the Committee better access to them, in a sense, than the Mexican state has.

Syncretism, Institutions, and the Ticuani Transnational Community

Yet, this does not explain why or how Ticuanenses developed transnational institutions; it only provides a functional basis for supposing the "need" or utility of such institutions. My answer to the question of how the New York Committee came to be in the position of donating most of the funds for Ticuani's potable water project is that they have engaged in a "syncretic institution building," drawing on indigenous traditions, while using contemporary communications technology, to create a transnational public life for Ticuanenses in Brooklyn and in Mexico. They combine "premodern" practices from the Spanish colonial era with telephones, jets and faxes—all "postmodern" technologies—to create transnational communities. These syncretic processes can be best understood within the context of a discussion of Ticuani's history and the Committee's history and composition, and the area's mixed indigenous and mestizo past (Carrasco 1963).

The "New York Committee" is formally the Comité Solidaridad Ticuani de Nueva York. Since their first project, the Committee has built or contributed to the building of two schools, re-building parts of the municipal palace and church after an earthquake, and a series of other smaller projects, culminating with the greatest one, the potable water project. They have been able to raise this kind of money in New York by adapting, throughout their migration, to the indigenous corporate institutions first analyzed by Eric Wolf (1957).[5] According to Wolf, the closed corporate peasant community was the step-child of the Spanish conquest and the Crown's struggle for control with the native creole elite in the New World. In fighting the creole elite's attempts to make wage workers out of the indigenous population, the Crown "gave" the indigenous population communal lands with certain rights in perpetuity. However, the end result was only to make indigenous people poor enough that they had to do wage work— which was organized communally, not individually—while producing nearly enough to support themselves. These practices resulted in a wide-spread social form privileging the communal over the individual. This value is reinforced by a set of religious practices and a religious cargo system in which religious and political authority are fused in varying degrees, and positions of authority are attained through the rotating discharge of one's duties to pay for various parts of the Feast for the entire village, as well as through other kinds of communal service (Kearney 1995; Neiburg 1988; R. Smith 1995; Carrasco 1963). The emphasis is not on individuality, but rather, on how one relates to and fulfills his or her obligations to others in the group (Rouse 1995).

In the Mixteca region of Puebla, these corporate forms co-exist with *caciquismo* (*caciques* are political bosses who have extensive influence in their towns; *caciquismo* is literally "boss-ism") and a violent political localism, in which central state authority has never been completely established and local caciques exercise a great deal of autonomy and power. The Mixteca region's history is full of recourse to violence in response to unjust conditions on its haciendas, in support of the Cristero movement (Maroni 1993), in resistance to central state authority or, especially, *due to competition between or internal divisions within municipios* (Jaramillo 1985; Joachim 1979). This violent tendency was exacerbated by the fact that the Mixteca's caciques are "large in number but small in resources," according to a local *Diputada* (state representative). Current Puebla Governor Manuel Bartlett created a special army team to dislodge recalcitrant caciques and their supporters who refused to yield power after losing elections (Silva 1993), as happened in Ticuani's neighbor, El Ganado. Ticuani has a long history of political violence, including a string of assasinations from the 1930s through the 1970s, which were important causes of migration.

This history sets the stage for understanding some of the Ticuanenses adaptation of particular traits of the closed corporate peasant community, and other issues regarding their ethnicity. Ticuanense ethnicity is a hybrid indigenous-mestizo ethnicity (which exists throughout the Mixteca) emerging in this case from the competition between Ticuani and its richer neighbor, El Ganado, and reinforced through experience with U.S. ethnic and racial hierarchies. On the one hand, Ticuanenses embrace their indigenous identity and social forms when comparing themselves with El Ganadenses, saying that they are "more authentic" and have more "pure Indian blood," while Ganadenses are derided as being "immigrants" from Spain, and are said to have whiter skin. Historically, Ticuani was a point of passage (*lugar de paso*) for indigenous tribes in the area, while El Ganado was one of the first Spanish towns in the area settled to convert the natives. Much of Ticuani's land was owned by large landowners in El Ganado before the Reparto Agrario in the 1930s, and conflicts between the two towns have led to many deaths (Pantaleon 1991). Even in New York, Ticuanenses and Ganadenses have strong rivalries, though usually with less severe consequences. Yet despite their identification as being indigenous, hardly any young Ticuanenses speak an indigenous language (Nahutl was most common a generation or more ago), and they often make fun of the "indios" from neighboring Oaxaca. Hence, Ticuanense ethnicity is indigenous in relation to more powerful forces, but is mestizo in most other contexts, including in relation to speakers of indigenous languages. This hybrid identity can be seen as a "relational ethnicity" and is important later in the incorporation in the United States.

Ticuanense migrants have drawn on all these traditions and history in creating transnational institutions. A first corporate form has been crossed with the caciquismo and localism of the region in creating the Committee. In the *consejo de ancianos* (council of elders) or *principales* (principals) system described by Neiburg (1988), leadership results from participation in the religious cargo system wherein a group holds power and exercises it collectively. The New York Committee's collective procedures and internal dynamics match this form, though its single President (Don Manuel) in 30 years suggests something more like a cacique. The 30 or so Ticuanense notables, who usually assemble for political meetings in Brooklyn, have participated for long periods in the collective work of the Committee. In Ticuani, the Feast Commitees which organize the important business of the annual feast, have compadres and other *personas de confianza* of the New York Committee—including the teachers—as well as of the local elite.

As with the *prinicipales* system in general, all of the New York Committee members and 30 or so Ticuanense notables are men, though women sometimes participate (Neiburg 1988). One woman with business experience served briefly as the Committee's Treasurer, but was dislodged from that post when she attempted to institute changes in how they did business.[6] Women do often serve as Mayordoma of the Mass of the Feast, and do most of the work of preparing the actual feast, but have in my experience never been included in the intimate planning or strategizing sessions, and the politics that gets done in those meetings.

Who participates in the Committee's work and activities also reflects Ticuani's 50 plus years of migration. Many of the central characters have some kind of important involvement in Ticuani history in the pre-migration pasts. One Committee member's father was murdered in Ticuani's political violence. The Committee's President was a secretary under at least two (opposing) municipal presidents. Moreover, many of the central members, all men in their late-40s to early-60s by now, were friends in Ticuani as young men, playing basketball together, with some even running together in the first Antorcha para Padre Jesus (Torch Run for Jesus our Father). Indeed, the Committee President carried the torch into Ticuani for the first Antorcha. Yet, the membership of the Committee and its group of notables is broader than this. Among the most active and important members, the Committee also has younger Ticuanenses, some relatively recent arrivals and some born or raised in New York, who participate fully and have an impact on what the Committee does. Beyond these central members, the Ticuanense notables are drawn from several groups, and include all men, with rare exceptions. Ticuanense entrepreneurs are prominent participants who are often asked to donate funds or, more often, to sponsor some event. It is interesting that these entrepreneurs are not the main leaders of the group—as they are for example, among state-level federations in California (Guarnizo 1995)—but their opinions are carefully considered. Moreover, the main leaders are almost all wage-workers in the blue collar middle class (cooks, mechanics), but also include some undocumented people holding low paying jobs (e.g., busboys). The membership of this broader group is flexible, and includes those with some more recent link to Ticuani politics, leaders of Ticuani sports or cultural clubs in New York, and even sometimes those men who are casually interested.

The nature and extent of community wide participation among Ticuanenses also requires some attention. The Committee has what it claims is an exhaustive list of all the independent Ticuani households outside Ticuani, mainly in New York, but also in Houston and Los Angeles, though in much smaller numbers. One form of community participation comes through attendance at social functions. At the wedding of the daughter of one of the main Committee members, the management of the place where the wedding was held counted 1,600 people coming through the doors! While not all of these were Ticuanenses, many (perhaps half) were. In a community where there are about 2,000 Ticuanenses in New York, that so many had come to this wedding conveys some impression of how extensively the Committee serves as a center to Ticuani public life in New York. The Commitee members are also seen at picnics in Prospect Park in the summer, at basketball games in the winter, and other public gatherings of Ticuanenses. Hence, while Ticuanense public life in New York is not democratically participatory, it does include many Ticuanenses, and those at its center are well known in the community.

The participation of second-generation, New York-born or -raised Ticuanenses requires brief note here because of how it spans a generation, and how it reflects the important role of both American racial and ethnic hierarchies and the hybrid indigenous-mestizo ethnicity in constructing membership in the Ticuani community. Young Ticuanenses have formed the Ticuani Youth Group, among whose main activities is to organize sports tournaments with two objectives: raising funds in New York for public works projects in Ticuani, and through this activity, protecting Ticuani youth in New York from the vices which the Group's president sees befalling their Black and Puerto Rican neighbors. He expressed this sentiment to me at a volleyball tournament, when he pointed around earnestly and said, "Look at this group. Do you think that Blacks and Puerto Ricans have this kind of community? This kind of culture? ...No, they do not and this is the problem." According to the president, the "better culture" of the Ticuanenses enables them to simultaneously avoid urban vices while living in urban areas. This "better culture" is increasingly linked to remembering Ticuani's indigenous past— through talk and such activities as making a video, "Ticuani in history," depicting this past—which becomes more important to "remember" within the context of a low place in the American racial and ethnic hierarchy (Smith 1995; Anderson 1983). Hence, embracing American racial and ethnic hierarchies helps immigrants both feel like they are fuller members of American society, and reproduce in some form a transnational community and identity that draws on its links to an indigenous past (Smith 1995, 1996). It also points to the multiple identities of these migrants, and the importance of recognition in constructing such identities and communities (Calhoun 1994).

This reinforcement is not just in response to external boundaries, but internal dynamics as well, especially status. Ticuanense migrants and their children often re-enter Ticuani at the very top of its social hierarchy through such activities as building big houses there, attending the most important social events that would have been impossible for most of them to afford without money earned in the states, and even for a Brooklyn-born Ticuanense to be elected the Queen of the Mass, a highly prized ceremonial position for a Ticuanense youth who embodies the town's best virtues. Both the migrants and their children gain in status within the New York Ticuanense community for their public work in Ticuani; and similarly, their children's success in the United States increases their status in Ticuani and in New York. In going to college, these young Ticuanenses are seen as their having done well for Ticuani and due to their being Ticuanenses (Smith 1995).

A second and most important corporate form whose adaptation to the context of migration has helped the Committee become the institution through which transnational life is organized is that of *faenas* or communal labor obligation. *Faenas* require one to donate a certain amount of one's time to work on a communal project, such as a water project. Within the context of 50 years of migration to New York, most Ticuanenses now dispense with their *faenas* by donating money to the Committee.

How the Committee has been able to become the institution through which one's *faenas* are satisfied, and to reinforce the persistence of the tradition of *faenas* is also important theoretically. There are at least two ways this happened. First, it is the result of a conscious strategy by the Committee to become an important player in Ticuani public life, to "exit" and, adapting Hirschman's (1971) language, to "(re)-enter" with "voice". From the beginning, the Committee hoped to gain the *confianza* (deep trust) of the Ticuanenses in New York and in Ticuani, and build on it, to parlay it into the acknowledged right to participate in Ticuani public life. Secondly, the Committee serves as a moral center of Ticuani public life in New York in another way, as its members visit, in groups of two or three, all Ticuanense households to gather money for a project. Over the course of more than 20 years, the Committee has developed a context in which people contribute, both because of the *confianza* they have in the Committee, as discussed above, and because a kind of "social coercion" has developed. Ticuanenses know that the Committee asks everyone to contribute, and that there will be *chisme* (gossip) about them if they do not contribute to a project widely understood to be a fulfillment of their *faenas*. Not everyone views this social coercion positively, and there is gossip directed at the Committee to the effect that they use the donated money to buy drinks.

Technology and Transnational Life

Technology plays an important role in transnationalizing Ticuani public life. Technology facilitates the emergence of a sense of simultaneity which, as Benedict Anderson (1991) posits, is essential to the formation of community. Anderson points to the emergence of national print-markets as crucial in fostering a sense of simultaneity, the unspoken knowledge that one's own experience (in, for example reading national news in the newspaper) is like that of others doing the same thing at more or less the same time. In the case of Ticuani, technology has worked in several important ways, the most general being that it has devolved the power to create simultaneity into the hands of migrants whose lives are largely structurally determined. Put differently, technology has

made it possible for migrants and their children to have simultaneous and on-going participation in their communities of destination
and origin, nurturing multiple identities in the process. One clear
example is the use of conference calls that enable the Committee
and its notables to sit in a basement in Brooklyn and negotiate with
the municipal authorities sitting the Municipal Palace in Ticuani.
Another example is the return of New York Committee members
to Ticuani for the weekend to inspect the potable water project and
negotiate with the municipal authorities. That these Committee
members with full time jobs in New York can be important politi-
cos in a Mexican village—either visiting it over the weekend and
being at their jobs in New York on Monday, or never even leaving
New York and conducting their business collectively by phone—
attests to the powerful, facilitating role of technology in transnationalizing migrant life.

Many uses of technology promote simultaneity that have nothing to do with the negotiations between the Committee and the
municipio, but which, nonetheless, contribute to the transnationalization of Ticuani life in both public and private realms. For example, some migrants have purchased cellular phones for their
parents living in Puebla, so that they can call them easily and directly to arrange their visits to New York (CITE 1996). Videos and
telephones have substituted for letters for many, with friends carrying back videos featuring the successful lives of migrants in New
York. Also, videos of events taking place during the Feast of the
Patron Saint are taped and then played back again for those in
New York who could not go back. The Reina (Queen) of the Mass
in Ticuani, who of late have more frequently been born and raised
in Brooklyn, sell copies of videos about the Feast when they return
home. In a most deliberate attempt to create literal simultaneity,
tapes of the Grand Dance of the Feast from the previous year were
played in a dance hall in New York during the following year on
the same night as the Grand Dance was held in Ticuani. There are
many other examples, including many which are not political on
their face but often involve issues of contested limits to membership (R. Smith 1995).

Video tapes have played a particularly important role in the Ticuani case. The New York Committee has used videos to create a "we" in New York by creating a "they" in the Ticuani municipal authorities. Approximately seven hours of the day, and half of the meetings between the New York Committee and the municipal authorities in Ticuani for the potable water project, were taped by members of the New York Committee. These tapes were then shown in a "town meeting" with about 30 notable Ticuanenses in New York. While they were watching the tape, the President pointed out especially important parts of the meeting. Repeatedly in the tape, the New York Committee President invokes his responsibility to "nuestra gente en New York" (our people in New York) in responding to the municipal President's anger that the Committee was negotiating with them at all, instead of just serving as a conduit through which the money was being funnelled. In the several years since this scene took place, I have repeatedly observed such uses of videos, including requests for videos to clarify what had been said, done or promised in Mexico.

Contested Limits and Negotiated Settlements to Membership

Technology's power here is to facilitate the playing out and maintainence of a central tension in the relationship between the Committee and the municipio, and between those in New York and in Ticuani: their mutual and evolving interdependence. The New York Committee has the *confianza* (deep trust) of the Ticuanenses in New York more than do the municipal authorities. The New York Committee has never failed to finish a project, while the municipal authorities in Ticuani have a long history of corruption, including the stealing of public lands and funds. The municipal authorities cannot extract this money because its economically active population is almost all in New York. Hence, the Mexican state in the form of the municipio depends on a civil society organization in another country to perform one of its essential functions— extract revenues to re-produce the state and perform public works. However, the New York Committee also depends on the legitimacy conferred on it as the representative of the municipio, and hence of the Mexican state. Without this mantle, and the knowledge that the money collected would be translated into public works projects in Ticuani, the Committee would lose much of its legitimacy. The relationship is like a tempestuous romance: they can't live with each other, they can't live without each other.

This close relationship has led to the joint generation of municipal authority between the municipio and the New York Committee. The most graphic illustration of this authority has been the administration of the potable water project. The administration works this way: One pays the $300 *cooperaciones* (cooperations) to the New York Committee (not the municipio directly), and one is given a ticket stub as a receipt. The other side of the stub stays in the receipt book of the Committee. Both pieces of the receipt had been previously stamped with the seal of the municipio before it was sent to New York. When one pays one's $300, the Committee then stamps both sides with its own seal. With both seals, the receipt serves as proof of payment, and the Ticuanense in New York can send the receipt to his family in Ticuani to show to the authorities to turn on their water. If one does not pay the $300, the municipio and the Committee have agreed that the water to that house will be turned off. The Committee and municipal authorities also perform joint inspections of public works projects in Ticuani, and requests for better service are sometime put to the former instead of the latter when both are present. The municipio and Committee not only jointly generate and exercise municipal authority, they sometimes jointly monopolize which activities can be legitimately organized transnationally, such as cooperating to exclude others who plan transnational activities (races, T-shirt sales, video production) related to the Feast not approved by them. What has been the end result of this transnational activity? On the one hand, the New York Committee has gained greater influence in the public life of the municipio, while on the other hand, the municipio has drawn an increasingly hard line on allowing the participation of New York-residing Ticuanenses in Ticuani public life. One of the most serious conflicts, and a catalyst for the setting and testing of limits, was the 1989 municipal elections, in which the Committee ran a candidate for the municipal President. Contested elections in this part of Puebla do not indicate a healthy democratic system in the minds of

Ticuanenses; rather, they indicate a crack in the local clique's cohesion and a return to *la violencia* (the violence) that plagued the town through the 1970s. Hence, the return of Don Juan to the municipio after more than 30 years in New York working with the Committee was not greeted by all with enthusiasm. While Don Juan did manage to get the preliminary support of the *Comisario Ejidal* (Ejido Commission), an important entity within the municipio, in the end, he was forced to drop out of the race. This badly planned entrance into Ticuani electoral politics bared (or at least it looked as if it bared) the intentions of the New York Committee: to gain control of the municipal Presidency.

A second and on-going conflict stems from the increased economic and social importance of the New York Committee itself, and how it affects the local political elite. Given the tremendous economic contributions that the Committee was making for the potable water project, the municipal authorities, the local *cacique*, and their supporters feared that the Committee would try to impose itself in other ways into local politics. Hence, the inauguration of the potable water project in January 1993, which brought a visit from the largest ever delegation of the New York Committee, became the occasion at which the issues were brought out into the open. As several hundred Ticuanenses, invited guests, state officials and journalists, stood outside in stunned silence, the New York Committee and the municipal authorities yelled at each other over a minor administrative point that had brought the issue of who had the real responsibility and credit for the project. The contestation continued in more muted but still open form throughout the inauguration ceremony itself. Speaking on behalf of the Committee, one member asserted publicly that this work was "brought to completion, in the first place, I repeat, in the first place, by the Committee from New York; in the second place, by the state and federal governments; and in the third place, by the people of the pueblo." For his part, the municipal President never directly thanked the Committee as such, but rather acknowledged the committed support of the Ticuanenses *en el norte* or in New York (R. Smith 1995: Chapter 6). Such symbolic and verbal battles continued through the week of the Feast.

These public contestations are symptoms of a larger problem of the emergence of parallel structures of power. The Committee has emerged as the most important provider of *cooperaciones* to the Ticuani municipal government, and this has threatened the position of the *cacique* and his supporters and other notables in Ticuani. Caciques derive their power from their function as gatekeepers to, or intermediaries with, the outside world, through their ability to offer employment, and/or through their myriad fictive kin relations, or *compadrazgo* (Pare 1975). In Ticuani, the local cacique has many fictive kin relations with local notables and runs the only construction materials business and government sponsored "supermarket" or CONASUPO store. While he is powerful within Ticuani, the *cacique* cannot match the Committee's ability to raise large sums of money. Hence, the cacique and other local notables refused to contribute their $300 *cooperaciones* and, through the municipal president, made an issue of the Committee's even demanding that they pay. The argument of the municipal President was that, while of course everyone should pay, the Committee was not in a position to make demands that certain people be made to pay—that was the job of Ticuani's elected municipal authorities. Hence, the cacique, notables, and the municipal President made an issue of the Committee's standing within Ticuani politics. They also questioned their authenticity as Ticuanenses by suggesting that the Committee's concern with timely meetings and such things were the result of the corrupting influence of their time in New York.

These conflicts were addressed explicitly in a series of meetings between the Committee and the 1989-92 President and President-elect for 1993-95 (the change of municipal administration was to take place soon) regarding how the Committee and municipio should relate. Presented below in very abbreviated form are the terms of the settlement regarding the limits to participation by New York Residing Ticuanenses in Ticuani public life, and the standing of the Committee with respect to municipal authority:

1) There would be public acknowledgement and thanks for their sacrifices to the New York Committee by the municipal authorities.

2) Money for the projects would continue to be collected only in New York, so that the municipio and Committee could not be put in competition.

3) In order to run for municipal President, one must return and live in Ticuani at least one year, a sort of re-naturalization process.

4) Every Ticuanense household with the means would be made to pay the $300 "tax" for the potable water project. Those who do not pay will have their water cut off.

Points 1–3 were acted on or are in effect. Point 4 was a very contentious issue, because the only ones with means who had not paid were the *cacique* and local notables. While the President-elect settled the issue in the immediate context of the meetings by saying "We are not going to have to cut the water for a single one because we are going to convince them to pay," in fact the *caciques* and notables did not pay during the 1993–95 municipal presidency, nor do I think they will ever pay. This issue has been a central tension in the Committee-*municipio* relationship since then. While the President of the Committee had said that if everyone does not pay, you can "forget about us!", the Committee has not completely broken its relationship with the town. In the Spring of 1995 it did a small project—not involving the *municipio*—to illuminate the Church in Ticuani at night. Yet all planning for large future collaborations with the *municipio* stopped, and distrust of the 1993-95 President grew with his growing wealth (a new car and 40 animals) in Ticuani. One irate Committee member commented on this correlation this way: "you'd have to work *here* (e.g., New York) to get 40 animals!"

The Local State and National State in the Transnational Locality:
The Program for Mexican Communities Abroad and the Ticuanenses

Relations between the Committee and Ticuani have recently been rejuventated by two developments: the beginning in 1996 of a new three-year presidential term in Ticuani, and the entrance of the Mexican federal government into this relationship as part of its Program for Mexican Communities Abroad. The clearest expression of these two developments is the first-ever visit of a Ticuani municipal president to New York to visit the Ticuanenses there in July 1996. The trip was organized by the Program for Mexican Communities Abroad in the Secretary of Foreign Relations of the Mexican government, through officials in Governor's Office in Puebla, Consular officials in New York, and several municipal presidents from the Mixteca region of Puebla, including Ticuani.

The selection of a *compadre* of one of the main Committee members in New York as the new Ticuani President signals a desire on the part of the elite in Ticuani to redevelop this relationship, and the President said this in so many words in his visit. The Committee members are also excited at the prospect of working again. Their relative inactivity during the stand off underlined how much their legitimacy as a Committee stems from their relationship with the municipal authorities.

The Committee's position has been reinforced by the imperatives of the larger relationship between the United States and Mexico, as reflected in the Program for Mexican Communities Abroad. While offering a brief analysis of the reasons for the Program's creation in the next section, we can observe the increased interest and effects of the Mexican federal and state governments in such transnational micro-politics. The Program arranged for several municipal presidents to meet with their communities in New York. In the case of Ticuani, about 125 people showed up for this town meeting, to *"manifestar sus inquietudes"* ("express their dissatisfactions"), as it was advertised in fliers and in a radio show in New York hosted by a Ticuanense. This increased the leverage and importance of the Committee and Ticuanenses in New York *vis-à-vis* the municipio. The Ticuani President, Puebla state and Consular officials all visited the Ticuanenses and the Committee in these town meetings and in private meetings in their basement meeting place in Brooklyn over the course of the nine days they were in New York. The Ticuani President has promised to make at least one trip per year to New York to visit Ticuanenses, and has promised greater accountability to them and greater transparency in the handling of affairs. Regarding their requests to be included in the political process and public life of Ticuani, he commented at the town meeting: "It is

just, what you ask, perfectly reasonable...there is a political opening." He also said that everyone can participate in the electoral
process, though he repeated that candidates must return to Ticuani
for a year in order to stand for election for municipal president.
While such promises may be only words, this rhetoric is quite different than that of the negotiated settlement with the last two
presidents, where they challenged or only grudgingly accepted the
right of the Committee and the New York Ticuanenses to be
included in Ticuani public life. The position of the municipal
President is now the position previously held mainly by those most
closely associated with the Committee.

What has changed? There are several things, most related to the
PRI's domestic politics to the newfound realization of the importance and potential of links with *poblanos* in New York, and to the
political economy of United States-Mexico relations. One municipal president clearly stated his belief regarding why they were
brought to New York: the PRI is losing elections in some of
Puebla's cities like Cholula and Puebla, and hence is attempting to
shore up its base by cultivating its relationship with poblanos in
New York. He also said they have been given three times the normal muncipal budget. An official of the state of Puebla underlined
another compelling reason, in urging the municipal Presidents and
relevant Committee members to attend a meeting with Bancomext
(Mexican Bank of External Commerce) officials: the justification
for the entire trip was that it might increase the commercial links
between the Mixteca and Puebla and *poblanos* in New York, and
the northeast generally.

Domestic Politics Abroad, Diasporic Politics at Home:
The Mexican "Global Nation," Neo-liberalism, and Autonomous
Transnational Activity

Why would the Mexican state in the form of the federal government be so interested in developing relations with Mexicans in
the United States, and strengthening the relations between *oriundos*
or localities and states in the United States and Mexico? And how
will the Program's activities affect the transnationalization of political and social life between the United States and Mexico, such as

that seen in the Ticuani case? The short answer to the latter question is that the "autonomous migration" of the Ticuanense is happening within a changing context. In particular, the Mexican federal state in the form of the Program for Mexican Communities Abroad and its projects should affect how durable local transnational life is, and change how demands and social claims are made by providing a transnational public sphere within which to make them. The short answer to the former question is that the Program's activities seem to be an attempt to loosely organize local level transnational political and other activities within a federal umbrella, an attempt by the Mexican state to institutionalize a diaspora that has changed the meaning of citizenship and membership in the Mexican nation, in its global nation.

Why was the Program created and why in the early 1990s? A first reason was that the legalization of 3.1 million undocumented immigrants under the 1986 Immigration Reform and Control Act (IRCA)—more than half of whom were Mexican—shocked the Mexican elite out of its cozy "bracero" assumptions, and urged them to consider more closely the importance of relations, especially economic ones, with Mexicans in the United States. Migrant remittances from the United States are conservatively (U.S.) $2 billion per year, about equal to Mexico's earnings from agricultural exports, and to 56 percent of its *maquila* earnings (Durand et al. 1996).

Secondly, from the mid-1980s onward there emerged increasingly autonomous transnational political linkages between Mexicans and Mexican Americans in the United States and local- and state-level authorities or groups in civil society in Mexico. While protest groups in the United States had made such links before, perhaps the most important impetus for the Mexican state to act was the unexpected support for Cuauhtemoc Cardenas's 1988 national presidential campaign in the United States, and the extensive organizing in the United States on his behalf (de la Garza and Vargas 1992; interviews 1993). However, it was not just fear of loss of control but also a response to demands being made on the federal government by state and local authorities in Mexico and their corresponding groups in the United States that led to the

Program's creation (interviews 1995). For example, the Zacatecas Federation of Southern California has annually hosted the Governor of Zacatecas since 1985 (five years prior to the creation of the Program), had shown great potential for remitting funds for public works, and had lobbied the Mexican government for, and got, a better program (Paisano) to safeguard the rights of returning migrants. Hence, the Mexican government created the Program, at least partly in response to a transnationalization of political life by immigrants, attempting both to control and channel and this activity and to mute its potential to disrupt domestic politics. Kearney (1991, 1995) and Rodriquez (1996) analyze examples of such autonomous transnational activity.

Mexico's policy of closer relations and economic integration with the United States, or *acercamiento*, was another reason it created the Program at this particular historical juncture. Mexico's closer economic integration with the United States, consistent with the neo-liberal turn that began in 1982, with President de la Madrid, represented a break with the historic political pact which had been in effect for more than 50 years, and opened the PRI up to charges, such as Cardenas', that it had abandoned the Revolution. In the "peace for prosperity" pact, the PRI had traded labor peace in return for wage increases in some sectors, and political hegemony for some electoral competition; had subsidized the poor; and had assumed a nationalistic stance in the national economy and towards the outside, including the United States, IMF, and World Bank (Cornelius, et al 1994; Dominguez 1983). The Salinas administration created the National Solidarity Program to (among other things) attempt to soften the worst effects of neo-liberal adjustment policies, in what Dresser (1991) depicts as "neo-popular solutions to neo-liberal problems".

The Program can be seen as a part of this same strategy of *acercamiento* in several ways. First, according to one Program official, the passage of the North American Free Trade Agreement (NAFTA) was due in part to the Program, because it helped mobilize support for NAFTA among Mexican American organizations such as the National Council of La Raza. Second, these closening relations with the United States not only required that Mexico abandon the Estrada Doctrine and its hostile, nationalistic foreign-policy stance towards the United States, but also made it possible not to view as *Mexican* intervention in the United States the closer relations it was developing with its diaspora in the United States (interviews 1995, 1996; de la Garza 1995; Guarnizo 1996; Santamaria 1995). Evidence of this change lies in the elaboration of the "Mexican Nation" intiative in Mexico's National Development Plan for 1995-2000, that aims to "strengthen cultural links with Mexicans abroad and with people with Mexican roots outside Mexico...to recognize that the Mexican nation extends beyond its physical borders" (1995: 8).

Thirdly, within this context of acercamiento, the image of Mexico presented to the United States public became more important (de la Garza 1995; Smith 1995). Hence, the Program is an attempt to channel, co-opt and reorganize the disaffected energies of Mexicans in the United States who, for example, thought that the 1988 election results were fraudulent, or that the Mexican government had forgotten them. Conversely, this context also gave those groups protesting publicly in the United States more leverage. A leader of the Frente Indigenista Binacional Oaxaquena (Binational Indigenous Oaxacan Front) explained the situation this way: "If something happens in Oaxaca, we can put protesters in front of the Consulates in Fresno, Los Angeles Madera..." (interviews 1995; Kearney 1994: Nagengast and Kearney 1990 have previously analyzed this dynamic). Both Frente leaders and consular officials agree that the Frente gets much more attention paid to its demands because they are making them publicly in the United States, and especially since the emergence of the Zapatistas in 1994, because both groups are indigenous.

Given these reasons for the Program's creation, what has it done and how does that affect transnational life between the United States and Mexico? It has pursued four separate but related strategies aimed at institutionalizing a Mexican diaspora. First, it has attempted to institutionalize existing meaning creating practices under the aegis of the Mexican state. Hence, the Program has promoted the development of local-level clubs, such as that of Ticuani, and of federations similar to the Zacatecas Federation. It has also formed regional sports leagues in the United States, and national sports tournaments, thus organizing a central structure in immigrant communities through the Mexican state. A second strategy has been to create new programs aimed at increasing the links of Mexican Americans with Mexico, and increase their power within the United States. Among these efforts are youth exchanges between Chicano and Mexican youth, relationships with Bilingual Associations in California and other states, and efforts to foster links between Mexican and Mexican American groups within the United States. For example, the Program organized a meeting between the Zacatecas Federations of California and of Chicago, at which the latter donated (U.S.) $4,000 to Unidad Latino, a group in which many of the Los Angeles Zacatecanos were participating to fight Proposition 187. While the donation was small, it is theoretically very important: here are two groups organized within U.S. civil society based on their origin in a Mexican state, being brought together by the Mexican state, and then participating in American politics.

A third strategy has been to institutionalize the Program itself in two ways. The Program has established what can be called offices of emigrant affairs in the Governor's offices of major migrant states, and made routine the links between these offices and their oriundos in the United States. This attempts to reverse their status as "pochos" in Mexico (Smith 1993). Moreover, the Program has survived into its second *sexenio*, and is staffed by a cadre of foreign service officers many of whom have lived, served, or studied in the United States and understand the Chicano community (interviews 1995, 1996).

A final strategy is not the work of the Program itself, but is part of the same vision. This involves two developments: the first is an agreement among the major parties to make it possible to vote for the Presidential election from outside Mexico in the 2,000 elections; the second is agreement to remove the Constitutional clause mandating loss of Mexican citizenship upon acquisition of another kind of citizenship. Ironically, one of the factors causing the change in Mexico's stance on the issue of double nationality has been Pete Wilson's anti-immigrant politics, especially the passage of Proposition 187. This has made both the Mexican state and Mexican leaders in the United States more aware of the need for Mexican immigrants to become voting American citizens. Such changes would give stronger expression to the simultaneous memberships of Mexicans in the United States within a transnational context, and of Mexico's attempt to institutionalize a diaspora. However, some members, particularly businessmen, are likely to share more fully in this simultaneous membership via Program activities (Guarnizo 1995).

Models of Political Community and Transnationalization of Social and Political Life

What are theoretical implications of the foregoing analysis? What insights can it give us into the transnationalization of political and social life? One implication of the creation of transnational localities "from below" is that the kind of imagination and institutionalization of transnational community such as the Ticuani case are not an automatic, natural outgrowth of migration. Rather, they emerge from specific historical contexts, and their emergence is contingent and variable. Not all transnational localities look like Ticuani. In the case of Ticuani, a transnational community emerged as a result of negotiated settlements on the part of migrants on both sides of the border. A community can be said to exist because its members agree it exists, and because they use it as the "unit of discourse" (Walzer 1967) and emotion within which they feel they belong. However, to argue that such a sense of community exists is not to argue that equality reigns. Rather, communities are usually riven with inequalities and organized around hierarchies. In the Ticuani case, the formation of a transnational community is highly gendered, with men almost exclusively organizing the creation of a transnational public sphere. Moreover, transnational communities create public spheres in which differences in status and class, especially upward mobility or educational success of children, can be displayed, and in which they have special meaning (Smith 1995; Goldring 1996). Yet, despite the strong contradictions between the Ticuanenses in New York and in Ticuani, and internal differentiation, a community can be said to exist because there is at least public agreement on the common responsibility to work for the good of "el pueblo Ticuanense" (the Ticuani people/community).

Secondly, this analysis points to the essential role that technology plays in facilitating the creation of transnational localities such as Ticuani. Today's travel and telecommunications technology make it possible to simultaneously carry on significant public lives in more than one place. The simultaneity vital to community is sustainable, at least in the medium term, between Brooklyn and Ticuani. One result has been the emergence of parallel power structures, with the old *caciquismo* co-existing with the new "Comitismo" (i.e., Committee-ism). However, it is not that technology itself transnationalizes political and social life, but rather that it enables relationships—and the tensions within them—to be maintained and intensified despite geographical and temporal separation. And while technology's role in facilitating migration and building links between distantly placed people has been invoked before (e.g., Foerster 1919), it is quantitatively and qualitatively different now.

A third implication is that models of political community and immigration are either not asking the right questions to understand the transnationalization of political and social life, or are offering paths that lead only to partial understanding of it. Hence, one lesson we can draw from the Ticuani case (and the Program for Mexican Communities Abroad and Zacatecas Federation) is that the creation of political *community* need not be wedded to territory in the same way as is supposed in the citizenship model, *nor* divorced from it in the absolute sense posited in the post-national model. However, the physical, geographical locality *is* very important because it provides the site and emotional vocabulary for many community-forming practices, even if these practices are subsequently carried out in other sites, as with the Ticuanenses in New York.

Similarly, this analysis suggests that the generation of political *authority* need not be wedded to the state in the way posited in the citizenship model, nor evaded as in the post-national model. Rather, *migrant transnational organizations are forcing the state to engage them in new ways, either in kind or in degree; but engage the state still they must.* The "autonomous migration" analyzed by Rodriguez (1996) or Kearney (1991) does depict transnational activity carried out relatively autonomously from the national state, especially from American law, but we must recognize that "the state" is more than the federal government. Indeed, in the Ticuani case, negotiation and engagement with the local state, the municipio, is a central part of creating a transnational locality and sense of community. Moreover, the national state in the form of the Program for Mexicans Abroad is attempting to institutionalize links between itself and its diaspora in the United States. The involvement of local state and the federal or provincial state in such transnational activity can stabilize transnational political and social life, thus promoting the formation of a transnational civil society (Cohen and Arato 1992), even as the intent of such programs is to channel and control autonomous transnational activity (Smith 1995, 1996).

However, even given this assertion of the centrality of engagement with the state, we must also consider the existence of different kinds of engagement and different degrees of "relative autonomy" (Block 1981) from the state. For example, the members of the Binational Indigenous Oaxacan Front have an oppositional stance towards the Mexican state in Mexico and in the United States (*vis-à-vis* the Consulate and Program activities), while the Zacatecano Federation is much more closely aligned with the Mexican state, leading to different relations with the state and different degrees of autonomy. And even with such differences, there can be important and similar dynamics. For example, the Ticuanenses negotiate with the Ticuani authorities using much the same rhetoric as the powerful Zacatecano Federation uses in negotiating with the Mexican government: we are not obligated to do the work we do, and hence can walk away from it if we feel our sacrifice, status, and contribution are unappreciated. The point is that transnationalization calls for contextualized analysis.

The simultaneous holding of different forms of membership and identity—e.g., those linked to communities of origin, to state-level federations, to global nations—inherent in transnational life denies the all-encompassing, Americanizing experience supposed in the immigration paradigm, as well as the uniqueness and co-terminousness of nation-membership and state-membership, supposed in the citizenship paradigm critiqued by Brubaker (1989). The ethnic pluralist model can accommodate some of these memberships and identities in that immigrants and their children are indeed becoming Mexican-Americans or Chicanos or Latinos. However, their links to a living Ticuani or Mexico cannot be accommodated under this model, neither in the ways that immigrants attempt to retain these links, nor in the ways that sending states attempt to cultivate these links and form such entities as "global nations." The core of this new condition lies in the simultaneous memberships of migrants and their children, which we can describe as the creation of a transnational community or locality, a transnational civil society, or as a process of diaspora formation (Rodriguez 1995; Smith 1995).

The term "diaspora" is not usually used to analyze events on the micro-level, but it may have relevance here that links the micro and macro levels of transnationalization. A "diaspora" is usually understood as a people, usually a national people, who are dispersed, often after having been expelled from their homeland (Safran 1991). Under this definition, neither the larger Mexican case nor the micro-level Ticuani case can be properly seen as diasporic. Clifford (1994) has usefully recast this debate for us, pointing us to look where difference is manifest, where people understand themselves to be different, even while living among others—"to dwell differently." Following Clifford, we can understand what is happening at the macro-level (e.g., the Program), the intermediate (e.g., Zacatecas Federation) and the micro level (e.g., the Ticuanenses) as related. Practices and identities, such as those of the Ticuanenses, create the kind of membership, the kind of institutionalized transnational structures that make or define positively the space that nurtures the difference Clifford posits. They are the pre-existing, pre-diasporic capillaries through which a diaspora can be formed and can breathe. Micro- and macro-levels intersect here. The Program is a conscious attempt to create a diaspora, a Mexican global nation, by imposing and insinuating a flexible structure of meaning over and throughout these local practices. In the process, the Mexican state is helping to create a transnational civil society, to make transnational life more durable, and to make viable the long-term holding of simultaneous memberships.

This attempt by the state to order and organize these processes, and the existence of different forms of membership and political community suggests a dynamic at odds with the usual placement of migrants and states in the structure-agent problematic. Whereas states and markets are normally seen as the structures or forces to which migrants respond, in this case migrants have created transnational structures on local and state levels to which the state has responded (Smith 1993). Still, as noted above, states have not been superseded in this transnational world, even if social and political structures now transcend them. States are crucial structures of power to which transnational organizations are usually linked, and through which they often gain more influence, even if their initial power stemmed from their having been at least partially autonomous from the state.

We should note important differences in southern sending and northern receiving states on-going attempts to create "the nation." The latter are responding to immigration as a threat to their national political communities, and hence nationalistic, anti-immigrant political rhetoric and attempts to further control unauthorized entry are increasing (Cornelius et al, 1994; Sassen 1996). Sending states, with different relations to the economic globalization and political power that contribute to migration, are attempting to create "global nations" that transcend the state's territorial boundaries.

Finally, these new forms of membership indicate a re-emergence of the saliency of local identities and forms of community within a global context, particularly within the global economy organized along neo-liberal lines. Tilly et al. (1975) argue that, between 1830 and 1930, national structures of power displaced local ones, yet, not as a direct result of economic modernization as high functionalist modernization theory suggests. Rather, the eclipsing of local centers of power by national ones resulted from the long-range reorganization of solidarities that economic modernization and new political administration brought with it. This analysis informs my own. It is not the globalization of the economy that has directly brought about transnationalization of political and social life as its natural consequence, as is often posited. Rather, within the overdetermined circumstances of their lives—which *are* clearly caused in large part by the globalization of the economy (Grindle 1988; Portes 1985)—technology has made it possible for people to maintain and nurture, even foster new ties to their communities of origin. Hence, in this way, globalization and new technology have led to a resurgence of the salience of local forms of community and identity, that exist even while not displacing the predominant national forms. It is towards the analysis of the tensions between these that we must turn increasingly if we are to understand the meaning and course of community and identity formation, of political practice and belonging, within an increasingly migrant world.

Notes

1. The author gratefully acknowledges support for this research from the following sources: The Social Science Research Council, Program on the Urban Underclass, with funds provided by the Rockefeller Foundation; William and Flora Hewlett Foundation and the Institute for Latin American and Iberian Studies at Columbia; Tinker Foundation and El Colegio de la Frontera Norte; the National Science Foundation, Program in Sociology, and grants from Barnard College and Columbia University. Thanks also are extended to the following people for their comments and support: Michael P. Smith, Luis E. Guarnizo, Saskia Sassen, Alejandro Portes, Roger Waldinger, Douglas Chalmers, Mark Kesselman, Sarah Mahler, Katie Hite, Michael Kearney, Gaspar Rivera, Devra Weber, Luin Goldring, and the anonymous reviewers.
2. In very different contexts, Sassen emphasizes the importance of technology as crucially facilitating the communication and travel that are part of economic globalization. See Sassen, 1988; 1991; 1996; 1997.
3. This argument does not hold for the Philippines, which has about 70 million people and accounts for the second largest number of legal immigrants of any single country, behind Mexico. Most of Basch, et al. analysis is based on the Haitian and Caribbean cases.
4. That Don Pedro and his brother and cousin went to New York instead of California and Los Angeles is largely a historical accident. They had been living in Mexico City after having fled from the political violence in Ticuani, and were trying to bribe their way into labor contracts to the United States through the Bracero Program. Knowing of their trouble in getting such a contract, a friend of theirs introduced them to an Italian-American New

Yorker named Montesinos he knew who visited Mexico City every year for vacation. Montesinos drove them back to New York, put them up in a hotel, and found them jobs within two days. Don Pedro actually reported the date as July 7, 1942, but it is almost certainly 1943 because the Bracero Program only began transporting migrants north in September, 1942 (Garcia y Griego, 1995).

5.   Wolf's original conceptualization was of closed corporate peasant communities. While the Ticuani transnational community, and Ticuani itself, are no longer closed nor peasant, it they are both most certainly corporate in the communal sense of that word.

6.   I have been told that she wanted to modernize the book keeping and perhaps invest the money for a profit, while the Committee wanted to stay with their notebook listing of who has paid what, and keep the money in a simple account. There is more of a story here.

References

Anderson, Benedict. (1983). *Imagined Communities: Reflections on the Growth and Spread of Nationalism*. New York and London: Verso. Reprinted 1991.

Appadurai, Arjun. (1991). "Global Ethnoscapes: Notes and Quieries for a Transnational Anthropology." In Richard Fox (ed.), *Recapturing Anthropology*. Santa Fe, NM: School of American Research Press.

Basch, Linda, Nina Glick Schiller, and Cristina Szanton Blanc. (1994). *Nations Unbound: Transnational Projects, Postcolonial Predicaments and the Deterritorialized Nation-State*. New York: Gordon and Breach Publishers.

Bendix, Reinhard. (1964). *Nation Building and Citizenship* New York: Wiley.

Block, Fred. (1987). *Revising State Theory*. Philadelphia, PA: Temple University Press.

Bosniack, Linda. (1994). "Membership, Equality, and the Difference Alienage Makes" *New York University Law Review* 69: 6: 1047-1149.

————. (1988). "Exclusion and Membership: The Dual Idenity of the Undocumented Worker Under United States Law" *Wisconsin Law Review* 6.

Brubaker, W. Rogers, ed. (1989). *Immigration and the Politics of Citizenship in Europe and North America*. Washington DC: German Marshall Fund of the United States and University Press of America.

Calhoun, Craig. (1994). "Social Theory and the Politics of Identity." In Calhoun (ed.), *Social Theory and the Politics of Identity*. Oxford, UK, and Cambridge, USA: Blackwell.

Camilleri, Joseph, and Jim Falk. (1992). *The End of Sovereignty? The Politics of a Shrinking and Fragmented World*. Aldershot, England: Edward Elgar Publishing.

Castells, Manuel. (1975). "Immigrant Workers and Class Struggle in Advanced Capitalism: Western European Experience." *Politics and Society* 5 : 1: 33-66.

Castles, Stephen. (1984). *Here for Good: Western Europe's New Ethnic Minorities*. London: Pluto Press.

Castles, Stephen and Godula Kosack. (1973). *Immigrant Workers and Class Structures in Western Europe*. London: Oxford University Press.

Clifford, James. (1994). "Diasporas." *Cultural Anthropology,* 9: 3: 302-338
Cohen, Jean, and Andrew Arato. (1992). *Civil Society and Political Theory* Cambridge: MIT Press.
Cornelius, Wayne A. (1990). "Labor Migration to the United States: Development Outcomes and Alternatives in Mexican Sending Communities." Final Report to the Commission on the Study of International Migration and Cooperative Economic Development. Center for U.S. Mexican Studies, University of California, San Diego.
Corchado, Alfredi. (1996). "Mexican Immigrants Send Children Home." *Times Picayune Newspaper (*New Orleans). January 7, 1996.
Carrasco, Pedro. (1969). "Central Mexican Highlands: Introduction." In Robert Wauchope (ed.), *Handbook of Middle American Indians. Ethnology.* 8: 2: 579-602. Austin, Texas: University of Texas Press.
Cornelius, Wayne, Ann Craig, and Jonathan Fox. (1994). *Transforming State Society Relations in Mexico: The National Solidarity Strategy.* San Diego: Center for US-Mexico Studies, University of California, San Diego.
de la Garza, Rodolfo. (1985). "Mexican Americans, Mexican Immigrants, and Immigration Reform." In Nathan Glazer (ed.) *Clamor at the Gates.* San Francisco; Institute for Comtemporary Studies.
————. (1996). "Foreign Policy Comes Home: The Domestic Consequences of the Program for Mexican Communities Living in Foreign Countries." Unpublished manuscript.
de la Garza, Rodolfo, and Claudio Vargas. (1992). "The Mexican Origin Population of the United States as a Political Force in the Borderlands: From Paisanos to Pochos to Potential Political Allies." In L. Herzog (ed.), *Changing Boundaries in the Americas.* La Jolla: Center for US-Mexico Studies.
Dillon, Sam. (1996). "Mexico is Near to Granting Expatriates Voting Rights." *New York Times.* June 16.
Dominguez, Jorge. (1982). Mexico's Political Economy: Challenges at Home and Abroad. Beverley Hills, CA: Sage.
Dresser, Denise. (1991) *Neopopulist Solutions to Neoliberal Problems: Mexico's National Solidarity Program.* San Diego: Center for US-Mexico Studies, University of California, San Diego.
————. (1994). "Bringing the Poor Back In: National Solidarity as a Strategy of Regime Legitimation." In W. Cornelius, A. Craig, and J. Fox (eds.), *Transforming State-Scoeity Relations in Mexico.* The National Solidarity Strategy La Jolla, CA; Center for US-Mexico Studies.
Durand, Jorge and Douglas Massey. (1992) "Mexican Migration to the United States: A Critical Review." *Latin American Research Review* 27: 2: 3-43.
Durand, Jorge and Emilio Parrado and Douglas Massey. (1996). "Migradollars and Development: A Reconsideration of the Mexican Case." *International Migration Review* 30: 114.
Estrada, Richard. (1995). "The Dynamics of Assimilation in the United States." In Robert Earle and John Wirth, (eds.), Stanford*Identities in North America: The Search for Community.* Stanford University Press.
Falk, Richard. (1990). "Evasions of Sovereignty." In Walker and Mendlovitz (eds.), *Contending Sovereignties: Redefining Political Community.* Boulder and London: Lyne Rienner Publishers.

Feldman-Bianco, Bela. (1992). "Multiple Layers of Time and Space: The Construction of Class, Race Ethnicity and Nationalism Among Portuguese Immigrants." Glick Schiller, Nina, Linda Basch, and Cristina Szanton Blanc (eds.), *Towards a Transnational Perspective on Migration; Race Class Ethnicity and Nationalism Reconsidered.* New York: Annals of the New York Academy of Sciences 645.

Foerster, Robert. (1919). *The Italian Emigration of Our Times.* Cambridge: Harvard University Press.

Garcia y Griego, Manuel. (1995). Personal communication.

Glick Schiller, Nina. (1994). Comments on "A Caribbeanist's Perspective on Mexican Migration." Conference, "Creating New Political Practices and Spaces; Transnational Processes in Caribbean and Mexican Migration." New York Universty and Columbia University.

Glick Schiller, Nina, and Linda Basch. (1993). "Transnational Projects of Immigrants and Ethnographers, and the Cultural Politics of Nation States." Unpublished manuscript..

Goldring, Luin. (1992). "Diversity and Community in Transnational Migration: A Comparative Study of Two Mexico- US Migrant Communities." Unpublished Ph.D. dissertation. Department of Rural Sociology, Cornell University.

————. (1995). "Gendered Memory: Reconstruction of a Rural Place of Origin by Mexican Transnational Migrants." In Melanie Du Puis and Peter Vendergeest, (eds.), *Nature, Rurality and Culture: The Social Construction of Rural Development and Environmental Conservation.*

————. (1996). "Blurring Borders: Constructing Transnational Community in the Process of Mexico-US Migration." *Research in Community Sociology*, 6: 69-104.

Gonzalez Gutierrez, Carlos. (1993). "The Mexican Diaspora in California: The Limits and Possibilities of the Mexican Government." In A. Lowenthal and Katrina Burgess (eds.), *The California-Mexico Connection.* Stanford University Press.

Gordon, Milton. (1964). Assimilation in American Life: The Role of Race, Religion and National Origin. New York: Oxford.

Graham, Pamela. (1995). "Nationality and Political Participation in the Transnational Context of Dominican Migration." Paper presented at "Caribbean Circuits: Transnational Approaches to Migration." Yale University.

Grew, Raymond. (1986). "The Construction of National Identity." In *Concepts of National Identity: An Interdisciplinary Dialogue.* Baden-Baden: Nomos Verlgsgesellschaft.

Grindle, Merilee. (1988). *Searching for Rural Development in Mexico.* Harvard University Press.

Guarnizo, Luis E. (1994). "'Los Dominicanyorks': The Making of a Binational Society." *Annals of the American Academy of Political and Social Science* 533: 70-86.

————. (1995). "La economía étnica mexicana en Los Angeles: Acumulación capitalista, reestructuración de clase y transnacionalización de la migración." Paper presented at El Colegio de Mexico, Mexico City.

————. (1996). "The Nation-State and Grassroots Transnationalism: Comparing Mexican and Dominican Transmigtration." Paper presented at the American Ethnological Association Meetings, San Juan, Puerto Rico. April 17-21.

Habermas, Jurgen. (1981). "Modernity and Postmodernity." *New German Critique* 33 Fall.

Hagan, Jacqueline. (1995). *Deciding to Be Legal: A Maya Community in Houston.* Philadelphia: Temple University Press.

Handlin, Oscar. (1951). *The Uprooted.* Boston: Little, Brown.

Hinojosa Ojeda, Raul, and Sherman Robinson. (1992). "Labor Issues in a North American Free Trade Area." in N. Lustig, B. Bosworth. and R. Lawrence (eds.), *North American Free Trade: Assessing the Impact.* Washington, DC: The Brookings Institute.

————. (1994). "Regional Integration in a Greater North America: NAFTA, Central American and the Caribbean." Paper presented at the International Studies Association. March.

Hirschman, Albert O. (1970). *Exit, Voice, and Loyalty.* Cambridge: Harvard University Press.

Huerta Jaramillo, Ana María de. (1985). *Insurreciones Rurales en el Estado de Puebla, 1868-1870.* Puebla, Mexico: Universidad Autónoma de Puebla, Centro de Estudios Históricos y Sociales.

Immigration and Naturalization Service, Statistical Yearbook, 1992.

Joachim, Benoit. (1979). *Perspectivas Hacia la História Social Latinoamericana* Puebla, Mexico: Centro de Investigaciones Historicas y Sociales, Universidad de Puebla.

Kearney, Michael. (1991). "Borders and Boundaries of State and Self at the End of Empire." *Journal of Historical Sociology* 4.

————. (1994). Personal Conversations.

————. (1995). "The Local and the Global: The Anthropology of Globalization and Transnationalism." *Annual Review of Anthropology* 24: 547-566.

Kyle, David Jane. (1995). "The Transnational Peasant: The Social Construction of International Economic Migration and Transcommunities from the Ecuadoran Andes." Ph.D. dissertation. Department of Sociology, The Johns Hopkins University.

Keely, Charles. (1995). "The Effects of International Migration on US Foreign Policy." M.Teitelbaum and M. Weiner (eds.), *Threatened Peoples, Threatened Borders.* New York: Norton.

Levitt, Peggy. (1996). "Transnationalizing Civil and Political Change: The Case of Transnational Organizational Ties Between Boston and the Dominican Republic." Ph.D. Dissertation, Department of Sociology, MIT.

Maroni de Velasquez, Maria de Gloria. (1991). "Estrategia de Supervivencia y Bracerismo en las Familias Campesinas Poblanas." Puebla, Mexico: Universidad Autónoma de Puebla.

Massey, Douglas and Audrey Singer. (1995). "New Estimates of Undocumented Mexican Migration and the Probability of Apprehension." *Demography* 32: 2.

Massey, Douglas, Rafael Alarcón, Jorge Durand, and Humberto Gonzalez. (1987). *Return to Aztlan: The Social Process of International Migration From Western Mexico.* Berkeley: University of California Press.

236 Transnationalism from Below

Massey, Douglas and Nancy Denton 1994 *American Apartheid* Harvard University Press.

Massey, Douglas, and Brooks Bitterman 1985 "Puerto Ricans and Segregation." *Social Forces* 64: 2: 307-331.

Mendlovitz, S. H. and Walker, R.B.J. (1990). "Interrogating State Sovereignty." In Walker and Mendlovitz, (eds.), *Contending Sovereignties: Redefining Political Community.* Boulder and London: Lyne Rienner Publishers.

Mines, Richard. (1981). "Developing a Community Tradition of Migration: A Field Study of Rural Zacatecas, Mexico, and California Settlement Areas." Monograph, No.3 San Diego: Center for US-Mexican Studies.

Nagengast, Carole, and Michael Kearney. (1990). "Mixtec Ethnicity: Social Identity, Political Consciousness and Political Activism." *Latin American Research Review.* 25: 2.

Neiburg, Federico G. (1988). *Identidad y Conflicto en la Sierra Mazateca: El Caso del Consejo de Ancianos de San José Tenango.* Instituto Nacional de Antropologia e Historia. Mexico, D.F.

Nelli, Humbert S. (1979). *Italians in Chicago, 1880-1930: A Study in Ethnic Mobility.* New York: Oxford University Press.

⸻. (1983). *From Immgrants to Ethnics: The Italian Americans.* New York: Oxford.

Panteleon, Dr. Oscar. Interview, 1991.

Pare, Luisa. (1975). "Caciquismo y Estructura de poder en la Sierra Norte de Puebla." In Roger Bartra (ed.), *Caciquismo y Poder Político en el Mexico Rural.* Mexico D.F.: Instituto de Investigaciones Sociales, U.N.A.M.

⸻. (1972)."Diseño teorético para el estudio del caciqusimo en Mexico." *Revista Mexicana de Sociologia* 34: 2.

Piore, Michael. (1979). *Birds of Passage: Migrant Labor and Industrial Societies.* Cambridge: Cambridge University Press.

⸻. (1986). "The Shifting Grounds for Immigration." In *The Annals of the American Academy of Political and Social Science.* Beverly Hills, CA: Sage.

Plan Nacional de Desarollo, 1995-2000. Poder Ejecutivo Federal, Gobierno de Mexico,

Portes, Alejandro. (1996). "Global Villagers; The Rise of Transnational Communities." *The American Prospect,* March-April.

⸻. (1995). "Transnational Communities: Their Emergence and Significance in the Contemporary World System." Working Paper, No. 16. 19th Annual Conference on Political Economy of the World System: Latin America in the World Economy. North-South Center, University of Miami.

Portes, Alejandro and Ruben G. Rumbaut. (1990). *Immigrant America: A Portrait* Berkeley: University of California Press.

Portes, Alejandro, and John Walton. (1981). *Labor, Class and the International System.* New York: Academic Press.

Portes, Alejandro and Luis E. Guarnizo. (1991). "Capitalistas del trópico: la inmigracion en los Estado Unidos y el desarollo de la pequeña empresa en la República Dominicana" Santo Domingo: Facultaad Latinoamericana de Ciencias Sociales.

Redfield, Robert. (1955). *The Little Community and Peasant Society and Culture.* Chicago: University of Chicago Press.

Rodriguez, Nestor. (1996). "Autonomous Migration, Transnational Communities and The State." *Social Justice* 23: 3.

———. (1995). "The Real World Order: The Globalization of Racial and Ethnic Relations in the Late Twentieth Century." In M.P. Smith and J.R. Feagin (eds.), *The Bubbling Cauldron: Race, Ethnicity and the Urban Crisis.* University of Minnesotta Press.

Roediger, David. (1991). *The Wages of Whiteness.* New York: Routledge.

Rouse, Roger. (1989). "Mexican Migration to the US: Family Relations in a Transnational Migrant Circuit." Unpublished Ph.D. dissertation. Stanford University.

———. (1991) "Mexican Migration and the Social Space of Postmodernism." *Diaspora* 1: 1: 8-24.

Safran William. (1991). "Diasporas." *Diaspora* 1.

Sanchez, Arturo Ignacio. (1996). "Grassroots Organizing and Colombian Transnational Politics." Paper presented at the American Ethnological Association Meetings. April.

Santamaria Gomez, Arturo. (1995). *La Politica Entre México y Aztlan.* Universidad Autónoma de Sinaloa and California State University, Los Angeles.

Sassen, Saskia. (1988). *The Mobility of Capital and Labor.* New York and London: Oxford University Press.

———. (1991). *The Global City: New York, London, Tokyo.* Princeton: Princeton University Press.

———. (1996). *Losing Control? Sovereignty in an Age of Globalization.* The 1995 Columbia University Leonard Hastings Schoff Memorial Lectures. New York: Columbia University Press.

———. (1997). "Cities, Foreign Policy and the Global Economy." In Margaret E. Crahan and Alberto Vourvoulias-Bush (eds.), *The City and The World: New York in the Global Context.* New York: Council on Foreign Relations.

Schuck, Peter. (1984). "The Transformation of American Immigration Law." *Columbia University Law Review* 84: 1: 34-90.

Schuck, Peter, and Rogers Smith. (1985). *Illegal Aliens and the American Polity.* New Haven CT: Yale University Press.

Silva, Enriqueta. Personal Communications. January 1992 through September, 1993.

Smith, Michael Peter. (1994). "Can You Imagine?: Transnational Migration and the Globalization of Grassroots Politics." *Social Text* 39: 15-33.

Smith, Robert C. (1995). *Los Ausentes Siempre Presentes: The Imagining, Making and Politics of a Transnational Community.* Unpublished PhD dissertation, Political Science, Columbia University.

———. (1996). "Domestic Politics Abroad, Diasporic Politics at Home: The Mexican Global Nation, Neoliberalism, and the Program for Mexican Communities Abroad." Paper presented at the American Sociological Association Meetings. August.

———. (1993) "De-Territorialized Nation Building: Transnational Migrants and the Re-Imagination of Political Commuity by Sending States." Seminar on Migration, the State and International Migration, *Occasional Papers Series*, New York University, Center for Latin American and Caribbean Studies.

Smith, Robert C. and Luin Goldring. (1994). "Transnational Migration and Social Citizenship." Proposal to the National Science Foundation.

Soysal, Yasemin N. (1994). *Limits to Citizenship: Migrants and Postnational Membership in Europe* University of Chiacgo Press.

Suttles, Gerald. (1968). *The Social Construction of Community.* Chicago: University of Chicago Press

Tilly, Charles, Louise Tilly and Richard Tilly. (1975). *The Rebellious Century 1830-1930.* Cambridge; Harvard University Press.

Walker, R.B.J and Saul. H. Mendlovitz. (1990). "Interrogating State Sovereignty." In Walker and Mendlovitz, (eds.), *Contending Sovereignties: Redefining Political Community.* Boulder and London: Lyne Rienner Publishers.

Walzer, Michael. (1967). "On the Role of Symbolism in Political Thought." *Political Science Quarterly* 82 (June).

Warner, W.L. and L. Srole. (1945). *The Social Systems of American Ethnic Groups.* New Haven CT: Yale University Press

———. (1994). "Ethnic and Racial Identities of Second Generation Black Immigrants in New York City." *International Migration Review* 28: 4.

Wolf, Eric. (1957). "Closed Corporate Communities in Mesoamerica and Java." *Southwestern Journal of Anthropology* 13: 1: 1-18.

Zazueta, Carlos. (1983)."Mexican Political Actors in the United States and Mexico: Historical and Political Contexts of a Dialogue Revisted." In Garcia y Griego and Vasquez (eds.), *US-Mexico Relations: Conflict and Convergence* Los Angeles; UCLA Chicano Studies Center and Latin American Center.

Zendejas, Sergio. (1994). "The ejido as a structure organizing transnational political life." Conference paper.

———. (1995). "Appropriating Governmental Reforms: The Ejido as an Arena of Confrontation and Negotiation." In Sergio Zendejas and Pieter de Vries (eds.), *Rural Transformations Seen From Below: Regional and Local Perspectives from Western Mexico.* Transformation of Rural Mexico Series. San Diego: Center for US-Mexico Studies, University of California, San Diego. Pp. 23-48.

Zolberg, Aristide. (1991). "Bounded States in a Global Market: The Uses of International Migrations." In Pierre Bourdieu and James Coleman (eds.), *Social Theory for a Changing Society.* Boulder: Westview Press/Russell Sage Foundation.

———. (1989). "The Next Wave: Migration Theory for a Changing World." *International Migration Review* 23: 3.

———. (1983). "Contemporary Transnational Migration in Historical Perspective: Patterns and Dilemmas." In Mary Kritz (ed.), *U.S. Immigration and Refugee Policy.* Lexington, MA: Lexington Books.

———. (1988). "International Migration and International Economic Regimes: Bretton Woods and After." Unpublished manuscript.

IV

Transnational Practices and Cultural Reinscription

8

Narrating Identity Across Dominican Worlds[1]

Ninna Nyberg Sørensen

> *As I see it, Dominicans are in exactly
> the same situation as any other foreign-
> ers in this city. Bueno, we have one
> thing in common. We are migrants. But I
> don't know if that makes us more alike.*
> —Male shopowner
> Washington Heights 1991

Dominican migrants[2] are currently evolving into a social group whose economic, political, social and cultural territory transcends national borders. As 'natives' to the transnational world, Domini-can migrants produce local knowledge of the social space of migration. As inhabitants speaking and acting in this transnational space they constitute "the only fully valid source" for ethno-graphic field work (Barth 1993: 25). But their knowledge is neither necessarily shared (since differences in practice and expe-rience as well as in positioning and experience are profound), nor privileged (since a variety of perspectives need to be taken into ac-count). To paraphrase Edward Bruner (1986), the only experience they share is their common participation in migration.[3] This, of course, is an important point of departure for our analytical entry into the Dominican identity space.

Since the beginning of the 1960s, hundreds of thousands of Dominicans have boarded thousands of flights, primarily between the Dominican Republic and New York City. Some have travelled with a green card attached to their passports; some with time-limited tourist visas but perhaps boundless intentions; and a small number with 'borrowed' or 'purchased' papers in their pockets.[4] As time has gone by, more Dominicans have even travelled as U.S. citizens. Among those determined to leave their country without any papers at all, other routes have been established. Thus, numer-ous Dominicans have risked their lives on the 75-mile hazardous sea journey to Puerto Rico, often in small yawls. More than 10 percent are estimated to have drowned in their attempts to reach the Puerto Rican coast. In 1990, U.S. coastguard patrols intercepted 3,800 Dominicans in Puerto Rican waters, still another 20,000 were estimated to have succeeded in reaching Puerto Rico as undocumented migrants as compared to approximately 40,000 documented entries (Duany 1989, 1992; Rey-Hernández 1991).[5] During the first 10 months of 1996, 4,226 Dominicans were detained by the coastguard. Having reached Puerto Rico, many Dominicans continued their travels toward New York. From San Juan to New York no papers are requested.[6]

Other destinations increasingly travelled to in the United States, are e.g., Miami and Massachusetts, various Caribbean islands (among which Dominicans most often mention Aruba, Curaçao, and St. Thomas), and Latin American states, such as Mexico and Venezuela. Recent Dominican migration has been directed toward Europe. From the late 1980s an increasing number of Dominicans have migrated first and foremost to Spain, but also to the Netherlands, Switzerland, Italy and Greece. While New York City remains the dominant destination for the majority of Dominican migrants, Europe seems to be a new and growing attraction for Dominicans looking for a better future.[7] Toward the end of the paper I will include this new migration experience.

How are we to understand this multifaceted transitional migration experience and the identities it produces? In a world characterized by enhanced spatial mobility and formation of transnational flows of people and meaning, the correspondence between physical worlds and social realities among people differently situated is neither simple nor understandable with bounded concepts (Ardener 1993; Moore 1994). In this world, the Dominican cultural identity space is occupied by transnationals and locals whose lives and experiences are interweaved with the questions of *aqui? or allá?*, of here? and there? Whether Dominicans relate to, interpret, or themselves articulate on the price and quality of consumer products, weather conditions, gender relations, electricity supply or racism, they construct their world views by constantly contextualizing and interpreting events and acts in "here's"and "here's." Such geographic shifts in locus are more often than not communicated and enacted in terms of gender. Thus, gender plays a powerful part in the staging of migrant communities.

This paper offers key examples of how identity is voiced in contemporary Dominican transnational landscapes, and the gendered forms transnationalism takes. It uses various types of material—ranging from personal migration narratives and "native" novels, written about Dominican experiences from a US-based room with a view, to local commercials, using the view to boost their products. I shall use these examples to discuss the negotiation of political and cultural identities among members of Dominican worlds and the local cultural politics of consumption in contemporary global ethnoscapes.[8]

The discussion is divided in four separate but mutually interconnected parts. The first discusses transnationalism as a metaphor for the lived-experiences of Dominican migrants. I, then, proceed by approaching different Dominican identity narratives. The paper, finally reflects on the relationship between spoken, written and read identities. I argue for a differentiated conceptualization of transnationalism that focuses, not only on relationships between North American or European 'mainstream majorities' and Dominican "minority Others" but also on the counter narratives *within* transnational groups. My reflections are based on field work among Dominican locals and transnationals.[9]

Although this paper focuses on the relationships between Dominican migrations and Dominican identities, the analysis offered has, I believe, broader implications for migration research in general: implications for the ways we ought to understand the complex relationships between migration and identity in a variety of settings, as well as for the ways in which we understand and engage with transnationalism and its legacies.

Spatial Metaphors and Identity Narratives

In modern Athens, Michel de Certeau (1988) states, the vehicles of mass transportation are called *methaphorai*. When the people of Athens go to work or go elsewhere, they take a 'metaphor'—a bus or a train. Metaphors bring the Athenians to wherever they are. Stories or narrative structures, de Certeau continues, could also take this noble name. "Every day [stories] traverse and organize places, they select and link them together, [and] they make sentences and initiaries out of them" (de Certeau 1988: 115). According to de Certeau, then, every story is a travel story, a spatial practice, that organizes places through the displacements it describes. Space is practised place and stories carry out the labor that constantly transforms places into spaces and spaces into places (Ibid.: 118).

If we apply this view to the Dominican migration process we may say that the transnational space is a metaphor for the lived-experiences of Dominican migrants. This experience encompasses the whole of what individual migrants have lived through and therefore bears the potential for bringing experiences from different times and different locations into one single field of analysis. By being experienced, expressed, and performed, transnational spaces transform into different forms of places, or in another of Appadurai's neologisms, into various sorts of translocalities. Guarnizo has lately described the Dominican migrant experience/practiced place in a similar way:

> "...Dominican migrants, despite their social, educational, and regional heterogeneity and precisely because of their shared migratory and social experiences in the United States and in the Dominican Republic, have become a group whose territory is a borderless, transnational space. They are here and there and in between." (Guarnizo 1994: 78).

Individuals, communities, or states, however, rarely identify themselves as spatial craftsmen or transnationals, nor do they identify the places they inhabit as transnational spaces. All social processes are contextualized in particular places (Urry 1995). Migrants' identities continue to be voiced in terms of national origins (soy dominicana/o), and migrants usually talk about 'home,' 'apartment buildings,' 'work places,' 'neighborhoods' and 'communities' just like anyone else. Thus, to make it perfectly clear, my use of the transnational space metaphor neither refers to international air space or the crowds of travellers up there, nor to the erosion of national airspace by the advent of the satellite, as some postmodern analyses would have it. So far I limit myself to—and will elaborate a bit further on—a definition of the transnational space as practiced place among Dominicans involved in migration, as a space of social relations.

The anthropological concept of culture has often assumed that a natural, if not biological, identity exists between people and places, and that discrete peoples belong to specific, bounded territories, which demarcate their distinct cultures and fertilize their local identities. This view takes cultural difference and territoriality as the starting point, and tends to explain the dynamics of cultural and social change in terms of inter-cultural contact and acculturation. However, as Gupta and Ferguson (1992: 16) suggest, if we understand space as being culturally constructed, and already hierarchically ordered by a set of *difference producing relations*, that is, understand 'difference' as the end-product of analysis, rather than the starting point, then we may become able to see the attachment and fixation of people to places, as well as the construction of transnational communities and identities, as something worthy of explanation. We may also be able to distinguish migrants' projects in extra-territorial nationalisms (Appadurai 1993; Anderson 1994), and migrancy as a discontinuous state of being, a mobile habitat, in which neither the point of departure nor those of arrival are immutably certain (Chambers 1994).

The conceptualization of transnationalism, transmigrants, and transnational spaces allows us to analyze the "lived and fluid experiences of individuals who act in ways that challenge our previous conflation of geographic space and social identity" (Basch et al. 1994: 8) at the same time that it enables us to understand both the ways in which transmigrants are transformed by their transnational practices, and the various social relations they engage in.

Several authors have called for an anylysis of the relationship between identity, culture, and power in relation to the movement of people across space. Such analyses have become pressing, it is argued, as cultural politics have emerged as a means of either maintaining or resisting domination in a globally inter-connected world. Here the transnational perspective furnishes a focal point for both analyzing and theorizing issues at the interface of social identities and the multiple processes by which cultural representation, domination and resistance interrelate and are embedded in social relationships (Goldberg and Zegeye 1995; Schiller 1994).

Exploring different kinds of transnational linkages interrupts traditional multicultural constructions. Such constructions are more often than not based on simplified relations between dominant and subordinate groups in a given society without accounting for the differences between and *within* minority groups. We must therefore explore the complex ways in which transmigrants negotiate differences in their daily lives and how these differences are *told* in different stories.

I have elsewhere argued that if the task is to get beyond mobility, and understand how migration effects people's sense of belonging and identity, it is necessary to listen to how migrants themselves interpret their situatedness, and how they culturally construct 'histories' and 'herstories' (Sørensen 1993, 1994, 1996). It follows from this argument that identities by themselves do not exist. Identity is constructed by identity narratives "which attempt at imagining communities to lock up human groups within fantasmatic boundaries" (Martin 1995: 17)—but also to transgress them. As is the case with the 'migrant community,'[10] identity narratives cannot be understood as expressions of social or cultural homogeneity.

In the case of Dominican transnational migrant identity, several identity narratives are in competition. By underscoring difference and competition, I hope to work against what Kobena Mercer has called the race-class-gender mantra—a new kind of pluralism "that posits that a serial acknowledgement of various sources of identity is sufficient for understanding how different identities get articulated into a common project or don't," (Dernersesian 1994 289).

In the following I shall dwell on a specific arena for identity competition, namely that of gender. This is not to merely divide a gendered world into feminine and masculine identities. Rather, I shall on the one hand interpret culture through a gendered prism, and on the other hand interpret gender through a 'cultured' prism. Thus, the concept of gender is my analytical tool for dealing with Dominican identity formation and maintenance.

The Production of Space: Gendered Identity Narratives

Entering the transnational space as told in different travel stories confronts us with the problem of reference as well as representativity. Or, put differently, which transnational spaces and whose transnational experiences are narrated in which Dominican discourses—and why?

In previous works (see e.g., Sørensen 1994) I have isolated two layers of Dominican travel stories, or two layers of representations of Dominican migration experiences. I have distinguished between the *migratory legend* and *individual migration narratives*: master narratives and individual experiences that seldom fit the 'master.'

The *migratory legend* does to a large extent offer national politics as an explanation for migration and is the travel story most often offered by Dominican 'community leaders.' The legend serves to contruct a common history and a collective experience in which Dominican migrants can place themselves. The legend is not necessarily used to tell *who* Dominican migrants are but rather to tell *how* Dominican migrants as a collectivity differ (positively) from other migrant groups in North American society.

During a conversation with one of the board members of *Associaciones Dominicanas*—an umbrella organization for a variety of New York-based Dominican organizations that claims to represent the 'Dominican Exile Community' and direct their efforts towards giving this community a voice in U.S. politics—I was told about the many ways in which Dominican migrants contribute to both North American and Dominican worlds. When I asked if there was a tendency toward changed gender-relations within the Dominican migrant community he told the following story:

"[In New York] women become more independent. But is it positive? Traditionally, women are the backbone of the Dominican family and the extended family concept is the basic element of Dominican society. The American system is selling awareness—not knowledge—and what follows is chaos. The great American welfare program is terrible because it provides women with a second avenue...In the Dominican Republic the level of dependency holds the family together...here economically independent women seek divorce."

Gender relations—and in particular conflicts between women and men—are central to any understanding of how and why women and men experience changing social, economic [and cultural] practices differently from each other, says Henrietta Moore (1988: 95). "Which women and which men?" We should ask this question with a view to the transnational class restructuring Dominicans undergo abroad. Another example of how gender serves as the dynamic focus in articulating relations between the American welfare system and Dominican values can be extracted from one of the *individual migration narratives* I taped in New York City. A middle-aged female migrant expressed her experience quite differently:

> "In New York City women may loose everything because of men. In the Dominican Republic things are different. We don't have welfare. When welfare is available men can have two or three wives. Since the state supports single mothers, men are no longer responsible for paying the bills. Men are no longer the sole providers when women are protected by the government. Welfare is sometimes a poor help. Since men are *machistas* this easily happens. It ruins family life and welfare contributes to all these family interruptions."

Migratory legends are often part of a masculine construction in and around whose body, social location and ideological purview particular Dominican constructions converge and are diluted (Dernersesian 1994). Though gender may not be the issue discussed, it pops up in narratives about "distinguishing behavior that constitutes acceptable forms of 'assimilation' into the dominant culture and that which constitutes a 'failure to preserve one's cultural identity'" (Narayan 1995: 74). The interesting point is that Dominican 'culture' and Dominican 'identity' are portrayed differently in the two expressions. In the first, women are blamed for not maintaining their culturally decisive role in the Dominican family, for not being the 'backbone' of a homogeneous Dominican culture. In the second, American 'culture' is blamed for enabling Dominican men to further develop 'traditional' *machista* practices. These two examples should not be reduced to, respectively, the male and the female perspective. Rather they describe different experiences of displacement and relocation.

According to Basch, Schiller and Szanton Blanc, organizational practices differ from other domains in that they give transnationalism a public face. Transmigrants look to organizations to provide ways and means for building relationships across national borders, at the same time that transnational organizational practices provide a vehicle for individual transmigrants to obtain and reinforce their social position (Basch, et. al. 1994). Because migrant organizations are engaged in constructing meanings and identities, they are an arena of active hegemonic contestation for the political loyalty of migrants.

Women in contemporary transnational landscapes, such as New York City, Madrid, or Santo Domingo, often risk dismissal as a symptom of "Americanization" or "Europeanization" if and when they organize for their particular needs and rights. We therefore need to pay particular attention to how gender continues to be implicated in the scripts of gender roles' respective "nationalisms" and 'cultural identities' (Narayan 1995). Without an awareness of the gendered ways in which transnational organizations construct and reinforce social positions through gendered politics, and the places constructed by these politics, migrant women become relegated to the domain of assimilation and "westernization."11

But gender may also be implicated in other discourses, e.g., discourses of race. In the Dominican organization *Esclavas del Fogon* (a women's organization based in the Dominican Republic) female activists blame national Dominican identity politics for neglecting African cultural heritages in Dominican culture. National politics, these activists say, are based on an exclusion of blackness. However true this may be, a gender-sensitive analysis reveals that more than racial questions could be at stake. In the Dominican Republic women are granted higher status in Afro-Caribbean family practices than in the nationally promoted 'Hispanic' patriarchal family. Women, therefore, have a lot more than racial equality to gain from a racial struggle. Political discourses and/or practices by activists in *Esclavas del Fogon*, therefore, bear the potential of transgressing the gendered and racialized boundaries of nationalisms.

Spoken, Written and Read Identities

Anthropology has distinguished itself from other social science disciplines by "its particular focus on the lived-experience of the people studied and by given an authoritative status to the oral, to what people say, and to agency, what people do" (Melhuus 1994: 65). Careful recording of people's "story tellings" and extended periods of participant observation in "cultural settings" have constituted the anthropological field for data collection.

But anthropologists working in complex societies are not only confronted with a variety of discourses, but also with a variety of *texts*. In literate societies, Archetti writes, anthropologists must face the fact that informants not only speak, tell stories, dance, pray or sing. Informants also *consume* different types of written products. "Once the written word becomes an acceptable means of communication, it is difficult to contrast orality and literacy as opposing orders" (Archetti 1994: 23). The present spread of television and other forms of electronic communication further complicates the picture.

If most transmigrants have neither fully conceptualized nor articulated a form of transnational identity, contemporary fiction is increasingly written from the margins of hybridity and 'in-betweenness' (Basch et. al.: 8). Salman Rushdie, Hanif Kureshi and Bharati Mukherjee have vividly described transnational experiences between India, England and the United States. Latin American/Caribbean authors such as Michelle Cliff, Esmeralda Santiago, Christina Garcia, Oscar Hijuellos, Sandra Cisneros and many more, have dedicated their literary production to coming to terms with historical, geographical and emotional displacements. Thus, informants not only consume different types of written products, they also *produce* them.

In the introduction of *Writing Across Worlds*, the editors suggest that "for those who come from elsewhere, and cannot go back, perhaps writing becomes a place to live" (Russell et. al. 1995). Migratory experiences occur within personal biographies that neither start nor end at those events, but which provide the context for them (White 1995: 2). Migrant literature, then, offers an entry into the subjective migrant experience. Russell, Connell and White challenge the conventional ethnographical focus on *told* rather than *written* accounts of experience by a new genre of work linking geography with literature, and humanities with social science. While the geography-literature genre so far has concentrated on exploring place rather than movement, the humanities-social science genre bears the potential of offering new insights of migratory processes and the experience of migration (Russell et al. 1995).

The Dominican diaspora has produced its own 'literary hybrids' concerned with origin, nation, migration and belonging. Among them Julia Alvarez, whose two novels I shall use to discuss the negotiations of political and cultural identity among members of Dominican worlds. By doing so I will also stress the novels' place in Dominican migrants' public discourse.

Producing Places: Transnational Literary Products

During a field visit to New York City, *The New York Times Book Review* praised the first of Alvarez' two novels *'How the Garcia Girls lost their Accents.'*[12] I bought the book and read on the cover that this novel was "a representation of lived experience as perceived by a native author." Seventeen dollars seemed a reasonable price for a source of cultural knowledge about a Dominican experience of migrancy.

The writer is native to the Dominican worlds on which she critically reflects. She was ten years old when she arrived in New York City on August 6, 1960. After receiving her undergraduate and graduate degrees in literature and writing, Alvarez spent 12 years teaching poetry in schools in the US. At present she is a professor of *English* at Middlebury College and, as is written on the covers of both novels, lives with her husband in Vermont. Presumably, she preserves her duty as the backbone of the family.[13]

Her family was and is well-known by Dominican locals and transnationals alike and belongs to the upper pale layers of Dominican society. While still in the Dominican Republic, her father participated in an underground plot against Trujillo. The plot was cracked by the SIM, Trujillo's infamous secret police, and it was only a matter of time before those who had already been captured and were held at the notorious torture chamber of La Cuarenta (La 40), gave out the names of other members. The family escaped and was exiled to New York. Alvarez' first novel, however, is *not* about political exile, but is a perspective on a past national identity-space that can never be reclaimed. It takes us *aquí, allá* (here, there), but 'home' remains uncertain.

How the Garcia Girls lost their Accents tells the story of four Dominican girls—Carla, Sandra, Yolanda and Sofia Garcia—who experience displacement from the Dominican Republic to New York City as a result of their parent's migration. In this chronicle of a family in exile, the cultural differences between two nations are described through the eyes of the four daughters. Upon their arrival, New York City is described as foreign and mysterious: Laundromat, cornflakes, subway, snow. Foreign words, foreign places. During the girls' teen-age years the Dominican Republic becomes 'old hat,' hair and nails, chaperons, itchy boys with macho strutting unbuttoned shirts, hairy chests with gold chains and teensy gold crucifixes...a whole island of FAMILY! But it also becomes the home of a hot, sultry paradise of swiftly fading childhood memories. Stories filled with separations, exiles and longings.

The Garcia girls—or the story about them—is a story of the clash between worlds—the incompatibility of being an emancipated young woman from New York in the Dominican Republic and the hardships and losses of being a Dominican woman in New York City.[14] These are represented by the girls' presence on analysts' couches and in divorce courts. Back 'home' on a holiday visit one of the sisters considers that return would be the solution to her *split* identity. She never returns, though, and the story about the Garcia girls concludes as follows: The girls' struggle toward womanhood is inseparable from their struggle to understand their own multifaceted identity, and to come to terms with it. This identity is neither Dominican nor American, but both and in-between.

How did Dominican transmigrants respond to this novel? Well, actually quite a few welcomed it, and saw it as a sign of another homecoming, a homecoming to Dominican worlds in plural. These people used the novel as providing them with a critical social mirror in which they could reflect their 'Dominicanness.' Some Dominican women, moreover, saw Alvarez' novel as a challenge to the hegemony of views of gender roles in migration, deriving largely from male accounts. But Alvarez did not escape rejection from long-distance nationalists who criticized not only her novel but also her person for being totally assimilated to "North American culture" whenever they met at "community" celebrations in New York. "Dominica-nada" [dominican nothing], "is what she is," a male, Dominican lawyer told me between two glasses of champagne at a reception given by *Asociación Americana de Abogados Dominicanos.* "She has forgotten who she is. Her work is of no interest for your work!"

A Dominican acquaintance of mine told me exactly how Americanized Julia Alvarez had become:

> "I was at this wedding downtown. And Julia Alvarez was there. We used to know each other, you know. And I greeted her in Spanish, but do you know what she did? She looked at her watch and said, 'oh, hi(!),' and then she went over to talk to some American friends of hers."

While the lawyer probably stems from the same upper-class Dominican layer as Julia Alvarez' family, my female acquaintance used close to 20 years to gain a middle-class position in New York's Dominican community. So class undoubtedly has a lot to do with Alvarez' exclusion from the Dominican "we" in the latter case. But gender, or more precisely a failure to represent class-specific gender behavior, was what troubled the lawyer.

Julia Alvarez' second novel, *In the Time of the Butterflies,* was published in 1994, and was translated into Spanish in 1995 (and published in the Dominican Republic). In this novel, Alvarez leaves autobiography in favor of historical biography—a work of fiction based on historical facts. The novel describes the lives of four actually existing local Dominican women—Patria Mercedes, Minerva, Maria Teresa and Dedé Mirabel—of whom three were killed in 1960 by Trujillo's secret police. The voices of all four sisters speak across the times, from the 1940s to November 25, 1960, when the bodies of three of them were found near their wrecked Jeep at the bottom of a 150-foot cliff on the north coast of the Dominican Republic. The Mirabel sisters tell their stories, from hair ribbons to convent school; from faith in Trujillo (whose picture hung on the wall by the picture of "Our Lord Jesus" in the Mirabel's home), to coming to terms with what Trujillo's regime was really about; from political ignorance, to mobilization, prison. and torture. They describe the everyday horrors of life under Trujillo's rule. Minerva, once the object of the dictator's desire, had dared to publicly slap his face. Patria found her calling to the uprising through the church, and Maria Teresa joined the Guerilla in pursuit of romance. Only Dedé, the practical one, the most diligent in her duty to family and tradition, kept apart from the revolutionary movement. And only she survived to see that the names of *Las Mariposas* were remembered.

The novel is a construction of national heroines, but one that simultaneously challenges the national myth. Pre-marital sex and divorces scratch the picture of THE Dominican family. It is maybe therefore that Alvarez cautiously writes the following in the postscript:

> "I would hope that through this fictionalized story I will bring acquaintance of the famous sisters to English speaking readers. November 25th, the day of their murder, is observed in many Latin American countries as the International Day Against Violence towards women. Obviously, these sisters, who fought one tyrant, have served as models for women fighting against injustices of all kinds. To Dominicans separated by language from the world I have created, I hope this book deepens North Americans' understanding of the nightmare you endured and the heavy losses you suffered—of which this story tells only a few. *!Vivan las Mariposas!*"

Moving from literature to anthropology, Ruth Behar suggests that we all bring different burdens of memory, differently sanctioned ignorance, to the task of writing. "And there is a special burden that authorship carries if you have ever occupied a borderland place in the dominant culture, especially if you were told at some point in your life that you didn't have what it takes to be an authority on, an author of, anything. It means writing without entitlement, without permission." (Behar 1993: 340). Alvarez' first novel was written without permission, and certainly exiled her from male nationalist layers in Dominican worlds abroad. Crossing the border with the story of the Mirabel sisters is probably an impossible homecoming to this particular Dominican world. But it bridges the world of Latinas in "many Latin American countries." It describes another homecoming.

As de Certeau notices, every description is more than a fixation. It is a culturally creative act. Stories even have distributive power and performative force when an ensemble of circumstances are brought together. Then it finds space.

> "By considering the role of stories in delimitation, one can see that the primary function is to authorise the establishment, displacement or transcendence of limits, and as a consequence, to set in opposition within the closed field of discourse, two movements that intersect (setting and transgressing limits) in such a way as to make the story a sort of 'crossword' decoding stencil (a dynamic partitioning of space) whose essential narrative figures seem to be the *frontier* and the *bridge*" (de Certeau 1988: 124).

Both frontiers and bridges are observable in Dominican worlds. Frontiers are challenged every day by Dominican migrants who move across territorial borders for economic, political, and individual reasons. Cultural as well as political identity are constantly negotiated and reworked in these cross-national contexts. Literary products, their production and consumption, are part of this process. Other culturally creative products contribute other meanings to the Dominican identity formation.

Consuming Places: Transnational Metaphors in Advertising

Field work among Dominicans cannot be restricted to literature. It invariably involves watching television, which is not so bad after all since both national identity politics and migrant identity are highly communicated in this media and the conversations in front of it. Networks and channels transcend national boundaries while local and transnational audiences comment on and interpret whatever is on. Exposure to television is, therefore, an excellent way to enter into a dialogue on identity and sense of place. Places are, claims John Urry (1995), both figuratively and literally consumed, particularly visually. What Urry terms 'the sociology of place' is exactly about people's experience of social relations, both the relatively immediate, and the more distant ones, and how they intersect.

Migration has become a common Dominican reality to an extent, in which mass culture (defined as the cultural products put out by capitalist society) and popular culture (defined as the ways in which people use, abuse, and subvert these products to create their own meanings and messages)[15] have become enswathed with binational symbols. This is particularly the case with Dominican advertising which uses the image of "'he transnational Dominican" commercially.

During a stay in the Dominican Republic, one of the larger to-bacco companies introduced a new local cigarette. Marlboro had slowly taken over a large percentage of the Dominican market, and the tobacco industry had employed professional advertising experts to invent a splashing name for the 'new' product. Of course the cigarette was named *New York*. Who could not identify with that? Another large industry, the rum distilleries, quickly followed up with a new tele-commercial of an old product:

> The scene: A Dominican merengue band gives an open-air concert on a sunny Manhattan plaza. Inside a parked yellow cab, a male Dominican cab driver listens to the music. His face has a dreamy look. For a moment he is back on his island. A female (very blond) North American customer climbs into the back seat. Since the cab driver makes no move to drive, she asks, slightly annoyed, if the cab is actually free? The driver explains that the music is merengue from his home country. In the back seat the woman makes some clumsy dancing moves and says: "Oh merengue, mucho buena" (oh merengue, very nice [but grammatically incorrect]). As the driver starts driving he shakes his head and says: "Ay americana, no sabe nada" (hey American, you don't know anything).

> A few months later this commercial is substituted with a new one, like the continuation of a serial. This time the setting is in the Dominican Republic. The same North American woman (now dressed as a tourist) enters a Dominican cab, and the same cab driver (now in his 'native' environment) sits in his worn-out cab, listening to a merengue band playing outside the airport. The same conversation—with exactly the same words spoken (!)—goes on.

These two short film strips—produced by Brugal, one of the larger Dominican rum companies—were probably the most popular television spots in the Dominican Republic during 1992. Built up in the form of a *telenovela*, both strips pictured a stereotyped image of American culture as rich and ignorant, and of Dominican culture as proud tradition, despite poverty. Moreover, they pictured two very well-known forms of travel in Dominican society; that of New York-bound migration and that of tourism. The transnational character of Dominican migration was highly emphasized by having the same chauffeur installed in two different cabs in two different locations. Didn't he embark on *un pasaje de ida y vuelta* like so many other Dominicans had done before him? The global diffusion of Dominican culture was symbolized by merengue. First and foremost by merengue's world-music character but also by the fact that it was played in New York, whereby a Dominican-ization of the City was indicated.16

Brugal produced this commercial in 1992, the year in which the celebration of the quincentenary of Columbus' discovery of Hispaniola reached hysterical heights. While the majority of Dominican commercials included this event in one way or the other, Brugal commercialized a critical counter-view. At least Dominican viewers interpreted the commercial as a Dominican re-conquest of the First World, of New York City: *"Mira! All New York cab drivers are Dominican!"*

What does this commercial and its reception tell us about Dominican identity? In itself the commercial communicates a disjunction between state and nation. By a critique of the national policies together with an accentuating of national values of male and female behavior, the contradictions of transnationalism are made explicitly clear. From the homesickness on the cab driver's face on the first strip, it is obvious that he would rather be at home "where he belongs." The worn-out quality of the domestic cab nevertheless signals, that he does not really have a choice. A poor local economy apparently prevents people from staying permanently in the Dominican Republic. A certain critique of Dominican politics and standards is therefore implied. This is certainly a critique most Dominicans can identify with. The same critique can be read from the North American tourist's presence in the second strip. How can the government forward a development policy that allows for such an insult? She walks out from the airport as if she owns everything and, moreover, has the guts for insinuating that the cab driver is lazy. *Ay americana no sabe nada.*

But if national politics are discreetly challenged, 'traditional' values are simultaneously put in place. What does the female customer know? Neither merengue, nor Spanish, and certainly not the proper manner of approaching an honorable man. Though she acts as if she owns the cab driver (a woman in charge of a man— unthinkable!), his head shakings strongly indicate that she is in charge of absolutely nothing. He is the one who makes the cab drive when he pleases; however smart and professional she looks, she is subordinated to his will. *Ay americana, no sabe nada.* This is certainly the honorable edition of machismo. Moreover, some masculine ideas about relationships to women in general are communicated. As Dominican men continuously design their own autonomy as free mobility in encounters (note that the cab driver controls an auto*mobile*), a male control over female mobility is indicated by the cab driver's exercise of power. He has got the wheels!

Dominican TV viewers loved this commercial and always responded with laughter. Everybody asked each other if they had seen *la Brugal.* Moreover, the words of the cab driver: *Ay americana, no sabe nada,* almost totally substituted the frequent greeting, *hola gringo/gringa*, of American or European tourists in the streets of Santo Domingo. Those of us who were able to respond with a *merengue, mucho buena,* were given a great deal of credit. Having gotten the joke granted us with the status of *casi-dominicana*, of almost Dominican. *Ay ella sabe,* oh she knows (!), both friends and strangers commented, whenever I used the phrase.

Women laughed as much as men. But at least some women read the transnational message in quite a different framework. To them the taxi driver was a lover, a husband, a father. Out there—alone— surrounded by sexually emancipated, female and—very importantly, US visa holding—attractions. And contrary to some women's experience, this Dominican male resisted the temptation. He turned the *puta* down.[17]

Further research in the field of cultural aesthetization of local and transnational cultural values is in high demand. These studies should not be limited to cultural flows. Rather, the focus should be on how personal experience and performance with transnational worlds shape continuity and change within national and bi-national territories. A gendered analysis seems to be the perfect way to get about the complexities of local and transnational interpretations.

Michael Peter Smith has recently turned our attention to the insufficiency of reducing analyses of global mass communication to a question of who is sending and who is receiving these cultural flows. The interesting question is who consumes the flows and to what effect. He urges future research to concentrate on the images of men, women and gender relations that are being deployed in these flows and what effect these forms of imagined lives has on social gender relations:

> "Once women, whether motivated globally or locally, leave their old 'place' in the patriarchal domestic sphere to enter the public sphere and pursue new lives as transnational migrants, what specific risks do they face as border crossers who lack a 'public space' for acting on the basis of citizens rights?" (Smith 1994: 24).

Not all female Dominican migrants set out from a 'traditional' or 'patriarchal' social location (Sørensen 1993; 1994). This, of course, only makes the question more interesting, especially when researching various Dominican migrant destinations comparatively. 'Public spaces' may be produced in unforeseen ways, as the following description of Dominican placemaking strategies in Madrid will show.

Producing Places: New Dominican Territories

On Thursdays the Dominican housekeepers and nannies get the afternoon off. These afternoons in the plaza in Aravaca, a suburban district west of Madrid, is transformed concurrently with the arrival of the Dominican migrants. This could as well be Santo Domingo(!) The Spaniards withdraw and migrant women dressed up to the nines take over the benches. In less than an hour's time more than 200 women and a few men are gathered on the plaza. They indulge in ice creams and Dominican food, merengue brought along with ghetto blasters, and news from 'home,' from Madrid, from New York and elsewhere are exchanged. In the less noisy centre of the plaza, five mobile phones go round from hand to hand. On the phones, the women discuss everything from child upbringing to conceivable investments of money sent home, before the receiver is passed to the next in line. Towards the evening the women disappear in smaller batches, back to their Spanish middle class families and employers. When the last Dominican woman has left, the Aravaca square regains its Spanish character. The public image of this particular place in Aravaca nevertheless remains: The Dominicans have taken over the place.

By the end of the 1980s Dominican migration destinations have become more diversified, making Venezuela and Spain the quantitatively most important places after the United States and Puerto Rico. In times of high migration pressures in the Dominican Republic and severe restrictions on migration to the traditional destinations, Spain has represented a good alternative, first of all because of the relatively easy ways to enter the country—until July 1993 without visa requirements—but also because of the existence of a common language and a certain degree of cultural proximity. The presence of Dominican women in Madrid is now socially visible[18] and after 1992 Dominican migrants constitute the third largest group of Latin American immigrants in Spain.

Though Dominican migrants rank fourth among the documented migrants in Spain, their actual number may be much higher. According to *Asociación de Mujeres Dominicanas en España* (AMDE), 10-15,000 Dominicans were residing in Madrid in 1992. During my stay in Madrid in 1996, various Dominican migrant associations said that 30,000 to 40,000 Dominicans lived in Spain. Until 1992 the Dominican presence in Spain was fundamentally female. The actual gender composition among documented Dominicans is estimated to be some 25 percent males/ 75 percent females (Gallardo Rivas 1995). While some believe these migrants to be involved in prostitution (see e.g., Ferguson 1992), others assert that Dominican women primarily are employed in the unofficial Spanish labor market as domestics (Gallardo Rivas 1995). However that may be, a dual Dominican migration pattern is in the process of being established, a pattern in which Spain and Europe in general seem to be the attraction left for those who have not been able to link up (at least directly) to the New York-bound transnational circuits.[19]

Dominican Madrid-bound migration is not only distinct in its gender composition. The migrants also seem to originate from different places in the Dominican Republic: In New York City primarily from Santo Domingo and the relatively more affluent Cibao; in Madrid from the poorer village *Vicente Noble* and the Barahona region. The particularity of these places is not only socio-economic but also cultural. The experience of migrancy, belonging and identity in respectively New York City and Madrid as well as the economic, social, and cultural realities generated by migration is likely to contribute to a further diversified picture.

Whereas Dominican political participation in New York City has been rapidly escalating since the beginning of the 1980s, culminating with the 1991 election of Dominican-born Guillermo Linares to the New York City council, Dominican migrants in Madrid still lack representatives in visible positions in la *Comunidad Autónoma de Madrid* (CAM). Their massive presence in Madrid has nevertheless expanded their borderless transnational space. As Guarnizo suggests, it seems as though the stronger the attempts—in both countries of origin and destination—to control migrants' own spatial and social mobility and settlement, the stronger the migrants' resistance and consequently the stronger their cohesion and their binationalism (Guarnizo 1994: 86).

The Dominicanization of the Aravaca square may be viewed as a transformation of a public space into a particular place, a Dominican translocality. And it is a matter of fact that this place now serves as a gathering place in which new identities are constructed—from which new political organizations are in the process of being established. My understanding of this new phase of Dominican migration remains preliminary. It nevertheless suggests that specific forms of mobility articulate new experiences of gender and that a focus on the multifaceted relationship between dynamics of gender and migration may offer new insights into the ways in which identities are forged and negotiated in the daily lives of Dominican locals and transnationals.

Toward a Conclusion

As the refractions above have indicated, identity is voiced in a great variety of ways in contemporary Dominican transnational landscapes. In master narratives and counter narratives, in texts written with and without 'permission,' in mass cultural products and their popular consumption. Throughout the analysis I have showed that while Dominican migrants share a common participation in transnational migration, these migrants do not necessarily share a common experience, either in terms of their relations to North American/European society, or in terms of power within the Dominican 'migrant community.' Thus, we may identify the transnational space as a contested space. It contains several differentiated national and binational identities that are often expressed in terms of gender. An examination of different kinds of transnational linkages can hopefully challenge widely held assumptions of migrants as a bulk of undifferentiated, non-white, (non)peoples, a first step in the task of diversifying migrant identity.

Appadurai (1993) notices a disturbing tendency in the Western academy today to divorce the study of discursive forms from the study of other institutional forms such as the nation-state. Likewise, Stolcke (1995) has recently warned against those kinds of analyses that argue that transnationalism spells doom for the nation-state. "While capital and commodities nowadays know no national frontiers, the movement of people is quite another matter" (Ibid.: 21). According to Stolcke. the transnationalization of production has revitalized one crucial function of the nation-state, namely, that of controlling the movement of people across borders.

State policies also remain central to the understanding of the formation of transnational migrant circuits and transmigrants' social practices. As Hagan's recent study of a Guatemalan community in Houston suggests, evolving transnational relations between Houston and Guatemalan communities are importantly shaped by the acquisition of legal status. According to her study, legalized migrants are more likely than undocumented migrants to engage in bi-national social practices, strengthening both their social and economic ties to the United States as well as their successful reintegration as transnational rather than return' migrants into their 'home' communities (Hagan 1994). A first conclusion is, therefore, that transnational migration has not eroded state policies, and that individual transmigrants are not freed from the regulatory controls of the nation-state as if by postmodern magic. The *border* is out there!

Though more than one million Dominicans are involved in transnational migration, poverty and repression have not been eliminated in the Dominican Republic. While migration has helped relieve social pressures within the Dominican Republic, there can be no doubt that the enormous sums of money Dominican trans-migrants annually send home to their families, and—maybe even more important—the new and multifaceted world views they bring with them when they travel, have contributed to more than a preservation of an island on the margins. It has also produced links to feminist, social, political, and racial movements all over the world, and reconnected peoples of different colors, barrios, and borderlands to Latina/o movements and the 'Black Atlantic'—and in some cases even to both. Thus, if the Dominican nationalist earlier has noted that he is not as 'African' as the Haitian, nor as "Western" as the North Americans, as some Dominican historians will have it (e.g., del Castillo and Murphy 1987), involvement with a variety of diaspora movements in New York and elsewhere may have enlarged the cultural and racial identity repertoire from which national and transnational identities can be constructed. So *bridges* are observable as well.

A recent development in Dominican politics has been to allow US-naturalized Dominicans equal civil rights in the Dominican Republic, including their right to retain their original passports and opening the way for future domestic political participation.[20] This, together with the gendered transitions in recent Dominican migration, may very well change the spatial, the racial, and the gendered basis of the Dominican nation-state.[21]

Thus, a certain slippage between globalization from above and globalization from below (Clifford 1994) can be observed out there, *aquí/allá*. Hegemonizing economic, political and cultural world systems (including both instituting national or regional policies to control immigration and these politics' discriminatory practices against women) are constantly counteracted by people's transnational migratory movements and spatial practices. Such movements are both constrained by, but also exceeding, the politics of space.

In conclusion, I shall consider, in the words of Paul Carter, a future strategy for research in transnational migration.

"An authentically migrant perspective would, perhaps, be based on an intuition that the opposition between here and there is itself a cultural construction, a consequence of thinking in terms of fixed entities and defining them oppositionally. It might begin by regarding movement, not as an awkward interval between fixed points of departure and arrival, but as a mode of being in the world. The question would be, then, not how to arrive, but how to move, how to identify convergent and divergent movements; and the challenge would be how to notate such events, how to give them a historical and social [and I add cultural] value." (Carter 1992: 101).

To the extent that "critical thought is ultimately condemned to instability and movement, to be always on the margins of ironically subverting itself," then critical theory cannot rest content within any 'inherited discipline' of, for example migration studies, especially not if migration studies approach the acts of migration with a "fixed set of protocols" (Chambers 1994). New appropriate discursive terms for representing agencies and practices currently constituting bi-focal subjects, transnational social practices, and a globalized political space (Smith 1994) is in urgent demand. So is an understanding of migratory situations in which people migrate in order to maintain already-gained positions, the fact that not all people have access to transnational networks, and that people partaking in transnational realities may be differently situated and positioned.

Gender continues to pervade discourses on nationalism and cultural identity. The interplay between representations and practices of gender in transnational processes nevertheless produces new forms and visions of identity, drawing on social memory as well as aspirations for the future. The current making of transnational communities affects women and men differently and enhances particular images of masculinity and femininity that represent a challenge to states: to the efficiency of state boundaries (in promoting particular national identities) as well as to the politics of inclusion/exclusion and creation of national subject. To conduct research on transnational margins—empirically as well as theoretically—therefore reveals an opening and not a conclusion, or as Champers puts it, "it marks the moment of departure, never a homecoming" (op. cit.: 122). One departure could be to view culture as a migrant category, and identity as a mobility process, to engage in what Paul Gilroy has termed the dynamic of 'roots' and 'routes' (Gilroy 1993).

Notes

1. This is an expanded version of a paper delivered to the XIX International Congress of the Latin American Studies Association, 28-30 September 1995, Washington DC. The ideas presented here result from discussions and shared reflections with numerous colleagues and friends. I would like to acknowledge Dominican locals and transnationals who through various routes have shared their experiences with me, and Luis E. Guarnizo who has given insightful comments on the latest draft.
2. Although almost exclusively described as a traditional labor migrant population, early Dominican migration to New York consisted of a notable group of political exiles, who left the island in the turbulent years following the overthrow of dictator Rafael L. Trujillo in 1961. In this and following uses of the migrant concept I do not exclude the proportion of Dominicans whose mobility was informed by political decisions.
3. Bruner is concerned with performance. He writes: "We know that participants in a performance do not necessarily share a common experience or meaning; what they share is only their common participation" (Bruner 1986: 11).
4. In 1993, for example, 45,000 Dominicans received immigrant visas while 197,000 received non-immigrant visas, of which 145,000 were issued to "visitors for pleasure" (1993 Statistical Yearbook of the Immigration and Naturalization Service (1994), Tables 3 and 38).
5. Migrant and refugee labelling is a political matter. I choose to term the migrant without papers "undocumented," since this term neither implies that the host society not necessarily wants this migrant, nor has any criminal connotations. Finally the term "undocumented" comprises both that this migrant has no papers and that she is not included in any statistics (documents).
6. Puerto Rico has been a U.S. territory since 1898, Puerto Ricans have been U.S. citizens since 1917.
7. Whereas up to 90 percent of Dominican migrants were estimated to choose New York City as the port of entry in the 1970s (see Allen and Turner 1988, De Rege 1974), 60 percent of the documented US-bound migrants still settled there from 1982 to 1989 (Department of City Planning 1992). Estimates including undocumented entries to continental USA easily reach a figure over 500,000 Dominicans of whom 80 to 90 percent end up in New York or its immediate environs (Spalding 1989). For a discussion of the number of Dominicans residing in New York City, see Sørensen (1994).

8. Arjun Appadurai invented the term *ethnoscape* to refer to the dilemmas of perspective and representation in the changing social, cultural and territorial reproduction of group identity. He writes: "As groups migrate, regroup in new locations, reconstruct their histories, and reconfigure their ethnic 'projects,' the *ethno* in ethnography takes on a slippery, non-localized quality, to which the descriptive practices of anthropology will have to respond" (Appadurai 1991: 191).

9. Field work has been conducted in several locations. In the Dominican Republic: Rural villages in the Cibao region, 'nouveau riche' and not quite so rich migrant communities in and around Santiago, Santo Domingo, Puerto Plata and La Romana, and finally in the border areas close to Haiti. In the United States: Primarily in Washington Heights (Upper West Manhattan), but also in the Bronx, Queens, Brooklyn, and Yonkers. Finally, I have joined migrants on several air trips between their different 'homes'. These field visits took place between 1991-94. I am currently working on a research project including Dominican and Moroccan migration to Spain. Six months of field work was conducted in Madrid in 1996.

10. Here, I place the Dominican 'migrant community' in quotation marks to stress that the notion of *community* needs to be used with caution. The Dominican 'migrant community' is not a homogeneous and harmonious entity—and it does not encompass an organic wholeness or a given collectivity. This, on the other hand, doesn't mean that social and cultural collectivities are not constructed for strategic purposes and that they cannot be analytically identified in specific contexts.

11. See e.g. Grasmuck and Pessar (1991). See my critique in Sørensen (1994).

12. The novel was published in English. It was later translated into Spanish. Spanish-Spanish, not Dominican-Spanish, some Dominicans say. "No one would say *chicas* here, we say *muchachas*"(!)

13. It should perhaps be stressed that I have never met Julia Alvarez myself. I have enjoyed her novels enormously, but my knowledge of her is restricted to cover biography and various oral representations (gossip).

14. For a broader analysis of the experience of being perceived as foreigners in both locations, see Guarnizo (1994).

15. I owe this highly useful distinction to John Fiske (1989).

16. See Sutton (1987) for an analysis of the Caribbeanization of New York City.

17. *Puta* literally means whore. That some Dominican women call American or Puerto Rican women whores does not mean, of course, that these women are whores. It means that they represent a threat. As U.S. citizens they are attractive marriage partners for Dominican men in search of a visa and many Dominican women have lost a husband to a US citizen even when the marriage was only intended *de negocio*, to be a business arrangement.

18. After the murder of Lucrecia Pérez—a Dominican woman from Vicente Noble—in Madrid November 1992, the Dominican presence has been highly visible, not at least in the Press.

19. A few Dominican women in Madrid even report that they paid a broker to get them a visa (meaning a visa to the United States), but ended up with a visa to Spain. (Gallardo Rivas, personal communication).

20. The fact that U.S. law specifically prohibits citizens from voting in foreign elections may render this agreement inoperative for many (Betances and Spalding 1995:18).
21 For a discussion of a pre-dual-citizenship situation in the Dominican Republic, see Sørensen (1994).

References

Allen, James Paul and Eugene James Turner. (1989). *We the People—An Atlas of America's Ethnic Diversity*. New York: Macmillan Publishing Company.
Alvarez, Julia. (1991). *How the Garcia Girls Lost Their Accents*. Chapel Hill: Algonquin Books.
————. (1994). *In the time of the butterflies*. Chapel Hill: Algonquin Books.
Anderson, Benedict. (1994). "Exodus." *Critical Inquiry* 20 (Winter): 314-327.
Appadurai, Arjun. (1991). "Global Ethnoscapes: Notes and Queries for a Transnational Anthropology." In Richard Fox (ed.), *Recapturing Anthropology*. School of American Research Press: Santa Fe, New Mexico.
————. (1993). "Patriotism and Its Futures." *Public Culture* 5: 411-429.
Archetti, Eduardo P. (1994). "Introduction." In Eduardo P. Archetti (ed.), *Exploring The Written: Anthropology and the Multiplicity of Writing*. Oslo: Scandinavian University Press.
Ardener, Shirley. (1993). *Women and Social Space: Ground Rules and Social Maps*. Oxford and Providence: Berg Publishers. First edition, 1981.
Barth, Fredrik. (1993). *Balinese Worlds*. Chicago and London: University of Chicago Press.
Linda Basch, Nina Glick Schiller, and Cristina Szanton Blanc. (1994). *Nations Unbound: Transnational Projects, Postcolonial Predicaments and Deterritorialized Nation-States*. New York: Gordon and Breach Publishers.
Behar, R. (1993). *Translated Woman: Crossing the Border with Esperanza's Story*. Boston: Beacon Press.
Bentances E., and H.A. Spalding. (1995). "Introduction." *Latin American Perspectives* 22 : 3: 19.
Bruner, E. M. (1986). "Experience and Its Expressions." In Victor T. Turner E.M. and Bruner (eds.), *The Anthropology of Experience*. Urbana and Chicago: University of Illinois Press.
Carter, Paul. (1992). *Living in a New Country. History, Travelling and Language*. London: Faber and Faber.
Chambers, Ian. (1994). *Migrancy, Culture, Identity*. London and New York: Routledge.
Clifford, James. (1994). Diasporas. *Cultural Anthropology* 9: 3: 302-338.
de Certeau, Michel. (1988). *The Practice of Everyday Life*. Berkeley: University of California Press. First edition, 1984.
del Castillo, J., and M.F. Murphy. (1987). Migration, National Identity, and Cultural Policy in the Dominican Republic. *The Journal of Ethnic Studies* 15 : 3: 49-69.

Department of City Planning. (1992). "The Newest New Yorkers: An Analysis of Immigration into New York City During the 1980s." New York City: DCP # 92-16.

De Rege, C. (1974). "Dominicans are Coming to New York." *Migration Today*. July.

Dernersian, A. C. (1994). "Chicana! Rican? No Chicana-Riqueña!" In D.T. Goldberg (ed.), *Multiculturalism: A Critical Reader*. Oxford and Cambridge: Blackwell.

Duany, J. (1989). "De la Periferia a la Semiperiferia: La Migracion Dominicana Hacia Puerto Rico." *Punto Review* 2: 1: 26-64.

————. (1992). "Caribbean Migration to Puerto Rico: A Comparison of Cubans and Dominicans." *International Migration Review* 26: 1: 46-66.

Ferguson, James. (1992). *Dominican Republic: Beyond the Lighthouse*. London: Latin American Bureau.

Fiske, John. (1989). *Understanding Popular Culture*. Boston: Unwin Hyman.

Gallardo Rivas, G. (1995). *Buscando la Vida: Dominicanas en el servicio domestico en Madrid*. Santo Domingo: Coedicion IEPALA-CIPAF.

Gilroy, Paul. (1993). *The Black Atlantic*. London: Verso.

Goldberg, D. T., and A. Zegeye. (1995). "Editorial Note." *Social Identities* 1: 1:3-4.

Grasmuck, S., and Patricia R. Pessar. (1991). *Between Two Islands: Dominican International Migration*. Berkeley: University of California Press.

Guarnizo, Luis E. (1994). "'Los Dominicanyorks': The Making of a Binational Society." *The Annals of the American Academy*, AAPSS, 533 (May): 70-86.

Gupta, Akhil, and James Ferguson. (1992). Beyond 'Culture': Space, Identity, and the Politics of Difference." *Cultural Anthropology* 7: 1: 6-23.

Hagan, Jacqueline M. (1994). *Deciding to be Legal: A Maya Community in Houston*. Philadelphia: Temple University Press.

King, Russell, John Connell, and Paul White (eds.). (1995). *Writing Across Worlds: Literature and Migration*. London and New York: Routledge.

Martin, D.C. (1995). "The Choices of Identity. "*Social Identities* 1: 1: 5-20.

Melhuus, M. (1994). "The Authórity of a Text: Mexico through the Words of Others." In E.P. Archetti (ed.), *Exploring The Written: Anthropology and the Multiplicity of Writing*. Oslo: Scandinavian University Press.

Moore, Henrietta L. (1988). *Anthropology and Feminism*. Cambridge: Polity Press.

Narayan, U. (1995). "Eating Cultures: Incorporation, Identity and Indian Food." *Social Identities* 1: 1: 63-86.

Ry-Hernández, C.A. (1991). "La Identidad de lo Nacional: Una Reflexion Comparativa entre el Migrante Puertorriqueño y el Dominicano." *America Latina Local y Regional: Memorias del ll Simposio Internacional de la Universidad de Varsovia sobre América Latina*. Warszawa: CESLA.

Schiller, N. G. (1994). "Introducing Identities: Global Studies in Culture and Power." *Identities* 1: 1: 1-6.

Smith, Michael. Peter. (1994). "Can You Imagine? Transnational Migration and the Globalization of Grassroots Politics." *Social Text* 39: 15-33.

Spalding, H.A. (1989). "Dominican Migration to New York City: Permanent Residents or Temporary Visitors?" *Migration* 5: 47-68.

Stolcke, V. (1995). "Reply." *Current Anthropology* 36: 1: 19-24.

Sutton, Constance R. (1987). "The Caribbeanization of New York City and the Emergence of a Transnational Socio-cultural System." In Sutton, Constance. R. and E.M. Chaney (eds.): *Caribbean Life in New York City: Sociocultural Dimensions.* New York: Center for Migration Studies.

Sørensen, Nina N. (1993). "Ethnicity and Gender." In H. Lindholm (ed.), *Ethnicity and Nationalism: Formation of Identity and Dynamics of Conflicts in the 1990's.* Göteborg: Nordic Network of Ethnic Studies.

―――. (1994). "Telling Migrants Apart: The Experience of Migrancy Among Dominican Locals and Transnationals." Copenhagen: Institute of Anthropology, University of Copenhagen.

―――. 1996. "There are No Indians in the Dominican Republic." In K. Hastrup and K.F. Olwig (eds.), *Siting Culture.* London: Routledge.

Urry, John. (1995). *Consuming Places.* London and New York: Routledge.

White, Paul. (1995). "Introduction." In R. King, J. Connell, and P. White (eds.). (1995). *Writing Across Worlds: Literature and Migration.* London and New York: Routledge.

9

Belizean "Boyz 'n the 'Hood"?
Garifuna Labor Migration and
Transnational Identity[1]

Linda Miller Matthei
David A. Smith

More than 80 people were arrested in a week-long drive against drug-related gang violence last month; they were charged with possession of drugs, arms and ammunition. Members of the Belize Defence Force were brought in to patrol streets in Belize City. Several people have died in recent shooting incidents attributed to drug gangs (Caribbean Insight, June 1992).

New legislation to combat gang warfare in Belize was tabled in parliament last month, based on recommendations from a Crimes Commission set up by the government in September 1991. The bill proposed mandatory prison sentences for drug trafficking, tightened controls on possession of firearms, and a ban on the carrying of offensive weapons in public places. The commission also proposed that a meeting should be arranged between representatives of the two main gangs, the Bloods and the Crips, in an effort to "lower the flame of antagonism" (Caribbean Insight July 1992).

Tales of drugs, crime, and violent gangs are familiar to U.S. citizens in the 1990s. Our inner cities provide a familiar backdrop for horrific images of "drive-by shootings," "crackhouses," and "carjackings" that we see on the TV news and graphically depicted in books, movies, and music. And in the American imagination, perhaps no other place evokes as strong an association with murder and mayhem and street gangs than Los Angeles. Reality-based films like "Boyz 'n the 'Hood" depict this underside of life in "South Central" and science-fiction movies in the "Blade Runner" genre present grim images of Los Angeles' future. In *The City of Quartz*, Mike Davis notes that popular culture views Los Angeles as "the Nightmare at the terminus of American history" (Davis 1990:20) (and this was prior to the 1992 Los Angeles riots/uprising). He colorfully characterizes the racially charged shooting war between police and gangs as "Vietnam in the Streets" (Davis 1990:269). At first glance, Belize seems a most unlikely place to find Los Angeles-style urban problems.[2] This small country bordered by Mexico and Guatemala and facing the Caribbean Sea, is a land of rainforests, coral reefs, and tropical agriculture. Recently it has been touted as a destination for "eco-tourism," but throughout its history Belize has been viewed as an underdeveloped and isolated place. Following a visit to colonial Belize in the 1930s, Aldous Huxley wryly captured this sense: "If the world had any ends British Honduras would certainly be one of them. It is not on the way from anywhere to anywhere else." In some ways, the description seems apt even today. The physical landscape of Belize has changed little since Huxley's visit in 1934. Victorian-era mansions and public buildings stand crowded together with small, unpainted clapboard houses. Colorfully dressed women doing their marketing make their way through crowded streets with bundles perched atop their heads. In rural areas, the Maya still live in thatch huts and wash their clothes in tropical forest streams. Focusing on scenes like these, travel brochures often describe Belize as "quaint" and "picturesque," while visitors not so taken with their surroundings, often describe the country as the quintessential "colonial backwater." Belize is neither isolated from the outside world nor lost in time, however. One of our objectives in this paper is to explain the apparently paradoxical (and for most Belizeans unwelcome) transformation taking place in Belize. We will argue that this process is linked to the institutionalization of particular patterns of labor migration to the United States, which have, in effect, created a "transnational community" that is "neither here nor there," but simultaneously in *both* places (Portes 1996). Cultural identities, even in the small towns and villages of Belize, have been profoundly affected: One need only do a quick visual survey of the T-shirts worn by locals to discover where Belizean migrants live in the United States—the sports logos of the Chicago Bulls, L.A. Lakers, and New York Knicks are ubiquitous. Even the poorest home often has a color television and cable access to CNN and HBO. Today nearly everyone has some exposure to the United States, if not through personal experience, then through visits from kin, letters, home videos, and telephone calls. Indeed, 96 percent of international calls from Belize in 1987–88 were to the United States (Central Statistical Office 1990). Two points about this transformation need to be stressed. First, this is *not* a simple case, a la "modernization theory," of the generalized "diffusion" of American culture to a less developed society. Instead, it must be understood in terms of the inter-personal networks of real people—in this case, the migrants and their children who are moving back and forth between Belize and the United States. In other words this is an instance of the development of a "transnational community" which transcends international borders (e.g., Glick Schiller et al. 1992). Here, "transnationalism" denotes the processes by which immigrants forge and sustain multi-stranded social relations that link together their societies of origin and settlement. Transmigrants take actions, make decisions, and develop subjectivities and identities embedded in networks of relationships that connect them simultaneously to two or more nations (Basch et al. 1994:7).

Second, we must be clear that this reconstitution of identity is not a one-way process, but truly a contested terrain. In particular, this paper will illustrate the *generational* dynamics of this redefinition of cultural practices, as parents (and particularly mothers) attempt to insulate their children from what they see as the corrosive influence of U.S. inner-city lifestyles. So, rather than understanding changed identities as simple outcomes of globalization and the incorporation and immersion of new groups of people into the modern world-system, we must focus on "people's cultural responses to that system" (Georges 1990:10). And particularly in this case, it is crucial to understand that individual family members within the same household may respond very differently, as age and gender dynamics play themselves out. Though we are convinced that our story must begin with an understanding of international migration—conceptualized in terms of Belize's historical role in the global political economy—the research strategy and conceptual approach appropriate to this problem differs from typical macrostructural and statistical analyses that have dominated mainstream sociological studies of migration. While we appreciate (and use!) the seminal insights of structural analyses that argue that migration is a response to the penetration and expansion of global capitalism and the allocation of labor within the world-economy (Fernandez-Kelly 1981; Sassen 1988), we are also aware of the limits of these approaches. Extreme versions, which treat migrants "like empty grocery carts, wheeled back and forth between origin and destination under the hungry intentions of capital," provide little understanding of migration as a social process. Instead, taking a cue from social anthropologists doing community-level research (e.g., Georges 1990; Glick Schiller et al. 1992; Basch et al. 1994), we are interested in the more nuanced understanding possible through ethnographic research. We agree with John Lie (1995: 305) that "The immigration experience can no longer be safely ensconced in macroscopic generalizations," and that "distinct voices" of "class, gender, and ethnicity" need to be heard. This requires bringing active migrants and their narratives back in to our analyses, and considering that, even within households, different people may have different, and potentially contradictory, interests and goals. That is what this paper sets out to do. It is based on an extensive ethnographic study of a "transnational community:" the Garifuna ethnic minority in their native Belize and the Garifuna diasporic community in Los Angeles (Miller [Matthei] 1993). One author did field research at both the "sending" and "receiving" ends of this migration (although it turns out that these labels are much too simplistic). She spent three months in a mid-sized town in Belize which serves as a staging point for Garifuna migration, living with a Garifuna family and doing ethnographic work, and two years as a participant observer in the expatriate Garifuna community in South Central Los Angeles. A central theme of this research was the way the political economy of "global restructuring" and the sociohistorical forces in both Belize and Los Angeles promoted the distinctive pattern of labor migration that occurred. This is consistent with Portes' (1996) claim that "the emergence of (transnational) communities is tied to the logic of capitalism itself." But our primary thrust in this paper—as well as in a previous paper focussed on the gendered nature of Garifuna migration to Los Angeles (Matthei and Smith 1996)—is on the "micro" level of the personal experiences and actions of the Garifuna themselves, people actively building new lives for themselves in the face of changing global macrostructural circumstances. While this paper is also about "transnational communities/identities" here the central focus will be on how the "multistranded" personal networks of women migrants is changing Garifuna families and parenting, and making major impacts on communities back "home" in Belize.

The Historical-Structural Context of Garifuna Migration

The Garifuna are essentially a product of European colonial expansion into the Caribbean. They emerged as a distinct ethnic group during the eighteenth century after African slaves, being transported to Caribbean sugar plantations, escaped a ship wreck in 1635, and took up residence with the indigenous Carib Indians on the island of St. Vincent (Taylor 1951). After repeated skirmishes with the island's British colonizers during the 1700s, these "Black Caribs"—as the British called them—were finally exiled to Roatan Island in the Bay of Honduras in 1797. By 1800 they began to migrate to the Central American mainland where they established settlements based on horticulture and fishing along the Central American coast from present-day Nicaragua to Belize. For a short time, Garifuna villages remained relatively autonomous and economically self-sufficient. But this changed as colonial demands for labor grew with the declining availability of slaves in the early 19th century. The burgeoning forestry industry in Belize and the surrounding area was chronically short of workers, and the British increasingly turned to Garifuna men to supplement the limited supply of slave laborers (Grant 1976; Bolland 1977). Thus began a long history of Garifuna dependence on male labor migration (see Gonzalez 1969). Although men were eventually drawn into the labor markets of Central America's "banana republics," until the 1940s, their migration was by and large temporary. During off-seasons, most returned to their home communities, where women continued to carry out traditional horticultural activities. However, men's migration patterns changed during World War II. The U.S. Labor Department recruited large numbers of Garifuna men to take jobs vacated by U.S. workers serving in the armed forces. After the war ended about half of these men stayed (Vernon 1990), paving the way for a sustained flow of Belizean Garifuna to the United States. Today, there are small Garifuna communities in African American neighborhoods in cities throughout the United States, including New York, Chicago, Houston, and Los Angeles (Gonzalez 1979; Rodriguez 1987). The Belizean government does not compile emigration statistics, but a report in 1990 on government-operated Radio Belize estimated that on average 1400-1600 Belizeans have migrated to the United States each year for the past four decades, "more than half of them illegally." Unofficial estimates indicate that about 40,000-60,000 Belizeans currently live in the United States (EIU 1993; Vernon 1990). If reasonably accurate, these figures indicate that the number of Belizeans in the United States may represent nearly 30 percent of Belize's current population of 212,000. Although Belizean Creoles (descendants of Belize's slave population) make up the largest proportion of the immigrant population, the Garifuna are also well-represented. Most estimates indicate that the Garifuna (who represent only 6 percent of Belize's population) comprise about 25 percent of the total documented and undocumented migration to the United States (Vernon 1990; Everitt 1984). Based on these estimates, we believe the current population of Belizean Garifuna in the United States is about 10 to 15 thousand (cf. Gonzalez 1979; Everitt 1984; Rodriguez 1987). According to a U.S. consular official in Belize City, the Garifuna are the most "visa-wise" ethnic group in the country (personal communication 1990).

Women's Incorporation into International Labor Migration

Throughout most of the colonial era in Belize, Garifuna women's opportunities were sharply limited by an economic system which imposed a rigid division of labor by sex. As they did elsewhere, British colonizers (and later employers in the United States) cheapened their labor costs by recruiting and employing only men. Hence, while their mates spent extended periods working away from home, women continued to engage in traditional subsistence production—activities which served to reproduce laborers for capitalist enterprises and provide for their maintenance during periods of unemployment, illness, and retirement (cf., Meillasoux 1972, 1981; Portes and Walton 1981). As export agriculture began to displace subsistence farming in Belize, a small number of women found seasonal work in Belize's citrus and banana industries. But in recent decades this employment option has largely disappeared as employers in those industries have shown a marked preference for immigrant workers from Guatemala, Honduras, and El Salvador (Moberg 1996). Therefore, most Garifuna women must look to the informal sector to generate household income. During the 1960s, a shift in Garifuna migration patterns began to emerge as economic restructuring in the United States created a substantial demand for female labor in the rapidly expanding low-wage service sector (Sassen 1988). Garifuna women—with and without legal documents—wasted little time in joining their male counterparts to take advantage of the employment opportunities now available to them also (Ashcraft 1973). By 1968, females accounted for 58 percent of legal immigration from Belize, and they have consistently represented more than 50 percent of the legal flow since that time (Immigration and Naturalization Service 1968; Vernon 1990). Recent studies addressing female participation in labor migration frequently focus on young, single women "sent" by their families to work as household domestics or in multinational factories in various locales around the world (e.g., Thadani and Todaro 1984; Wolf 1992). Though single women do constitute a significant proportion of contemporary migration flows, mothers—both married and unmarried—also migrate (e.g., Chavez 1992; Hondagneu-Sotelo 1994). Moreover, the migration of women with children requires organizational strategies and produces consequences not found in the movement of single women nor in male-only migrations. In the following sections, therefore, we focus on the strategies Garifuna women employ to effect their own migrations and on some of the unintended consequences for sending communities in Belize of an emerging pattern in which both parents may leave to pursue employment abroad.

Economic Restructuring and the Dilemmas of Migrant Parents

Garifuna in Los Angeles describe the 1960s and the early 1970s as a boom period for immigrants of both sexes seeking work in the city. Not only were jobs plentiful, but employers were relatively unconcerned about the immigration status of prospective employees.[3] Thus, both men and women were able to find relatively high-paying, stable work shortly after their arrival in Los Angeles (and in some cases U.S. employment was pre-arranged before they even left Belize). By the late 1970s, however, economic restructuring was well on its way to transforming the Los Angeles labor market. Between 1978 and 1982, the Los Angeles metropolitan area lost some 75,000 mostly unionized, relatively high-wage manufacturing jobs to plant closures and indefinite layoffs (Soja 1987: 182). The deindustrialization of nearby cities where major employers including General Motors, Goodyear, Firestone, and Bethlehem Steel closed their operations devastated the South-central area, and the "median family income fell by the late 1970s to $5,900, $2,500 below the city median for Blacks" (Silverstein and Brooks 1991). Having grown accustomed to finding reasonably high-wage, blue-collar jobs, Garifuna men found it difficult to adapt to the transformed labor market in Los Angeles, while women continue to experience strong demand for their labor, even though many are employed in very low-wage domestic services and un-skilled nursing jobs. Despite the continuing market for female immigrant workers, by the mid-1980s economic conditions in South Central Los Angeles were worse than they were at the time of the Watts riots in 1965 (Soja 1987). A substantial change in the demographic make up of the South Central area also occurred between the 1970s and 1990. In 1970, when many Garifuna im-migrants settled in the area, the population of South Central Los Angeles was 79 percent black (Palacio 1982:15). By the 1980s, however, the city's rapidly growing population of Mexican and Central American immigrants began expanding into the area. At the same time, middle-class blacks began to move out. According to the 1990 census, South Los Angeles (which includes the South Central area) is currently 49 percent black, 44.8 percent Latino,

3.6 percent Anglo, and 1.8 percent Asian or Pacific Islander (Silverstein and Brooks 1991). In 1990, a Garifuna woman who has lived in South Central Los Angeles since the early 1960s described the changes in her neighborhood:

> It was predominantly white when we first bought here. Then the Mexican moved in and the black moved in and the white people move out—only three of them around here now. They all move out. ...Orientals [sic] own most of the businesses now. But up and down the street there are more Mexicans than there are blacks now.

As economic conditions in South Central Los Angeles worsened over the years, and as its neighborhoods underwent rapid demographic change, crime rates—especially those associated with gang violence and drugs—soared. In 1987, the Los Angeles Police Department's 77th Division, which oversees much of the area in which the Garifuna are concentrated, reported 155 homicides, "a per capita murder rate higher even than Washington, D.C., the nation's newly proclaimed murder capital" (Morrison 1989: 1). In 1990, the local NBC affiliate had begun to refer to the South-Central area as the "land of the drive-by shooting." In 1992, Los Angeles recorded 800 gang-related homicides (Hunzeker 1993). Given the dismal economic situation, and the proliferation of crime in their neighborhoods, few Garifuna residents were surprised when riots erupted in the spring of 1992.[4] Interviews with Garifuna men and women in Los Angeles often revealed fear and frustration with the worsening conditions in their neighborhoods. In an open-ended survey question, for example, which asked what respondents disliked most about living in Los Angeles, 34 of 51 individuals identified gangs, drugs, and drive-by shootings as major concerns. In informal interviews, they often spoke at length about their fears. The following excerpt from an interview with a woman in her fifties is representative:

> They [gang members] don't have no respect, that's why I'm afraid of walkin' up and down on the street. Because that's when the drive-by shootin'—when the gangs are out there—that's when the opposite ones—because in this area they are the Bloods, you see—and the Bloods shoot up where the Crips are, and the Crips come and shoot up where the Bloods are. There's certain colors you can't even wear. You can't wear red in this area because we're in the Bloods over here. I saw a Mexican guy

today with a bandana on his head, and I wanted to tell him so bad to take that red bandana off his head because they would kill him. I don't go out in the night. And I don't open the door. I don't open the door for *nobody* after dark—not even my own brother.

In another interview a woman recalled:

The year before last I have a roommate, and he was standin' close to one of the wall and a bullet came through. He was makin' tacos. He didn't eat no tacos that night! A man that time—a man was goin' to the store and he got shot when the bullet came through my wall. It was an innocent man goin' to the store, and he got shot.[5]

As the levels of violence intensified over the years Garifuna parents have become increasingly concerned about rearing children in South Central Los Angeles. Although some families have acquired the financial means to move their families out of the area, most have not. Even middle-class families often remain trapped because they purchased homes during the 1960s and 1970s. Most say that, even if they were able to find buyers for their houses, they cannot afford to purchase property elsewhere in Southern California. Hoping to reduce the influence of gangs and drugs in their children's lives, parents work diligently to limit their children's interactions with individuals outside the Garifuna community. Many parents who can afford the additional expense send their children to a Catholic school in nearby Compton which is operated by an order of nuns who also teach in Belize. Parents note that, in addition to providing the discipline lacking in public schools, some of the nuns speak Garifuna and encourage the students to learn the language. Several organizations also focus on the "preservation" of Garifuna culture, offering Garifuna history lessons and dance classes. A community-wide celebration each year seeks to foster transnational ethnic ties by featuring traditional and contemporary Garifuna music and dance, ethnic foods, and speeches by Garifuna dignitaries flown in for the occasion. The community even sponsors an annual Ms. Garifuna pageant, in which adolescent girls must display traditional dance and language skills, as well as their knowledge of Garifuna cultural history. An annual "Garifuna Career Day," which developed out of concern about increasing high school drop-out rates among Garifuna youth, includes a panel of speakers from the community who describe their own difficulties growing up in Los Angeles and the strategies they used to overcome them. The panelists offer advice about educational and career options, and encourage young people to seek skills that can be utilized in Belize as well as the United States. Despite these efforts, however, it is difficult to insulate children from the influences of drugs and gangs. As one young woman, who joined her parents in Los Angeles when she was eight, remarks:

> Up to today, my grandmother would say that the United States ruined us, because we had no focus once we came. Our parents were always working, which left us to do whatever the hell we wanted to do—including being a part of a gang, smoking marijuana, drinking. You name it we did it—at an early age at that.

The dilemmas of raising children in South Central Los Angeles are especially perplexing for female single-parents who lack technical skills and, as often as not, legal immigrant status:

> Some people they get these sleep-in jobs, you know, where they have to stay at the job. Well then the kids are home by themselves. They say they don't have any choice—they have to work. And because that's the only kinda work they could do, they do that. And the kids, once they are at least thirteen or fourteen, they're allowed to take care of themselves—maybe an adult will go check on them now and again. They're on their own. They really have access to go out and do what they want to do.

Although some parents do manage to juggle work and childcare, according to a local community leader, at least 10 Garifuna youths have been killed as a result of gang-related activity in recent years. Thus, many parents—but especially single mothers—opt to leave their children behind when they seek work in Los Angeles. Today, however, the social problems associated with migration and childcare needs are filtering back to Belize.

Child Fostering and Garifuna Migration

Child fostering is a long established cultural tradition among the Garifuna as it is throughout the Afro-Caribbean region (Clarke 1957; Sanford 1971; Soto 1987). For generations, Garifuna women in Belize have temporarily placed their children in the care of kin (usually maternal) in order to take advantage of the limited income-earning opportunities available to them. In an ethnography based on research in the 1940s, for example, Douglas Taylor noted "...if the father be away, the mother will not hesitate to accept employment a long way from home. She will shut up house, leave her children with her own mother or with a married sister, and go her way" (1951: 74). With this longstanding childcare system already in place, many Garifuna women were able, with minimal fuss, to join male counterparts already in the United States and take advantage of the relative abundance of employment opportunities opening for them there. The following excerpts from a letter received by Linda Matthei in 1990 is representative of the stories of unskilled, single mothers who leave their children with kin[6] in order to find work in Los Angeles. (The excerpts are reproduced here as they were written, though we have added punctuation marks and occasional spelling changes for the sake of clarity):

> I came to Los Angeles 1977 and live with my mother in New York. before I came to New York I had a hard time raising my kids[.] I have twelve kids[—]six boys and six girls[—]and it was very hard to raise them without a father[.] I used to work in a [citrus] farm. ...I get paid every two weeks and whenever I get paid I have to pay my bill for food. So I end up her[e] and when I get to New York I start work to get money to come over her[e] to Los Angeles. When I get her[e] I work to sent for my kids[,] but I like over here and I fix my kids papers and got ther green card.

Although this woman's family is unusually large, the critical role that fostering arrangements play in facilitating Garifuna women's migration is brought into sharp focus when one considers that in the southern districts of Belize where the Garifuna are concentrated up to 40 percent of households are headed by women (Ministry of Education 1984: 15). Moreover, since many Garifuna women have only limited skills and, as often as not, migrate without "proper" immigration papers, they often find that their opportunities in the United States are limited to domestic service in private homes. For women who find themselves doing "live-in" work in Los Angeles, the availability of childcare in Belize is critical. Mothers who seek to migrate rarely have difficulty finding a relative or friend to care for their children. With few employment opportunities available to them locally, non-migrant women in Belize seek every opportunity to forge strong ties to kin in the United States. Fostering the children of migrant kin not only ensures a regular flow of cash remittances, it also builds a network of potential support in the United States should they or a member of their household decide to migrate. Therefore, sisters and mothers of migrants often compete for the opportunity to provide child-care. As a woman in Belize explained, "Even a little job in the States can support two families"—one in the United States and another in Belize.

During the 1960s and 1970s, child fostering arrangements were typically temporary. Parents left their children in Belize for a year or two until they were well enough established to send for them, or until the children were old enough to attend school in the United States. However, as crime rates soared in Los Angeles over the past decade or so, more and more families began to extend their childrens' stay in Belize. In some cases, adolescents who have spent most of their lives in Los Angeles are returned to kin in Belize "under punishment" after they have become involved in gangs or drug usage in Los Angeles, or are arrested there. Still others are sent, not by parents, but by the United States government, deported after serving criminal sentences in the United States.

Transnationalism and Transformation in Belize

As we suggested in our introduction, the influence of U.S. culture is very strong in contemporary Belize. The institutionalization of labor migration to the United States has created a strong transnational orientation among Belizeans. Even tots play "goin' to States," a game which involves an imaginary journey to the United States and triumphant return with elaborate gifts for everyone. Not surprisingly, however, the "States orientation" in Belize is most apparent among teenagers and young adults—especially those with immigrant parents. An education official in one Garifuna community estimates that 80 percent of secondary school students plan to migrate to the United States—another says they all do. Some students, they say, intentionally fail exams in the misguided hope that their parents in the United States will become concerned and send for them to join them. Teachers say that it has become increasingly difficult to motivate students who are simply biding their time while they wait for an opportunity to leave Belize. "Right now," one lamented, "our schools are educating people for the United States." For decades remittances have formed a vital economic link between Garifuna migrants and their kin who remain in Belize. A local Garifuna community leader and a local social worker estimate that 80 percent of households in one Garifuna town receive some form of remittance (cash and/or material goods) from relatives and friends in the United States. Though a substantial portion of cash remittances provide basic economic support for elderly parents, and for dependent children left behind with local kin, the flow of remittances from "absentee parents" also has a down side according to local residents. In order to compensate in some measure for their extended absences, some migrant parents have begun to send their children larger sums of money along with expensive clothes and other consumer items. A local resident, himself a former U.S. migrant, provides his assessment of the disruptive influence of this recent trend:

> Now, some parents stop sendin' used clothes to their kids. They begin to send new clothes, expensive clothes. Now, if these are school children, they're goin' to the same school, we in the same class. Well here we are, your mother and father in the States, my mother and father in the States. You wearin' those things. Look at what I'm wearin'. That has its psychological effect. ...they don't feel happy, they look at it as neglect. Okay, so they hurriedly destroy [the used items], and they write their parents and they write their parents personal letters. And the next thing you know that the parents with this thing fresh in their minds they'll send new clothes, new outfits for a period of time, and stop. Then that create a new problem. Then, uh, this boy or this girl begin to feel something is not correct. Now if this girl is thirteen-fourteen she will decide to find her own clothes. Then, here comes a gradual build-up in prostitution. If it's a boy reaching that age ...he see that quick dollars are passin' from some other friend who is not goin' to school anymore by probably selling a few stick of weed for that man over there. Then he begins to think of start makin' his own money. Then that develops from sellin' it to usin' it, until that boy becomes worthless. ...It also happen to people [whose parents] do not go, who do not travel. These same children begin to see that other children are usin' expensive and good things.

Despite their growing concern, Garifuna officials see little like-lihood that they will be able to effect any real change locally. Because the national economy remains stagnant and many house-holds rely on remittances from the United States for basic survival needs, local residents are unwilling to turn down the opportunity to foster the children of migrant kin. Even when serious problems de-velop, they say, many foster families fail to inform the children's parents because they fear that the children will be taken from them and the flow of remittances will end. One might well assume that the foregoing discussion exaggerates the seriousness of a localized phenomenon. These are not, however, local issues confined to small pockets of Belize but national ones. Nor are the problems facing Belize limited to an increase in so-called "victimless crimes" like drug use and teenage prostitution. In fact, crime re-ports from Belize have begun to take on an eerie resemblance to those coming out of Los Angeles as gangs like the notorious "Crips" and "Bloods" emerge as an ominous by-product of Belize's transnational ties to the United States. The two reports from 1992 at the beginning of this paper, which included consid-erations by the national parliament, highlight the gravity of the problem in this small country. If anything, the problems appear to continue to build as the following news report suggests:

> Following months of increased gang violence in Belize City, including three gang-related murders in one eight-day period in May, police in June began "Operation Gang Bang" in an effort to take back city streets. They detained and then released some two hundred alleged gang members (Belize First 1995).

Indeed, in 1995, the transnationalization of the Crips and Bloods and their spread to Belize was brought to the attention of readers of the *Los Angeles Times* by California State Assemblyman Tom Hayden, in a column titled "L.A.'s Third World Export: Gangs." Unlike the reports emanating from Belize, Hayden's explicitly links the phenomenon to the United States demand for low-wage, immigrant labor, and he is clearly of the opinion that the United States has gotten the better end of the exchange:

> They [Belizeans] work mostly at sub-minimum wages. Many are illegal; others came here illegally and received amnesty. ...While Belize exports

people to Los Angeles, it imports Bloods and Crips. Some Belizeans become gang members in Los Angeles, then return home in their new colors. They become a new "family" option for many street youth whose parents have gone to Southern California. Some act as couriers for cocaine flown from Colombia to Los Angeles. Crack cocaine addiction is prevalent for the first time. Guns are shipped from Los Angeles to the streets of Belize City. Shootouts and funerals follow, unprecedented in Belizean history.

The stark reality is that gang graffiti, like that splashed across the concrete walls, signs, and underpasses of Southern California freeways, has also become commonplace in Belize. Even in small towns and villages far removed Belize City (which by the way is a city of only some 60,000) spray paint announces the presence of Crips and Bloods.

Solutions Through Transnational Community?

Portes' (1996) view of transnational communities stresses the potentially progressive effects that migrants living and working in prosperous countries like the United States can have for underdeveloped sending communities. For example, he describes a project to install a new water system in a rural community in Mexico that is funded, organized, and supervised by former village residents on weekends, who return to their jobs in New York City on Mondays. Transnational community, in this vision, becomes a possible instrument of social transformation. Portes finds this very encouraging because "the phenomenon is fueled by the dynamics of globalization itself...and offers a broader field for popular initiatives than alternative social structures" (1996) But what does this sanguine perspective offer for our analysis of the Garifuna case?

In Los Angeles, Garifuna immigrants often wistfully recall the simple, bucolic lives they left behind in Belize. "In Belize," one man repeatedly insists, "you can send a four-year-old to the store with a 20-dollar bill and she'll come back with the groceries and the correct change. Here you can't step outside your door without getting robbed or shot at." Most immigrants, however, are painfully aware that the serene existence they recall—and would like to return to someday—no longer exists. They are frequently reminded by visiting dignitaries that the problems facing their former communities are their problems also, and that they must share in efforts to resolve them. In 1990, the mayor of Dangriga, the largest Garifuna settlement in Belize, spoke to a large crowd celebrating the Fourth of July in Los Angeles. In her speech, the mayor asked those assembled for "a recommitment to Dangriga" after pointedly reminding them that her town's social problems are not local ones but those of the transnational community:

> One serious factor posing a continuous threat to the stability of our fami-
> lies and our community is the great percentage of absentee parents. ...and
> our society is beginning to reap the bitter rewards....I'm certain that my
> comments will solicit [sic] some criticism, but I want to make it clear
> that I am only commenting on the reality of the situation. So many of
> our young children are growing up without parental guidance and without
> any social or cultural values.

> ...I am aware of the problems that confront parents who are forced to seek
> a better life here in the United States and are forced at times to leave their
> children behind. Given the circumstances of life for some parents in the
> United States, it is sometimes difficult for these children to be with their
> parents. My appeal to you my dear people is to communicate with your
> children—not through clothes and other material goods, which seemingly
> have become a replacement for our love for our children, but to write to
> them and let them understand that you are close to them in your hearts. It
> will not be the answer to their problems but they will understand that
> there is a mother or a father who means more than a brand new pair of
> Adidas, Levis, and a stereo system.

Although she may have expected a decidedly negative reaction, the mayor's speech was greeted with rousing applause. Garifuna immigrants—especially those who plan to return—are deeply aware of the "reality of the situation." Many have invested their savings in houses and businesses in Belize and make substantial contributions to development projects back home. They recognize and identify themselves as a truly "transnational community." As such they share a sense of commitment to their community, including those who still live at "home." In this sense they are not so different from those former Mexican peasants in New York City organizing to better their village of origin. But this case of "Belizean Boyz 'n the 'Hood"—in both South Central and Belize City—illustrates that, just as transnational networks based on migration can operate as a collective force *against* structural forces of economic underdevelopment in Third World sending communities, they can also be the circuits along which less benign information, organization and "identity" can be transmitted as well. Los Angeles-based gangs like the Bloods and Crips, which arguably are also intrinsically tied to the "the logic of capitalism," are bringing new problems to the Belizean state and society and even introducing a new dynamic into the cultural practices of Garifuna families and households (both at "home" and "abroad"). The Garifuna immigrant community's efforts to contribute to the welfare of the Belizean homeland, ironically, will have to come to grips with a pernicious process that their migration to the United States inadvertently triggered. The "transnational" activities of Belizean youth provided with the "opportunity" to internationalize the operations of L.A. gangs presents formidable social costs to Garifuna families and the "sending" society. While the upstanding community members at the Independence Day celebration in Los Angeles may earnestly desire to make "a recommitment to Dangriga," they also realize that their efforts may only have a palliative effect. For they recognize that as long as uneven development in the world-system forces them to seek employment abroad, the problems facing Belizean families and society are likely to become even further entrenched. Until that time, the power of transnational gangs may outweigh the power of transnational community, and the transnational identities that emerge may include those of the Crips and Bloods.

Notes

1. Linda Miller Matthei gratefully acknowledges research support provided by a National Science Foundation dissertation grant (BNS-8918803) and by a Rockefeller Foundation Post-doctoral Fellowship at the Institute of Latin American Studies, University of Texas at Austin in 1992-93.
2. Belize is the most sparsely populated nation in Central America. Its current population is about 225,000 in an area slightly smaller than Massachusetts.
3. Although some early immigrants to Los Angeles found themselves in the midst of the Watts Riots, they seem to have had little impact on continuing migration from Belize. Despite the destruction of neighborhood stores and businesses in the South-central area, the job market for immigrant workers apparently remained relatively stable.

4. Although it is difficult to know if any Garifuna participated directly in the riots, several families lost their homes to the fires which swept their neighborhoods and those with whom Matthei spoke by phone during the unrest reported seeing numerous incidents of looting and violence. Despite the violence in Garifuna neighborhoods they seem to have had little impact on the continued flow of new migrants from Belize. Explaining why Belizean Garifuna continue to come to South Central L.A. despite the warnings of kin already there, a woman in Belize stated simply, "You have to compare hard here, to hard there."

5. Ironically, this interview was interrupted by a brief burst of gunfire outside. Matthei learned the next day that a young American girl had been shot during a drive-by shooting while celebrating her eighth birthday.

6. In this case, the children were fostered by the woman's sister.

References

Ashcraft, N. (1973). *Colonialism and Underdevelopment: Processes of Political Economic Change in British Honduras*. New York: Teacher's College Press, Columbia University.

Glick Schiller, Nina, Linda Basch, and Cristina Szanton Blanc. (1994). *Nations Unbound: Transnational Projects, Postcolonial Predicaments and the Deterritorialized Nation-State*. New York: Gordon and Breach Publishers.

Bolland, O. N. (1977). *The Formation of a Colonial Society: Belize, from Conquest to Crown Colony*. Baltimore: Johns Hopkins University Press.

Caribbean Insight (1992). "New Law Proposed to Combat Crime." *Caribbean Insight* 15: 7.

Central Statistical Office (1990). *Abstract of Statistics.* .Belmopan, Belize: Central Statistical Office.

Clarke, E. (1957). *My Mother Who Fathered Me: A Study of the Family in Three Selected Communities in Jamaica*. London: Allen and Unwin.

Chavez, Leo R. (1992). *Shadowed Lives: Undocumented Immigrants in American Society*. Fort Worth: Harcourt Brace Jovanovich College Publishers.

Economist Intelligence Unit (1992). *Belize, Bahamas, Bermuda Country Profile*. London: The Economist Intelligence Unit.

Everitt, J. (1984). "The Recent Migrations of Belize, Central America." *International Migration Review* 8: 2: 319-325.

Georges, Eugenia. (1990) *International Migration Review*. New York: Columbia University Press.

Glick Schiller, Nina, Linda Basch & Cristina Szanton Blanc (eds.). (1992). *Towards a Transnational Perspective on Migration: Race, Class, Ethnicity and Nationalism Reconsidered*. New York: New York Academy of Sciences.

Gonzalez, N. (1969). *Black Carib Household Structure*. Seattle: University of Washington Press.

———. (1979). Garifuna Settlement in New York: A New Frontier. *International Migration Review* 13: 2 :204-214.

Grant, C. (1976). *The Making of Modern Belize: Politics, Society and British Colonialism in Central America*. Cambridge: Cambridge University Press.

Hayden, T. (1995). "L.A.'s Third World Export: Gangs." *Los Angeles Times*, January 30.

Hondagneu-Sotelo, Pierrette. (1994) *Gendered Transitions: Mexican Experiences of Immigration.* Berkeley: University of California Press.

Hunzeker, D. (1993) "Ganging Up Against Violence." *State Legislatures* (May): 28-31.

Immigration and Naturalizatio Service (1968). *Annual Report, 1968.* Washington, D.C.: Department of Justice.

Lie, J. (1995). "From International Migration to Transnational Diaspora." *Contemporary Sociology* 24: 4: 303-306.

Matthei, Linda Miller, and David A. Smith (1996). "Women, Households and Transnational Migration Networks: The Garifuna and Global Economic Restructuring." In *Latin America in the World-Economy.* Westport, CN: Greenwood Press.

Meillasoux, C. (1981). *Maidens, Meal, and Money: Capitalism and the Domestic Economy.* Cambridge: Cambridge University Press.

————. (1972). From Reproduction to Production. *Economy and Society* 1: 93-105.

Ministry of Education (1984). *Belize Today: A Society in Transformationa.* Belmopan, Belize: Sunshine Books, Ltd.

Moberg, M. (1996). "Myths That Divide: Immigrant Labor and Class Segmentation in the Belizean Banana Industry." *American Ethnologist* 23: 2: 311-330.

Morrison, P. (1989). "In the 77th It's Life at Mach 2: City's Danger Zone." *Los Angeles Times.* May 14.

Portes, Alejandro. (1996). "Global Villagers: The Rise of Transnational Communities." *The American Prospect* 2: 74-77.

Portes, Alejandro and John Walton. (1981). *Labor, Class, and the International System.* Orlando, FL.: Academic Press.

Rodriguez, Nestor. (1987). "Undocumented Central Americans in Houston: Diverse Populations." *International Migration Review,* 21: 1: 4-26."

Sanford, M. (1971). Disruption of the Mother-Child Relationship in Conjunction with Matrifocality: A Study of Child-Keeping among the Carib and Creoles of British Honduras." Unpublished Ph.D. dissertation. Catholic University of America.

Sassen, Saskia. (1988). *The Mobility of Capital and Labor: A Study in International Investment and Labor Flow.* Cambridge: Cambridge University Press.

Silverstein, S., and N. Rivera Brooks. (1991). South Los Angeles Shoppers Need Stores. *Los Angeles Times.* November 24.

Soja, Edward. (1987). "Economic Restructuring and the Internationalization of the Los Angeles Region." In Michael Peter Smith and Joe R. Feagin, *The Capitalist City: Global Restructuring and Community Politic.* New York: Basil Blackwell. Pp. 178-198.

Soto, I. M. (1987). West Indian Child Fostering: Its Role in Migrant Exchanges. In *Caribbean Life in New York City: Sociocultural Dimension.* New York: Center for Migration Studies, Inc. Pp. 131-149.

Taylor, D. (1951). *The Black Carib of British Honduras.* New York: Wenner-Gren Foundation.

Thadani, V. and M. Todaro. (1984). "Female Migration: A Conceptual Framework." In *Women in the Cities of Asia: Migration and Urban Adaptation.* Boulder, CO: Westview Press. Pp. 36-59.

Vernon, D. (1990). "Belizean Exodus to the United States: For Better of For Worse." In *SPEAR Reports 4: Second Annual Studies on Belize Conference.* Belize City: SPEAR. Pp. 6-28.

Wolf, Diane. (1992). *Factory Daughters: Gender, Household Dynamics, and Rural Industrialization in Java.* University of California Press.

10

Forged Transnationality and Oppositional Cosmopolitanism[1]

Louisa Schein

A couple years ago I found myself in an unexpected position. As an anthropologist working with the Miao in China and with Hmong refugees from Laos, I had suddenly landed in the role of transnational marriage broker. Certain Hmong men, troubled by the unnerving Americanization of "their" women had begun to seek more "traditional" marriage partners among their putative co-ethnics in the romantic Chinese homeland. These men—who were steeped in dreamlike memories of a Laos they felt they had lost due to the United States' withdrawal from the anti-Communist effort they had fought passionately as their own—were turning now to an imagined China their ancestors had left many generations before. It was a China that, on the one hand, they abhorred, as the once-Imperial now-Communist oppressor of their people. But it was nevertheless this same China that purportedly housed the most archaic pockets of their tradition left on earth. This tradition could be had through an importing technique akin to the mail-ordering of brides from Asia by nostalgic "first world" men that has been interrogated elsewhere (Tolentino 1996, Villepando 1989, Wilson 1988). Wielding their Americanness, Hmong men could get culture back by playing on the desires of Miao women within China, desires for a liberation that their future husbands would both proffer and deny.

But it was not Hmong men who were asking me to be their agent. Rather, Miao women, during and after a trip I made to China in 1993, hoped that I would make introductions and convey photographs.[2] Moreover, if communication was initiated, language issues might arise. Some of the Miao dialects were so unintelligible with Hmong as to make telephone conversation nearly impossible. Beyond that, Miao knew Chinese and Hmong knew English, but that meant that courtship letters had to be painstakingly composed through interpreters. A final recourse was the American anthropologist, who could translate faxes and phone calls, paving the way for more intimate communications and expediting the crafting of an ethnic bond into a transnational marital union.

I want to begin my reflections on this and related stories yet to be told by exploring the potential space opened by Bruce Robbins in an essay on "Comparative Cosmopolitanisms" (1993). Robbins travels through critiques of multiculturalism, the problematic of situatedness, the commentary on global culture, through Mohanty, Spivak, Said and especially Clifford (and this is not a complete list), to arrive at a revision to our recoil from the notion of cosmopolitanism as nothing but a circumscribed site of privilege from which "free-floating intellectuals" reproduce their elitism through assertions of universality. The antidote for the queasiness of totalizing privilege, Robbins argues, cannot be as simple as valorizing the particularity of the local. Instead, Robbins builds on Clifford's notion of travelling cultures, on the latter's assertion that "the representational challenge is...the portrayal and understanding of local/global historical encounters, co-productions, dominations and resistances" (Clifford 1992: 101). The space Robbins makes is for cosmopolitanism to be more widely distributed, to be non-elite, situated and yet somehow worldly. "Instead of renouncing cosmopolitanism as a false universal, one can embrace it as an impulse to knowledge that is shared with others, a striving to transcend partiality that is itself partial, but no more so than the similar cognitive strivings of many diverse peoples" (1993: 194). Variant cosmopolitanisms could be located, then, among those who have long constituted elite cosmopolitanism's others: among migrant workers, for instance, or among indigenous intermediaries that intervene in the construction of ethnographies, or among diasporic groups imaginatively travelling toward "home." "The world's particulars" Robbins proposes, "can now be recoded, in part at least, as the world's 'discrepant cosmopolitanisms' (1993: 194).

From this point of departure I want to wander further, to consider the discrepancies between cosmopolitanisms as vital interstices from which oppositionality could be enunciated. I want to push beyond the recognition that cosmopolitanisms will vary predictably according to the degree to which they emerge, on the one hand, from power and privilege—as in the case of, say, tourists or mobile capitalisms—or, on the other hand, from constraint or economic disadvantage—as in the case of, say, refugees or guest workers. Cosmopolitanisms, in their multiple incarnations, ought instead to be thought of as processual and as *potentially* renegotiating precisely that nexus of privilege and constraint that conditions them. This is, obviously, an optimistic scenario, but one which, given what I will present below, may deserve to be examined.

In a recent essay, community studies specialist Michael Peter Smith affirmed the importance of looking at the kind of multilocal grass roots political activism that takes place in transnational contexts. This is a kind of activism that reflects what he calls the "polyfocality" (1994: 28) of human agents who reveal themselves to be capable of "thinking and acting simultaneously at multiple scales" (1994: 25)—particularly those of the sub-national and the supra-national. Translocal activism, Smith holds, not only evades state structures, but may in fact erode their sovereignty (1994: 31). Critical to this destabilization is the work of fashioning identities that accompanies or propels social movements:

> The reprocessing of identity by those who once saw their lives as more or less predictably constrained by the givenness of established orders may produce new emancipatory social movements with a high degree of political efficacy (Smith 1994: 31).

Smith's comments are provocative, especially for formulating transnational research agendas, but I would suggest that as anthropologists we may want to cast our nets considerably wider than the focus on social movements and overt activism would entail. I suspect that ethnographies attentive to multilocal linkages will turn up a great deal of subterranean activity which may not name itself as activism, may not focus around oppositionality, but may in fact have the *effect* of subverting the constraints of the territorially based state. As ethnographers, then, and interpreters of ethnographic data, let us attend not only to resistance *per se* but to oppositionality as an effect of translocal practices—especially those practices concerned with identity production.

Attending to cosmopolitanisms' effects, then, raises a number of questions at different levels. Specifically, how might the active forging of transnationality, to which diasporas have lately given rise, unsettle the logic of the nation-state and of superpower politics? Must the identity politics of such transnational moves inevitably devolve into re-invented particularisms, no matter how globalized? Is it conceivable that they could be anything other than complicit with and structured by global capitalism? When translocal identities defy particular states, how likely are they to instead be complicit with global capitalism?[3] And, finally, should the voluntary union of a Miao woman from China and a Hmong refugee man in the United States (through the less than voluntary brokerage of an American feminist anthropologist) be read as some form of critique, or only as the latest incarnation of a nostalgia-driven practice of raiding the "third world?"[4]

This essay will entertain these and other questions through looking ethnographically at what I call "identity exchanges" between Hmong and Miao across the Pacific. I intend my use of "ethnographic" to be provocative, since the character of this kind of research is necessarily divergent from a conventional sense of ethnography. Because it is siteless, and lacks any fixed duration, I have cast it as "itinerant." I will expand upon this issue of itinerant ethnography further after a brief introduction to Hmong-Miao transnationality. I will then explore Hmong refugee production of homeland videos along with an array of other cultural practices out of which identity is being forged along with the reciprocal interests that U.S. Hmong and Chinese Miao bring to their encounter. Finally, I will contextualize such interests in terms of the respective state constraints which may engender such maneuverings and explore the latter's significance for the notion of the postnational. Throughout, I will enact my own polyfocality, shifting rapidly between the perspectives of the minority and the state, and those of China and the United States, in order to demonstrate how densely articulated these positionings are.

Cultural Production and the Forging of Transnationality

The ethnic bond that Hmong and Miao agents have been avidly kindling in recent years is being forged virtually "from scratch." The cumbersome umbrella term "Miao," which became naturalized as a official category of ethnic agency in China's Maoist decades, refers to a number of disparate groups totalling 7.5 million people, speaking three mutually unintelligible dialects and scattered over seven provinces in southwest China. One to two centuries ago, several hundred thousand of these people migrated out of China into Vietnam, Laos, and Thailand after conflicts with the Qing state. These are the people that, by Southeast Asian and Western convention, are referred to as the Hmong. This migration took place enough generations ago that direct kinship ties and living memories of the Miao in China have been forgotten. What has not been forgotten is that China represents the homeland.

Several generations of Hmong migrants to Southeast Asia have assiduously kept the memories of China alive through folklore and oral history. In funerals, for instance, when a Hmong ritualist anywhere in the world guides the soul of a deceased person back to a place where it can be at rest, the ultimate destination is a mythologized China, shrouded in authenticity and the aura of origins. Those Hmong who left their subsistence agrarian lives in Laos to resettle in American cities long not only for the land they inhabited most recently. Like other refugees, their longing for the land of earliest origins has become hyper-acute as a consequence of what they now remember as an involuntary ejection from the peaceful, independent, pastoral lives they once led. The obsession with loss has inspired a tremendously productive array of cultural practices, many of which are directly concerned with recovering China. Hmong cultural producers have thrown themselves into reinventing both their homeland and their ancestors, unflinchingly creating ties of putative kinship out of the vacuum that was centuries of isolation. At the same time, the political and economic ramifications of this recuperative project are not lost upon them. Their practices constitute what Stuart Hall has so aptly called "identity as a 'production'" (1989: 68). The artifact that emerges from this identity production is a multivalent and potent transnationality.

What are the strategies through which Hmong refugees are crafting this transnationality? The players in this project are not the "transmigrants" that Basch et al (1994) have described, nor exemplars of the "flexible citizenship" identified by Ong (1994). Firmly based in territorial sites, Hmong-Miao identity production is heavily conditioned by the U.S.-China disparity. Periodic travel, as well as the movement of objects, images, and most recently brides, comprise the ground on which identity elaborations are being constructed. A general notion of fraternity as well as more particularized bonds of fictive kinship and marriage alliance are the idioms out of which a sense of mutual obligation is produced—as discussed further below. What does it mean to do research on a vagrant identity-in-production? Because of the mobility of the cultural producers and their products, my research on this process has of necessity been multi-sited and episodic. Indeed, to talk about "sites" seems not the point since there is no *place* one can go to watch this process unfold. Often, too, as in the case of the fax above, the encounter with "data" has been unplanned or incidental. This itinerant ethnography compels me to chase cultural products and events around the globe, and often to settle for their discursive traces in anecdote or written account. The story is assembled piecemeal, then, and on its own schedule. I must be consigned to stay home and answer the phone, or to collect representational objects and second-hand accounts of events. Sometimes, I travel great distances to do participant observation at international events as far-flung as California, Minnesota, or Hunan. I want to make a case for these nomad-like methods, not as second order or secondary, but as the legitimate primary sources for a research that works out of whichever margins its subjects are working within. These margins are akin to those which Anna Tsing (1994) has theorized as significant sites for new forms of cultural analysis, but unlike Tsing's, these margins are not situated only in what she calls "out-of-the-way places" (1994: 284).

What have been the consequences, then, for the once-idealized detachment of the researcher when she works in these shifting venues? In addition to itinerancy, my privilege has been called upon, as my resources and mobility have been targeted as vehicles for transpacific identity exchanges. Over fourteen years of research, I have been a porter, a translator, a keynote speaker, a networker, a broker. I have been a transmitter of messages, of

precious objects, of texts. I have been the link through which many
a transnational relationship has been inaugurated. Throughout, my
partisanship to Hmong-Miao unification has gone unquestioned.
How else could I better deconstruct my ethnographic authoriality
than to let myself be thus employed as a conduit for the agency of
the other? How contradictory, then, that I should embark on writing about it, as I am doing here.

Video Hegemony

One of the chief means by which the Miao of the Chinese
homeland are being recovered by Hmong in the West is the video
image.[5] Some Hmong businessmen who have saved money in
other enterprises have invested in video cameras and, upon
attainment of a U.S. passport, have jetted off to China as tourists in
search of roots. Touching down on homeland soil, their cameras
play lovingly over every detail: the curve of the mountains, the
costume of the young women, a toast of liquor from their hosts, a
villager's song. Shepherd children head up the mountainsides
straddling water buffaloes...women beat the filth out of clothing at
sparkling streams...families squat around a communal hot pot of
bubbling pork, bak choy, and chilies. Thick with nostalgia, this
type of video image is most marketable to the Hmong-American
elderly, who have lost the strength to travel themselves, but retain
an inviolable sanctuary in their memories for the pastoral lives
they lost.[6]

Pristine visions of their Miao co-ethnics are not the only images
they bring back, however. Some would-be documentarians never
make it to Miao villages since they travel under official tourist statuses. Instead, they turn their cameras onto China itself—the figure,
simultaneously, of the historically oppressive other, but at the same
time of an ancient, originary power with which to affiliate. Scenes
of the Great Wall, of city streets, of staged ethnic performances, of
the tour-buses themselves, fill these taped narratives of the travel
experience. Such visual musings seem to intimate a subtextual
wondering: "What would it have been like if we had never left?"
Here the "we" is distilled into an historical agent, the one who
took the giant step out of China which eventuated in their exile to

the West. The videos, then, simulate a traveling backward in time, a retracing of migratory paths—hence the interest in travel narratives themselves as subject matter.

Faye Ginsburg has proposed to look at indigenous, or more generally Fourth World, media production practices such as these as positive trends in the context of a global economy of representation that still leaves Fourth World peoples relatively mute:

> ...indigenous media offers a possible means—social, cultural and political—for reproducing and transforming cultural identity among people who have experienced massive political, geographic, and economic disruption. The capabilities of media to transcend boundaries of time, space, and even language are being used effectively to mediate, literally, historically produced social ruptures and to help construct identities that link past and present in ways appropriate to contemporary conditions (Ginsburg 1991: 94).

From this perspective, the video cassette, and its tremendous portability is a formidable medium for ethnic learning across great spatial divides. Produced in Hmong language, exclusively targeted for intra-ethnic consumption, the China tapes constitute means for the simulated reduction of the cultural distance engendered by history. The tapes circulate widely in the West and, for Hmong that lack the resources to travel themselves, they function as a salve to the wounds of their own war-induced dislocation. Voraciously consumed, they offer the next best thing to being in the homeland.

But there is more to be read in the manufacture of these cultural products. In most cases, their producers are not merely disinterested disseminators of cultural messages. They are entrepreneurs who have hit upon a means to derive profit from the relative disadvantage of their co-ethnics. They often have their own video companies—I know of at least 20 in the United States—with names such as Mong Enterprises Home Video (Minneapolis), S.T. Universal Video (Stockton), Southeast Asia Video Production (Chicago) and Hmong Traditional Video Cassette of China and U.S.A. (Minneapolis). In addition to China documentaries, these companies also produce a range of genres—love dramas, war and martial arts stories, music videos of Hmong bands—all intended for Hmong consumption. Their products, including the China tapes, are packaged slickly in illustrated, shrink-wrapped boxes with copyright warnings printed on the outside and repeated along with the credits on the leaders to the videos. The cultural material therein is transformed into the intellectual property of the video producers. Not for random copying, they are for sale only. They are distributed by mail order and at large-scale ethnic events such as the Hmong New Year fair in Fresno, California, where stall after stall of small vendors offers official copies of these tapes for $30.00 a piece. For the majority of less affluent Hmong refugees whose dreams may be limited to earning minimum wage, the homeland can be vicariously had, but only for a dear price.

This marketing of origins is also significant in terms of the relation it establishes between elite Hmong travelers and their land-locked objects of ethnic recuperation in China whose own prospects for travel are virtually non-existent. It is the Miao peasants in the southwest China highlands who are the source of the greatest fascination for the nostalgic eyes of Western Hmong refugees. For centuries, exoticizing dominant Han representations derogated the Miao as figures of wildness at the fringes of the Chinese empire. Then, in the Maoist and post-Mao decades their cultures were promoted and celebrated, but according to a pernicious logic that blithely conflated their essentialized "tradition" with the stigma of backwardness. From the perspective of Miao peasants, then, while the fascinated gaze of their own co-ethnics is undoubtedly far more welcome than that of a contemptuous majority other, it nonetheless preserves the asymmetry of the gaze—an asymmetry rooted in differential economic conditions. For Hmong-Americans, Miao co-ethnics are largely a leisure activity, spicing up their idle hours with spectoral entertainment while Miao peasants, on the other hand, don't have VCRs in *their* living rooms on which to watch reciprocal images of their migrant "cousins" going about their first world lives.[7]

Elite Hmong cultural producers, then, cannot be immune from the kind of cautions which Rey Chow has posed for the category of "third world intellectuals" in the West. For Chow, these discourse-producers, among whom she classes herself, "need to unmask [themselves] through a scrupulous declaration of self-interest" (1993: 117), in which their championing of minority discourse is no less implicated in what Spivak called "empire-nation exchanges" (1990: 90) than that of Euro-American intellectuals who would presume to speak for the voiceless other. For Chow, the identification with the "third world" implicit in diasporic claims, harbors special dangers:

> Physical alienation...can mean precisely the intensification and aestheti-cization of the values of "minority" positions that had developed in the earlier struggles and that have now, in "third world" intellectuals' actual circumstances in the West, become defunct. The unself-reflexive sponsorship of "third world" culture...becomes a mask that conceals the hegemony of these intellectuals over those who are stuck at home.

> For "third world" intellectuals, the lures of diaspora consist in this masked hegemony...Their resort to "minority discourse,"...veils their own fatherhood over the "ethnics" at home even while it continues to legitimize them as "ethnics" and "minorities" in the West (1993: 118).

The production of Hmong video, then, is a powered practice that cannot circumvent some form of first world-third world asymmetry. The fact that its circulation is intentionally and almost entirely intra-ethnic, however, also positions it to be deployed otherwise in ways that potentially foil dominant appropriation. When contextualized in light of the practices of Miao cultural producers *within* China, its power appears more multi-vectoral. The unilateral character of Hmong production of the romanticized Miao other is tempered by the ways in which Miao are deploying *self*-representation. I will use the term "identity exchanges" to describe the multiple agencies that comprise this overall, yet, fragmented project out of which transnationality is being forged. After describing some other ways in which Hmong are consuming Miao images, I will turn to a consideration of respective imagings and the particular linkages they effect.

Identity Exchanges

Hmong refugees come to the encounter with homeland Miao with multiple intentionalities, the most salient of which are the quest for roots and the quest for profits. In addition to video and travel, however, there are additional ways that Hmong in the west have been consuming the Miao of China. Hmong ethnic style, for instance, has begun to bear the mark of the recent encounter with Chinese origins: at festivals and on special occasions on which Hmong refugees dress in ethnic garb, imported clothing from the Miao in China has become quite fashionable. Although the variation from their original Southeast Asian style of festival dress may be minimal, these imported styles are instantly recognizable to Western Hmong as prestige emblems because of their association with the homeland. The adoption of an obviously differing style of dress than that of one's own sub-group is a decisive announcement of pan-ethnic identity and of a disregard for intra-group distinctions. In the context of the Hmong becoming an American minority this dress practice could also be seen as symbolizing what Kobena Mercer called a "reconstitutive link" (1990: 253) with the homeland—one that asserted a pristine unity prior to segmentation by the political borders of modern states.

Beyond adopting imported dress, Hmong refugees are also importing actual Miao from China, especially as objects of entertainment at festivals. The craving to gaze upon a homeland native and putative bearer of one's most ancient traditions has inspired Hmong refugees to collectively put up funds for all-expenses-paid visits to the United States for Miao who have particular cultural resources to offer. At the 1993 Fresno Hmong New Year fair, for instance, three young women from China's Yunnan province were brought over. Bedecked in multi-layered embroidery and silver, weighted down with cumbersome headdresses, they were asked to appear on stage over and over again to sing the songs of courtship, hospitality, and folk history that U.S. Hmong longed to hear. As emblems of authenticity, they were paraded about in costume, drawing stares and whispers from Hmong fairgoers who imagined themselves to be witnessing their very past incarnate.

So far, the sketch I have drawn of U.S. Hmong consumption of their homeland co-ethnics is one that smacks of unilateral objectification. Celebratory as it is, it amounts to a production of the other as both other and constitutive of the self, but not as an autonomous agent. The Miao in China who encounter this appropriation, however, do not resent, it, but on the contrary, welcome it as a fraternal embrace. Their own cultural practices are highly complicit with Hmong representations of them as less "modern" and as bearers of tradition. In fact, they offer themselves, and their purported cultural expertise, almost as prestations in an ongoing exchange that they hope will have other consequences. What strategies are Miao pursuing in their nurturing of identifying bonds with diaspora communities?

The recent years of the post-Mao reform experiment have seen significant political and regional realignments for the people who inhabit China's remote interior. Reform policy since 1979 has consistently been one of what I have called "scripted difference" (Schein 1996) in which relative economic stasis is what has been prescribed for the subsistence producers of the hinterland while capital is relentlessly extracted for joint-venture investment in Special Economic Zones along the coast. Minority peasants were particularly set up for exclusion from the putative economic miracle that has transformed the coast and many urban sites; their economic marginalization was rationalized precisely by their imposed and valorized role as cultural conservators. With few resources for household enterprises, many families have resorted to sending their teenaged children to labor for wages in farms and factories in more rapidly developing regions. In addition to their omission from China's grand prosperity schemes based on enforced uneven development, minorities and others in the interior have seen decentralization, structural reform, the responsibility system, and other reforms smash the iron rice bowls on which many had come to depend. Concomitantly, reduced state intervention in affirmative-action type policies which had insured minority places in education, jobs and government has likewise resulted in their progressive exclusion and impoverishment.

Miao elites—intellectuals and party cadres—alarmed and angered at the acute consequences of recent reforms for their people, have turned to the embrace of identity politics as a vehicle for voicing their concerns.[8] Many of these elites who, during the Maoist and early post-Mao days were well on the way to a kind of intra-ethnic class formation in which they would have constituted the upper stratum, have done an about face and become passionate advocates for less advantaged members of their ethnic group.

Ironically (since many of them are still speaking from within the state), it is precisely the withdrawal of state presence from their lives, the decline in state planning, protection, and redistribution that they are protesting. The overarching objection is to the velocity with which their region and their people are being pushed to the ever more distant margins of Chinese economic life. Their requests, then, are addressed to the state, and are comprised of demands for greater inclusion in the national economy and what are perceived as its newfound riches, for representation in advocacy positions in the government, and for protected opportunities in education and employment. But these requests, in the assessment of Miao proponents, go largely unheeded.

The arrival of what appear to them as tremendously prosperous overseas Hmong has coincided with the formation of this increasingly organized and oppositional Miao elite. Hyper-aware of the way in which Chinese state policy has circumscribed their futures, Miao see an opening up of alternative possibilities embodied in these roots-seeking co-ethnics who hail from the first world. If Miao peasants represented an object of nostalgic longing for urban American Hmong, the latter likewise have come to represent a focal point for the desires of Chinese Miao who seek to circumvent the limits imposed upon them by a Chinese national plan that allocates to them only sacrifice and patient labor.

These Miao elites, then, have elaborated myriad ways of enmeshing the U.S. Hmong with them culturally and economically. Some are purchasing or manufacturing ethnic costumes to be shipped or carried overseas for sale through Hmong brokers for what constitute high returns by Chinese standards. Some organize international Miao studies conferences to which overseas Hmong are graciously invited as the most special of guests. Some record and send audio tapes or develop pen pals in order to foster long-term communication. Some have designed language or culture classes which they hope to market to Hmong travellers-turned-pupils who will stay in China long enough to embark on a course of study to learn where they came from culturally. In 1996, the Institute of Cultural Research of the Miao Nationality in Hunan offered an eight-week course promoted through contact persons in the United States. The preamble to the course description went as follows (note the language of "compatriots" and that the Miao authors do not use "Hmong"—the preferred ethnonym in the United States):

> Through two international seminars on the Miao nationality, we understand many scholars mentioned that they didn't know much about the history and culture of the Chinese Miao nationality, and hope to have an opportunity to come to China for studying the history and culture of the Miao nationality. In order to meet the demands of our compatriots of the Miaos in foreign countries, we decided to run a class for advanced studies of the Miao's history and culture. Our compatriots of the Miaos in America are welcome to take an active part in the class.

With a tuition of $400, the course offered not only classroom instruction in history and culture, but also training in Chinese language for those interested in widening their ventures in China, and "on the spot" investigation for those interested in first-hand visits to their rural origins. In this way, through a structured and academicized medium, culture was delivered and the homeland saw returns.

These ventures are not reducible, however, to the instrumentality of economic transactions. Central to this project is the cultivating of Hmong obligation based on appeals to common cultural idioms of indebtedness. Miao elites hasten to host Hmong visitors to China offering conveniences such as arranging their touring and accompanying them at every moment. Most common is the banquet thrown to enact Miao hospitality rituals, bestowing the glow of cultural intactness on the nostalgic travelers. No matter how limited their means, Miao hosts struggle to put on lavish spreads of high-prestige food, and to assemble an entourage to dine along with the guests. The proffering of liquor to the guests' lips, accompanied by ceremonial welcoming songs, constitutes the most significant offering. In the course of these meals an aura of kin-bonding is created; brothers are constituted out of strangers through partaking in the ritual feast. Kin-obligation comes to function very powerfully in these forged familial ties. To the dislocated Hmong, Miao offer identity; in exchange, they hope for concrete returns in the form of sponsorship for overseas study or travel, joint-venture investment in Miao-run enterprises, charitable donations for the Miao poor, subsidies for education and academic publishing.

But immediate concrete returns are not the only aim of these offerings. On the contrary, as I've said, they are better seen as prestations which, according to the age-old logic of reciprocity, put the Miao in long-term positions to make claims on their privileged co-ethnics overseas. The Miao elites who enter into these identity exchanges envision a growing thicket of linkages which will consolidate the Miao in China with the Hmong in the West in a potent alliance of mutual aid, an ethic of reciprocal commitment born of their shared lot as minorities wherever they are located. I turn now to examining the process by which such cultural and economic exchanges come to assume political valences.

Oppositional Cosmopolitanism

There is a noteworthy dissonance in the intentionalities that Hmong in the West and Miao in China bring to their enthusiastic reunion. While the former seek a territorial centering, a return home, a recovery of the land of origins, the latter envision themselves detached from the land, despite their boundness to it in terms of livelihood and legal citizenship. Dislocated Hmong in diaspora feel flung to the farthest reaches from what they consider home. The direction of their movement, both psychic and spatial, is centripetal—toward an imagined locus both of the steadfastness of culture and of a potential wellspring of political vitality. When anomic youth gangs began to form in refugee Hmong communities, some Hmong elders invited a visiting Miao intellectual from China to meet with the young gang members to instruct them in how to be upstanding members of their ethnic community. As well, some U.S. Hmong leaders have strategized for the loyalties of Hmong refugee followers by invoking whatever ties they have forged with Chinese Miao as a basis for their claim to power. That inalienable territory of the homeland, then, constant and stalwart, has become a leitmotif in the social imaginary of Hmong "out of place."

Meanwhile, Miao desires for transnational identification aim to defy space. Their strategy is to fan out over the globe through diasporic ties, to derive political strength precisely from their irreverence for national borders. This represents a significant realignment in their conceptualization of belonging. I hold that, for the post-1949 era at least, it was not until the last few years of the reform period (i.e. the 1990s) that Miao developed this acute sense of oppositionality toward China. In the Maoist (1949-1979) and early reform (1979-1989) periods, they were caught up in nationalist projects, building a strong sense of Chineseness *vis-à-vis* the West, throwing their cultural essence into the amalgam that was to constitute the multi-ethnic Chinese people. The Chinese state, for the most part, was seen as their patron, their benefactor, their protector from the vagaries of economic caprice, to which both nature and the market had subjected them in centuries past. Deeply disaffected with the trajectory post-Mao reform took, however, they then turned away from a Chinese national project which had devolved into the proliferation of invidious difference. They have turned instead toward a transnational source of identity which could yield the possibilities for development that the reform process had denied them.

The coalescence of interests that impels the Miao-Hmong's forging of transnationality has permitted the elaboration of common identity despite communication barriers and cultural disjunctions. An article in a newsletter of the Hmong American Partnership aptly exemplifies the coevalness of concrete exchanges and identity production. I quote at length to reveal the interweavings in the text:

> The gap between Hmong Americans and Hmong Chinese became a little narrower last spring, when HAP had the honor of briefly hosting Mr. Wu Zi Ming (Nom Kav Vwj), a Chinese-Hmong government official...to explore the possibility of developing formal relationships with organizations...to promote educational, economic and cultural exchange between Hmong communities of our two nations...The brief meeting was a momentous occasion for all who were there...Everyone who was there walked away enriched by the experience and the opportunity to reach back in time and connect with Hmong history and Hmong heritage. It is hoped that there will be more contact with our fellow Hmong in China and elsewhere as Hmong Americans continue to strive for prosperity and the world becomes an increasingly smaller place (Hmong 1996: 3).

Similarly, idioms of kinship are elaborated not on the basis of spatial proximity, but precisely on the basis of their ability to bridge the vastness of space and the gulfs between cultures. When a Miao intellectual from China visited a Hmong family in Washington, DC, they had no one to translate their mutually unintelligible dialects. They called me in New Jersey to act as interpreter and passed the phone back and forth for a brief interchange. The Hmong-American host asked whether the food they cooked was palatable. Yes, if I stick to Hmong food and stay away from Western food and raw vegetables, he offered back, stressing ethnic solidarity. Would he like them to place an international call so he could talk to his family in China? That would be nice, but not necessary, he demurred, highlighting his hosts' role as surrogate kin: he was happy just to be visiting with them. The host then made a short speech, proclaiming his joy at being able to receive a cousin from such a distant land right there in Washington D.C. The invention of this type of extended kin network, I propose, has its lure precisely in its de-territorialized character, in its cosmopolitanism. While the space of the homeland comprises an alluring trope to be deployed in the crafting of common essence, it is, on the contrary, the *multi-site* feature of this new-found identity that makes it so compelling.

Both Hmong in the West and Miao in China have encountered, both historically and in the present, a relentless marginalization at the hands of large states that would incorporate them as others, even as they maintain their difference. And both groups have been the targets of venomous national discourses—discourses which may exemplify the nationalist "pedagogy" that Bhabha (1990: 297) identified—which construct them as part of the nation-people either by exacting their selfless contribution, or by chastising them for withholding it. In the current period, Miao have been expected to enact their loyalty to China by laboring patiently at eeking subsistence rice out of scrappy mountain terraces while entrepreneurs on the coast prosper unimaginably. Hmong in the United States have been challenged to prove themselves worthy of the American citizenship they were promised by exchanging the everyday autonomy they retained on federal cash assistance for subjection to the wage work process.[9] And those who have "failed" to do so have in turn contributed inadvertently to their groups' imaging by journalists and social scientists as culturally "unfit" for U.S. society. An American anthropologist, for instance, pronounced with authority: "Taking into account their traditional existence...of the various Southeast Asian refugee groups the Hmong are culturally the most disparate from the receiving society" (Scott 1982: 146). *Newsweek,* resorting to racializing discourse, sneered, in a classic social-evolutionist slur: "The gene for adaptability is an elusive one; those who have it survive, those who lack it may not...[the Hmong embroidered squares] don't quite fit in, like Hmong themselves" (July 7, 1980: 34).

Remaining as they do on the cultural and economic margins of the states in which they reside, the choice to travel the postnational, translocal trajectory that Appadurai (1993) has described seems almost ineluctable. An alternative identification, forged out of cultural production and what I have called identity exchanges, appears to Hmong and Miao as a potent antidote to a state loyalty gone sour. This identification defines itself, as Clifford noted, against both the "norms of nation-states" *and* those of "indigenous, and especially autochthonous, claims by 'tribal' peoples" (1994: 307). It can be viewed as oppositional precisely because of the way it mocks the constraints and exclusions that the state would impose envisioning instead a plethora of linkages across the globe.[10]

Several qualifications must be raised, however, in entertaining this notion of oppositionality. First, it should not be conflated with secessionist impulses and with a diversion of interests entirely away from the state and from the national base in which each group is operating. Indeed, both Hmong in the United States and Miao in China juggle their transnational strategies and their local ones, striving, despite exclusions, for greater integration at home.[11] Second, as I have argued elsewhere (Schein 1997), the forging of transnationality may be not simply a set of autonomous moves, but may in fact be or appear consequential for the respective states. Certainly, China has been proactive in promoting the soliciting of donations, investments, and remittances from overseas Chinese

(Ong 1996: 174-5). Hmong of Lao origin, because of their homeland attachment to China, could conceivably come to occupy this position as well. Hence, oppositionality needs to be conceived in part as a product of involvements with the state, both consistent with and resistant to state aims. Third, this is an oppositionality, the effects of which remain to be seen. Christoffersen holds that for the region of Xinjiang, "transnational forces contributed to Xinjiang's closer integration into the Chinese polity" (1993: 132) through a "bargaining" process in which strength gained through economic ties abroad enabled this peripheral region to achieve more of its economic aims within the domain of Chinese policy. It is early to assess whether Hmong-Miao transnationality will be so consequential—either in China or the United States—and certainly it is by no means comparable with global pan-Islamism or, for that matter, the economic might of the "Greater China" alliance (Ong 1996). But it is conceivable that bonds could strengthen to the extent that they gain significant state notice.[12]

What emerges out of a close reading of the Hmong-Miao's forging of transnationality is a sense of a solidarity complexly fraught with inequality and difference. What to make of this difference? Is the necessary endpoint of this inquiry a recognition that Miao in China remain subjugated through their third-world status, remain the playful consumption objects of a set of globally travelling Hmong-American entrepreneurs tantamount to a leisure class? Or worse, that they can only be consigned to occupying the box of cultural exotica, functioning as emblems of the kind of difference that sells in late-capitalist modernity? Or is it possible to also think otherwise, to see this process of what Stuart Hall reluctantly dubbed "diaspora-ization" (1996: 447) as one which productively spans differences, without obliterating them, in a counter-move to the globalization that connotes homogeneity? This encompassing of difference has been a key to much minority politics—fought at the site where class meets ethnicity and coalitions may form. Coalitional thinking is what Radhakrishnan (1995: 821) seeks to transpose to the transnational scale through his vision of "eccentric cosmopolitanism." His call is for a radical imagining of a "postrepresentational space where one group will have earned the right to speak for the other in a spirit of equal reciprocity" (1995: 821). This speaking for the other is conceivable as oppositional when it is counterposed to the economic pragmatism of capitalism, when it defies the type of capitalist boundarilessness that fractures community.

This kind of ethnic mobilization, then, exemplifies Appadurai's escaped "nationalist genie," one which is out of the bottle of "ideas of spatial boundary and territorial sovereignty" (1993: 413). It is a mobilization that locates its strength precisely in its cosmopolitan character. It is not entirely free of some of the more pernicious features of colonial and nationalist discourses— the objectification of others in exoticizing nostalgia, the battling over women as the putative sites of tradition, the seizing upon cultural traits as essences—but it does replace some of those earlier logics. As an identity production, its inventiveness with regard to social forms and its unfixity with regard to cultural content, enable it to transgress disempowering localisms in ways that should not be ignored.

Notes

1. I am indebted to many local people, scholars and levels of government within China and the United States for their support of my research. For funding for a research trip to China in 1993 and for ongoing research in 1996-97, I thank the Rutgers University Research Council. I am grateful to the Rutgers-Princeton Interdisciplinary Conference "Placements/Displacements: The Politics of Location" organized by the Rutgers Center for the Critical Analysis of Contemporary Culture and the Princeton Theory of Literature and History Group and to Neil Smith for the first opportunity to present a version of this piece. For inspiration or comments during the development of the article, I would like to thank Michael Moffat and Bruce Robbins. I remain solely responsible for the final result.
2. See Tsing (1993) for a pertinent exploration of the initiative and narratives of Meratus Dayak women in Indonesia in seeking transnational relationships with men from other parts of Asia.
3. See a recent essay by Ong (1996) that interrogates narratives of "Greater China" as articulations of a modern identity wholly identified with the fluidity and global efficacy of late capitalism.
4. Despite its problematic effect of binarizing and overly homogenizing the two "worlds" (and conventionally leaving the "second" world under erasure), I retain the terminology of "first" and "third" worlds here for two reasons. First, it connotes a prestige structure that is very much in place in the transnational strategies of Hmong and Miao. Second, it positions these

transnational moves within a larger context of ongoing global asymmetries that substantially condition and resonate with the particularities of this instance.

5. Comments in this section address the following two aspects: 1) social, political and economic relations enacted in the production of videos and 2) the forms of representation revealed in the contents of the videos. These are componenets of a larger study of what I call the "China tapes" which will include interviews with video producers and reception studies among Hmong audiences.

6. See Litzinger (n.d.) for a comparable example among the Yao. He offers a trenchant critique of the over-privileging of hybridity in transnational identity production, emphasizing instead the equally significant impulse toward "cultural protection."

7. This stands in stark contrast to the situation reported by Hammond (1988) in which Tongan immigrants to Salt Lake City used video to create images of themselves. These videos of their lives and special ritual events were often sent back to relatives in their islands of origins as a means of communication and self-representation. To my knowledge this trajectory of communication is not found in the Hmong-Miao case, although photographs are often sent to China, especially as part of matchmaking ventures.

8. The resonance here and below with U.S. minority politics is striking, and suggests not only parallels but perhaps also transnational flows influencing the framing of identity political strategies.

9. See my argument (Schein 1987) that Hmong secondary migration to and relatively high dependency on federal cash assistance in the California Central Valley in the 1980s was part and parcel of an enclavement strategy that had everything to do with social and cultural autonomy and with community formation. For an analysis of recent conditions intensifying economic and cultural marginalization of immigrants in California, see Smith and Tarallo 1993.

10. This kind of move also warrants attention for its possible impact on the analytics of the national. As Gupta points out: "The displacement of identity and culture from 'the nation' not only forces us to reevaluate our ideas about culture and identity but also enables us to denaturalize the nation as the hegemonic form of organizing space" (1992:74).

11. Powerful organizations such as the Minnesota-based "Hmong American Partnership" dedicated to advancing "self-sufficiency" and economic integration while retaining cultural "pride" epitomize this philosophy in fund-raising statements such as "Your contributions will provide Hmong American Partnership with critical resources to overcome barriers that restrict Minnesota's Hmong from being *equal partners* in society" (Haus 1995:5, emphasis added).

12. See my discussion in Schein 1997 of the decision on the part of the Chinese state to deny exit visas to a couple hundred Miao scholars who wished to attend an international Hmong-Miao conference in Minnesota. I hold that the government's attempt to block this burgeoning alliance itself bespeaks the state's recognition of the potential for significant opposition.

References

Appadurai, Arjun. (1993). Patriotism and Its Futures. *Public Culture* 5(3): 411-429.

Basch, Linda, Nina Glick Schiller, and Cristina Szanton Blanc. (1994). *Nations Unbound: Transnational Projects, Postcolonial Predicaments and Deterritorialized Nation-States*. New York: Gordon and Breach.

Bhabha, Homi K. (1990). "DissemiNation: Time, Narrative and the Margins of the Modern Nation." In *Nation and Narration*. Homi K. Bhabha (ed.), New York: Routledge. Pp. 291-322.

Chow, Rey. (1993). *Writing Diaspora: Tactics of Intervention in Contemporary Cultural Studies*. Bloomington and Indianapolis: University of Indiana Press.

Clifford, James. (1992). "Traveling Cultures." In *Cultural Studies*, L.. Grossberg et al (eds.), New York: Routledge. Pp.96-116

———. (1994). "Diasporas." *Cultural Anthropology* 9: 3: 302-338.

Christoffersen, Gaye. (1993). "Xinjiang and the Great Islamic Circle: The Impact of Transnational Forces on Chinese Regional Economic Planning." *China Quarterly* 133 (March): 130-151.

Ginsburg, Faye. (1991). "Indigenous Media: Faustian Contract or Global Village?" *Cultural Anthropology* 6: 1: 92-112.

Gupta, Akhil. (1992). "The Song of the Nonaligned World: Transnational Identities and the Reinscription of Space in Late Capitalism." *Cultural Anthropology* 7: 1: 63-79.

Hall, Stuart. (1996) "New Ethnicities." In D. Morley & K. Chen, (eds.), *Stuart Hall: Critical Dialogues in Cultural Studies*. London: Routledge. Pp. 441-450. First edition, 1989.

———. (1989). "Cultural Identity and Cinematic Representation." *Framework* 36: 68-81.

Hammond, J. D. (1988). "Visualizing Themselves: Tongan Videography in Utah." *Visual Anthropology* 1: 379-400.

Hmong American Partnership. (1996). "HAP Visited by Chinese Officials." *HAP Voice* (Fall): 3.

Haus, J. (1995). "An Invitation to Donate to HAP." *The HAP Voice: Hmong American Partnership* 6: 1: 5.

Litzinger, R. A. (1995). "Narratives of Identity in Yao 'Post-National' Cultural Discourse." Paper presented at the Annual Meetings of the American Anthropological Association.

Mercer, K. (1990). "Black Hair/Style Politics." In R. Ferguson et al. (eds.), *Out There: Marginalization and Contemporary Culture*. Cambridge, MA: MIT Press. Pp. 247-264.

Ong, Aihwa. (1996). "Chinese Modernities: Narratives of Nation and of Capitalism." In A. Ong & D. Nonini, (eds.), *Ungrounded Empires: the Cultural Politics of Modern Chinese Transnationalism*. New York: Routledge. Pp. 171-203.

———. (1994). "On the Edge of Empires: Flexible Citizenship among Chinese in Diaspora." *Positions* 1: 3: 745-778.

Radhakrishnan, R. (1995). "Toward an Eccentric Cosmopolitanism." *Positions* 3: 3: 814-821.

Robbins, Bruce. (1993). "Comparative Cosmopolitanisms." In *Secular Vocations: Intellectuals, Professionalism, Culture*. London: Verso. Pp. 180-211.

Schein, Louisa. (1997). "Importing Miao Brethren to Hmong America: A Not So Stateless Transnationalism." In Bruce Robbins and Pheng Cheah (eds.), *Cosmopolitics*. . Minneapolis: University of Minnesota Press. Forthcoming.

———. (1996). "The Other Goes to Market: The State, the Nation, and Unruliness in Contemporary China." *Identities* 2: 3: 197-222.

———. (1987). "Control of Contrast: Lao-Hmong Refugees in American Contexts." In S. Morgan & E. Colson (eds.), *People in Upheaval*. Staten Island, NY: Center for Migration Studies. Pp. 88-107.

Scott, G. M. (1982). "The Hmong Refugee Community in San Diego: A Conceptual Framework for the Analysis of Dislocated People." *Anthropological Quarterly* 55: 3: 146-160.

Smith, Michael Peter. (1994). "Can You Imagine? Transnational Migration and the Globalization of Grass Roots Politics." *Social Text* 39: 15-33.

Smith, Michael Peter. and Bernadette Tarallo. (1993). "California's Changing Faces: New Immigrant Survival Strategies and State Policy." *California Policy Seminar Briefs* 5: 15: 1-10.

Spivak, Gayatri. (1990). "Gayatri Spivak on the Politics of the Subaltern: Interview with Howard Winant." *Socialist Review* 90: 3: 81-97.

Tolentino, R. B. (1996). "Bodies, Letters, Catalogues: Filipinas in Transnational Space." *Social Text* 48: 14: 3: 49-76.

Tsing, A. L. (1993). "Alien Romance." In *In the Realm of the Diamond Queen*. Princeton: Princeton University Press. Pp.213-229.

———. (1994). "From the Margins." *Cultural Anthropology* 9: 3: 279-297.

Villapando, Venny. (1989). "The Business of Selling Mail Order Brides." In Asian Women United of California (eds.), *Making Waves: An Anthology of Writings by and About Asian-American Women*. Boston: Beacon Press. Pp.318-326.

Wilson, Ara. (1988). "American Catalogues of Asian Brides." In J. B. Cole (ed.), *Anthropology for the Nineties*. New York: The Free Press. Pp. 114-125.

Contributors

André C. Drainville is an Assistant Professor of International Political Cconomy, Laval University, Québec City (tenured as of June 1997) and has taught political science at York University in Toronto, Ontario, at McMaster University in Hamilton, Ontario and in the department of International Relations and International Public Law, University of Amsterdam. He teaches courses on "International Relations" as well as on "Critical International Political Economy," "Internationalism and Resistance in the World Economy," "Travels in the World Economy." Published in *Review of International Political Economy* (U.K.), *Studies in Political Economy* (Canada), *Alternatives* (U.S. and India), *Social Justice* (U.S.). He is currently working on a book, tentatively entitled *Cosmopolitanism against Internationalism? Global Civility, Transnational Urbanism and Sustainable Capitalism in the World Economy*.

Georges E. Fouron is an Associate Professor of Social Sciences at SUNY-Stony Brook. He grew up in Haiti and migrated to the United States in 1969. His research is on Haitian bilingualism and has transnationalism. His publications include: "Schooling for limited opportunity: The Haitian migrant experience," in Benesh, S. (Ed.) *ESL in America: Myths and possibilities* and "Migration and identity: Haitian immigrants in the United States," in Macero, J. D., Agor, B. J., and Tumposky, N. (Eds.) *Proceedings of the Annual TESOL Conference, Buffalo, New York.*

Luin Goldring is an Assistant Professor of Sociology at York University, Canada. She has published research on Mexico-U.S. transnational migration and ejido reform in Mexico. Her current research focuses on state-transmigrant relations.

Sarah J. Mahler is an Assistant Professor of Anthropology at the University of Vermont. She received her Ph.D. in Anthropology from Columbia University. Her research has focused on Latin American and Caribbean migrants to the New York Metropolitan region and is currently studying transnational linkages between Salvadorans living on Long Island and their communities of origin. Among her most recent publications are *American Dreaming: Immigrant Life on the Margins* (Princeton, 1995) and *Salvadorans in Suburbia: Symbiosis and Conflict* (Allyn and Bacon, 1995).

Linda Miller Matthei is an Assistant Professor of Sociology and Anthropology at Texas A&M University—Commerce. Her ongoing research interests include immigration and transnational network building and the role of women in international migration. Her recent publications include an article on gender and transnational networks in *Social Justice.*

Nina Glick Schiller is an Associate Professor of Anthropology at the University of New Hampshire. She has done work on the construction of racial and ethnic identities for over 25 years. Her work on transnational migration includes *Nations unbound: Transnational projects, postcolonial predicaments and deterritorialized nation-states* (co-authored with Linda Basch and Cristina Szanton Blanc) and *Towards a transnational perspective on migration: Race, class, ethnicity and nationalism reconsidered* (co-edited with Basch and Szanton Blanc). She is editor of *Identities: Global Studies in Culture and Power.*

Alan Smart is an Associate Professor of Anthropology at the University of Calgary. He has conducted research in Hong Kong and China since 1982. He is the author of *Making Room: Squatter Clearance in Hong Kong* (Hong Kong: Centre of Asian Studies, 1992) and articles in *International Journal of Urban and Regional Research, Society and Space, City and Society, Critique of Anthropology, Cultural Anthropology, International Journal of the Sociology of Law,* and numerous edited volumes.

Josephine Smart is an Associate Professor of Anthropology at the University of Calgary. Her research is on informal economy, foreign investment in China, migration of Hong Kong Chinese to Canada, gender relations and development in post-1978 China and more recently NAFTA and its impact on the social and economic restructuring of three North American cities. She is the author of *The Political Economy of Street Hawkers in Hong Kong* (1989) and has published in *The International Journal of Urban and Regional Research, Critique of Anthropology, The Anthropology of Work Review, The Asian Journal of Public Administration* and in numerous edited volumes.

David A. Smith is an Associate Professor in Sociology and Urban Planning at the University of Southern California, Irvine.

His recent research focuses on comparative urbanization and development, global city networks, and the political economy of industrializaion in East Asia. He is the author of *Third World Cities in Global Perspective* (Westviwe 1996), co-editor of *A New Westview World Order? Global Transformations in the Late Twentieth Century* (Greenwood 1995), and has published numerous articles in sociology, urban, and development studies.

Robert C. Smith is an Assistant Professor in the Sociology Department at Barnard College, and directs the Transnational Migration module of the Hewlett Program on Mexico at the Institute of Latin American and Iberian Studies at Columbia University. His Dissertation "Los Ausentes Siempre Presentes: The Imagining, Making and Politics of a Transnational Community Between Ticuani, Puebla, Mexico and New York City" (Columbia, 1995), was nominated for the Bancroft Prize. He has held fellowships from the Social Science Research Council, the National Science Foundation, and other institutions.

Ninna Nyberg Sørensen is a Cultural Sociologist who received a Ph.D. in Anthropology from the University of Copenhagen, Denmark. She is currently employed as a researcher at Centre for Development Research in Copenhagen, with research concentrations in the linkages between development and international migration. She has carried out research on intra-national migration in the Dominican Republic, transnational migration between the Dominican Republic and the United States, and broader cultural aspects of the Caribbean. Her current research interest is the experience of Moroccan and Dominican migrants in Spain linked to transnational social networks in their countries of origin and to fellow nationals in other European countries.

Louisa Schein teaches Anthropology at Rutgers University and specializes in ethnicity, gender, sexuality and transnational processes. She has conducted fieldwork in China since 1982 and is presently writing a book on cultural politics in China's post-Mao era. Her articles have appeared in *Social Text, Identities* and *Modern China* and her ongoing research includes a multi-site study of Hmong-Miao transnationality.